DAMNED FOOLS IN UTOPIA

DAMNED FOOLS IN UTOPIA

AND OTHER WRITINGS ON ANARCHISM AND WAR RESISTANCE

NICOLAS WALTER

EDITED BY
DAVID GOODWAY

2011

ISBN: 978-1-60486-222-5
Library of Congress Control Number: 2010927836

PM Press
PO Box 23912
Oakland, CA 94623
www.pmpress.org

Printed in the United States on recycled paper by the Employee Owners
of Thomson-Shore in Dexter, Michigan. www.thomsonshore.com

Cover and internal design: Josh MacPhee | justseeds.org

CONTENTS

ABBREVIATIONS

APCF	Anti-Parliamentary Communist Federation
ARP	Air Raid Precautions
ASLEF	Associated Society of Locomotive Engineers and Firemen
BBC	British Broadcasting Corporation
CND	Campaign for Nuclear Disarmament
CNT	Confederación Nacional del Trabajo
CO	Conscientious Objector
DAC	Direct Action Committee against Nuclear War
FAI	Federación Anarquista Ibérica
GLC	Greater London Council
HO	Home Office
ILP	Independent Labour Party
IUDA	Industrial Union of Direct Actionists
NATO	North Atlantic Treaty Organization
NCF	No Conscription Fellowship
NHS	National Health Service
NLR	New Left Review
NVC	Non-Violent Commission
OECD	Organization for Economic Co-operation and Development
POUM	Partido Obrero de Unificatión Marxista
PPU	Peace Pledge Union
PRO	Public Record Office
ROC	Royal Observer Corps
RPA	Rationalist Press Association
RSG	Regional Seat of Government
SDF	Social Democratic Federation
SIGINT	Signals Intelligence
TUC	Trades Union Congress
VND	Voice of Nuclear Disarmament
YCND	Youth Campaign for Nuclear Disarmament

PREFACE

TWO OR THREE DAYS AFTER NICOLAS DIED IN 2000, I TELEPHONED Freedom Press to say I'd like to select a collection of his articles as a tribute. I'd always been surprised they'd never published such a volume and knew Nicolas had felt the same. I was given the go-ahead and was even sent copies of some of his longer pieces. I'd already worked with Vernon Richards on editions of Alex Comfort and Herbert Read for Freedom Press and felt Nicolas's best articles would hold their own alongside Comfort—a major influence on him and enormously admired to the end—and Read, for whom in contrast (as will be seen) he had little time, probably largely because of Read's un-anarchistic conduct when a member of the Committee of 100.

I proceeded to go through my voluminous files of newspaper cuttings and runs of *Anarchy*, *Solidarity*, *Inside Story*, *Wildcat*, and *Raven*, as well as partial holdings of *Freedom* for the 1960s. After six months, I forwarded a memoir to Angel Alley, together with the suggested contents of two volumes, one essentially what was published in 2007 as *The Anarchist Past* and the other, the present volume, centred on the 1960s, nuclear disarmament, the Committee of 100 and the Spies for Peace. I hoped that Freedom Press would publish both but was entirely prepared to reduce my selection to a single volume. Yet after much delay—and to my great disgust given Nicolas's decades of commitment to *Freedom*, *Anarchy*, and *Raven* (see "Thirty Years' War")—I was eventually informed that Freedom Press considered they would be commemorating him adequately by bringing out a new edition of *About Anarchism* and they didn't intend to do any more.

I thereupon contacted AK Press in Oakland, California, already the leading anglophone anarchist publisher, who replied that, although NW was a good writer, a book of his articles wouldn't sell well enough for

AK to publish it. In an aside I'd mentioned the possibility of doing the same for Maurice Brinton (i.e., Chris Pallis), yet that, I was assured, was a book would AK would definitely want in its list. Hence followed, in 2004, *For Workers' Power*, the title Ramsey Kanaan tells me he is proudest to have published.

That, I thought, sank the prospects of a Nicolas volume, if even AK couldn't anticipate making a success of it. It was therefore extremely tentatively that I mentioned the possibility to Ross Bradshaw, whose Five Leaves Publications had brought out the English-language edition of my conversations with Colin Ward as *Talking Anarchy* as well as several reprints of Ward titles. His immediate response was the very proper one that such a book needed to be published, although the print run would have to be short since he didn't expect it to make money. I fought off the suggestion to include rationalist material but considered *The Anarchist Past*, almost a history of anarchist thought and practice, would sell better than one laden with 1960s material—even though that was what most interested me (having a great impact on me at the time) as well as being the work in which I believe Nicolas was at his most distinctive and original.

When AK got to hear about the Five Leaves book, its publication was imminent, but their reaction was entirely different to the response of 2001 (and why I still don't understand), now wanting, at too late a stage, to co-publish *The Anarchist Past*. So I told Ramsey, then about to launch this new imprint, PM, that there was another book, *Damned Fools in Utopia*, which he was more than welcome to have. I still doubt its saleability—although a number of people have lamented *The Anarchist Past*'s lack of nuclear disarmament material—but continue to be impressed by its contents.

The selection of both volumes, as I've indicated, is skewed towards what especially interested me, by what I was moved to preserve at the time of publication. On the other hand, repeated requests over the years to relatives, comrades, and admirers of Nicolas have not resulted in a single addition—or exclusion—from the provisional list of contents.

A condition of PM's publishing *Damned Fools in Utopia* was that it would have a lengthy introduction by me. Well it has, but it is still essentially the memoir I wrote in 2000, a revision of which serves as the introduction to *The Anarchist Past*, and which I've slightly changed again. Obviously quite a few readers will only read, even buy, just one of the books and I feel this outline and appreciation of Nicolas's career needs to be in both. Similarly, I have also included for a second time "Thirty Years' War," an important autobiographical statement which also details his relations with Freedom Press. I apologize to readers of both volumes for the duplication of the introduction; but, once I've written on a given subject, to date I've found it impossible to come up with a significantly different treatment. Should this be seen as a strength or a weakness? It's a strength in that I've obviously thought hard about the appropriate issues in the first place and now see no reason to change my interpretation. But I appreciate it's a weakness since I try the patience of and disappoint publishers, editors, reviewers, academics and ordinary readers (and it is the latter, by the way, for whom I always write).

I have, though, made a small but important correction. Nicolas's first wife, Ruth, objected strongly to my describing him at the time of his association with the Solidarity group as a "pacifist." She points out that, while both of them were committed to non-violence as a means to certain ends, they didn't regard it as the only way of attacking the State and hence—unlike the pacifists—see non-violent direct action as "a kind of religion." They both disagreed politically with the pacifists in the Committee of 100 who (like Read) believed property should never be damaged, the Walters advocating instead the use of wire-cutters to cut the fences enclosing airbases. I would add that, if such pacifists had been involved in the Spies for Peace, they would have opposed secrecy and have been sentenced to many years of imprisonment.

Ruth also remarks that "The Committee of 100: Ends and Means" was the first article Nicolas had printed in the *Guardian*, that he was "incredibly chuffed" about this—and that the entire payment went to buy her an engagement ring.

Finally, I have not, for obvious reasons, attempted to eliminate the repetition that occurs between some of the original articles, particularly those written during 1961–63. This may annoy the few who read the collection from cover to cover; but most readers will, I suspect, dive in and sample individual chapters, here and there.

INTRODUCTION

IT WAS TYPICAL OF NICOLAS THAT WHEN I ASKED HIM TO CHECK THE references to himself in a brief memoir I had written of the historian Raphael Samuel and commented that it must have been at a meeting I described at Raphael's Spitalfields house in the early 1970s that we had first met, he retorted, without pause for reflection, that on the contrary that had occurred at the History Workshop at Ruskin College, Oxford, in 1969. I say it was typical because he was, of course, entirely right. But although we did not meet until the end of that memorable decade I had known, and indeed been in awe of, his name since its beginning. A callow eighteen-year-old from a small Midlands town and still a member of the Labour Party, I was among the hundreds arrested in Trafalgar Square on September 17, 1961, at the great Committee of 100 sit-down. In London again a fortnight later, this time to appear at Bow Street, I bought *Anarchy* no. 8 at Collet's in Charing Cross Road and read Nicolas's "George Orwell: An Accident in Society" (incorporated in 1998 in "George Orwell and Anarchism," which is reprinted below). I still have what I must have purchased on the same occasion and would have been my first copy of *Freedom*—for September 23, 1961—and this contains a long article, "Literature and the Left," signed by "NW," the initials soon to become excitingly familiar, and reviewing "one of the most inept books I have ever come across" (yet there were to be many more): John Mander's *The Writer and Commitment*. I proceeded to spend the winter of 1961–62 in London, attending the Sunday-evening meetings of the London Anarchist Group at The Two Brewers, Monmouth Street, and monthly meetings at Laurens and Celia Otter's Notting Hill flat; becoming a lifelong reader of *Freedom* (which in those months I normally bought at Solosy's, the little newsagent's shop across the road from Collet's); and eventually reading in the spring Nicolas's major essays in *Anarchy*, "Direct Action and the New Pacifism" and "Disobedience and the New Pacifism" (revised the following year as *Non-violent Resistance* and included in that form in this volume). It was in 1963, during my second year at Oxford, that I concluded an essay on Lloyd George by asserting that he had done more to lay the foundations of the Warfare State than of the Welfare State and was interrogated unsympathetically by my tutor, the historian Paul Thompson, as to what I meant by the term "Warfare State." (Yet equally I remember Paul congratulating Nicolas—it would have been at that same History Workshop—for his part in the Brighton Church Demonstration of 1966, although it emerged that he had written to him at the time).[1] Nicolas's two essays had a tremendous effect on me, contributing powerfully to my continuing belief in the easy superiority of non-violent direct action where it is at all feasible (but without my ever having become an absolute pacifist); and indeed it was Nicolas's articles in both *Freedom* and *Anarchy* which I most admired and was most influenced by in the early 1960s, long before I came to appreciate the originality and importance of Colin Ward's editorship of *Anarchy* and own writing. (Nicolas, on the other hand, came to disavow his advocacy of non-violence as the most appropriate means of struggle, merely saying, when I questioned him about his view of violence, that he had changed his mind.

* * *

Nicolas Hardy Walter was born in South London, where his father was researching at the Maudsley Hospital, on November 22, 1934, and was rightly proud of his dissenting family background over several generations. His paternal grandfather, Karl Walter (1880–1965), a journalist, had as a young man been an anarchist, known Peter Kropotkin and Edward Carpenter, and with Tom Keell was one of the two English delegates to the International Anarchist Congress at Amsterdam in 1907. Three years before he had married Margaret Hardy, an American woman he had met in Italy; and between 1908 and the First World War they lived in the States, where he worked on the Kansas City *Star*. In the 1930s they settled in Italy, Karl Walter as a sympathizer of Fascism, an ideological gravitation common to other erstwhile libertarian revolutionaries and later to be maliciously seized upon by Albert Meltzer; but in old age he returned to both anarchism and London and in the last years of his life was writing occasionally for *Freedom* at the same time as his grandson.[2] Nicolas's father, W. Grey Walter (1910–77), was a brilliant neurologist who created ingenious electro-mechanical robots (one of which was to be displayed in the Millennium Dome), wrote *The Living Brain* (1953)—widely read in its Pelican edition—was Director for many years of the Burden Neurological Institute in Bristol, and appeared, as I well recall, on television in the BBC's Brains Trust. In the 1930s and 1940s, like so many of his contemporaries, Grey Walter was a Communist fellow-traveller, but later he moved towards left libertarianism, prodded I suspect by his son, becoming a member of the West of England Committee of 100 and contributing a piece on cybernetics to *Anarchy*.[3] Nicolas's maternal grandfather was Samuel Kerkham (S. K.) Ratcliffe (1868–1958), another journalist, who had also known Kropotkin and Carpenter (at whose funeral he was a mourner) and had served on the executive of the Fabian Society alongside Charlotte Wilson (whose anarchist essays his grandson was to edit). Although acting editor of the daily *Statesman* of Calcutta, 1903–6, and editor of the *Sociological Review*, 1910–17, he was essentially a freelance journalist—and a liberal rationalist rather than a socialist—but he was also a formidable lecturer, undertaking no fewer than twenty-eight lecture tours of the USA and Canada. He served for forty years as "an appointed lecturer" of the South Place Ethical Society, the history of which he was to write, and Nicolas followed him in this role from 1978. On S. K.'s death Kingsley Martin wrote in the *New Statesman*:

> I have never known anyone so meticulous about accurate detail since I was taught Greek by a scholar whose interest in particles was as enthusiastic as mine was indifferent. I have always regretted that I did not send SK the manuscript of each of my books before publication; instead of awaiting his inevitable list of errors.[4]

S. K.'s brother, William Ratcliffe, became a painter and was a member of the Camden Town Group. Nicolas's mother, Monica, had been one of Ninette de Valois's dancers at Sadler's Wells. Grey Walter (who was three times married) and Monica Walter divorced when Nicolas was nine or ten and he was brought up by his mother and her second husband, A. H. W. (Bill) Beck, who was to become Professor of Engineering at Cambridge.[5]

Nicolas was sent to private schools in the Bristol area and then boarded at a minor and semi-progressive public school, Rendcomb College, Cirencester (and to which E. D. Morel and John Middleton Murry had sent sons). On leaving school he did his two years' National Service in the RAF as a Junior Technician in Signals Intelligence. He was one of those bright young men who were taught Russian as part of the Cold

War effort; and it was on Russia, second only to British history and anarchism, that he was to write most extensively and percipiently—for a considerable period he was contemplating a biography of Kropotkin—and a selection of his articles on Russian themes constitute the core of *The Anarchist Past*. In 1954 he went up to Exeter College, Oxford, as an exhibitioner to read Modern History. His tutor for Political Thought was in later years to be taxed for having unleashed not only Nicolas, an anarchist, on to the outside world but also the National Socialist Colin Jordan and Trotskyist Tariq Ali. From his Oxford years there is a very early letter to *Encounter* in which he defends Hugh Trevor-Roper's assault on Arnold Toynbee and *A Study of History*.[6]

At Oxford he was a member of the Labour Club—he had been "brought up more or less as a Labour Party supporter - an extreme left-wing Labour Party supporter"[7]—but in the autumn of 1956 the twin upheavals of the Suez Crisis and the Hungarian Revolution jolted him into a questioning of the accepted ideologies (as he explains in "Thirty Years' War"). An even earlier letter on Suez to the *Manchester Guardian* resulted in Colin Ward sending him a sample copy of *Freedom*, although this collective letter betrays no indication of incipient anarchism.[8] On graduating from Oxford in 1957 he left for London where he was to spend his entire working life, initially as a schoolteacher—among his first pupils was Christine Barnett, nine years his junior, who would later become his second wife—but soon moving on to political research, publishing (he was responsible for Duckworth advertising in an early issue of *Anarchy*) and journalism. He participated in the political and cultural ferment of the first New Left, frequenting the Partisan Coffee House in Carlisle Street, and being a supporter of nuclear disarmament before the actual formation of the Campaign for Nuclear Disarmament (CND) in 1958. He would recall seeing Doris Lessing being cuddled at a meeting by Eric Hobsbawm (the great Marxist historian who became one of his *bêtes noires*, as for so many anarchists, and "Frogspawn"). Late in 1958, Karl Walter was responsible for introducing him to Lilian Wolfe, who had been Tom Keell's companion and continued to live at Whiteway colony—a fine, affectionate tribute to her is to be found in *The Anarchist Past*—and he began to visit Freedom Bookshop, which was still in Red Lion Street, and to attend the London Anarchist Group's weekly meetings. From 1959 he became a contributor to *Freedom*, an association only to be terminated by his death.

When in the autumn of 1960 dissatisfaction with CND's legal methods and constitutional agitation spawned within it the direct-action Committee of 100, Nicolas had his first letter published in *The*

Times defending the dissidents, and as a consequence was invited to become a member of the Committee to help round up the well-known names to the all important figure of one hundred. As he was to write in the 1979 postscript to the republication of *Non-violent Resistance* (and retitled below "An Autobiographical and Textual Note"): "I was never at all important in the Committee of 100, but it was very important to me." The Committee of 100 was the leading anarchist—or at least near-anarchist—political organization of modern Britain; and Nicolas, in the grip of the events of 1960–62, and spending as much time as possible during the winter of 1961–62 outside of work and his consider-able political activity in the Reading Room of the British Museum, was also engaged, in "Damned Fools in Utopia" for the *New Left Review* and especially in the two *Anarchy* essays, "Direct Action and the New Pacifism" and "Disobedience and the New Pacifism," in attempting—and with considerable success—to work out the historical lineage and above all the political theory of the Committee of 100. (This was a task performed for the preceding Direct Action Committee by April Carter.) The *Anarchy* essays won him the greatly valued friendship of Alex Comfort, whom he properly concluded was "the true voice of nu-clear disarmament, much more than Bertrand Russell or anyone else" and who was their principal theoretical influence, as well as of the novel-ist Colin MacInnes.[9] For many years he was intending to write a history of the Committee of 100 and of all his unrealized books this is the one I most regret (although its outline may be inferred from chapters 2 to 11 of the present volume).

In June 1961 Nicolas had resigned from the Committee on account of "disagreement with its rhetoric and tactics which had worried me from the beginning." The failure of the demonstration at the Wethersfield airbase on December 9 led the following year to the decentralization of the committee into thirteen regional committees (several of which were already existent). Although there was a nominal National Committee of 100, the dominant body now became the London Committee of 100, which Nicolas joined at its inaugural meeting in April 1962. Another member was the twenty-year-old Ruth Oppenheim, a microbiologist at Sainsbury's, who also worked whenever she could in the Committee's Goodwin Street premises, and Barbara Smoker remembers that Nicolas and Ruth at the meetings always sat at the front and together—and in September they married.

The long, harsh winter of 1962–63, one of the century's worst, saw renewed crisis, now acted out in the London Committee. The radi-cals, mainly from or close to *Solidarity*, circulated the arrestingly titled discussion document, *Beyond Counting Arses*, advocating radical, subversive action: "we must attempt to hinder the warfare state in every possible way." It was essentially this group, joined by Nicolas and Ruth, who constituted the Spies for Peace, locating and breaking into the Regional Seat of Government at Warren Row, producing the pamphlet, *Danger! Official Secret: RSG-6*, and thereby diverting many of us on the Aldermaston March of Easter 1963 to explore the sinister surface buildings of the subterranean bunker (it was Ruth's twenty-first birthday). The disclosure of the preparations to rule the country, in the event of nuclear war, through fourteen RSGs represented, of course "a substantial breach of official secrecy" and caused, as one had assumed, Harold Macmillan's ministry real concern.[10] Nicolas, the only member of the Spies for Peace ever to have declared himself publicly, did so unambiguously as early as 1968, remarkably, and on the radio at that[11] (as well as in 1986 in "Thirty Years' War"). His account, "The Spies for Peace Story," was unattributed in 1973 in *Inside Story*—and continued so in "The Spies for Peace and After," the *Raven* version of 1988 in which it is reprinted here. For a short time he regarded himself as belonging to the impressively innovative Solidarity Group, participating in the homelessness agitation which they largely initiated, yet as a dedicated anarchist who was then committed to non-violent direct action—and perceived by them as a "pacifist"—he was remote from their Trotskyist origins and continuing Marxist perspectives, though he remained on cordial terms with the leading members, Chris Pallis (or "Maurice Brinton"—and previously "Martin Grainger") and especially Ken Weller, to whom he would eventually speak on the telephone most weeks.

At the time of the Spies for Peace Ruth was pregnant with their first child, Susannah; and a second daughter, Natasha, followed shortly. Considerably influenced by her increasingly proud father, Natasha Walter has become a prominent literary journalist and author of *The New Feminism* (1998). Her tender, admiring obituary in the *Independent* indicates the kind of man Nicolas was.[12] In 1963 he became Deputy Editor of *Which?* and a staff writer for the *Good Food Guide* and from 1965 Press Officer for the British Standards Institution. It was while working for the British Standards Institution that he underwent his only spell of imprisonment. The Labour Party Conference was held in Brighton in 1966 as the Vietnam War grew in intensity, as did the Labour government's complicity, and the Vietnam Action Group planned to disrupt the traditional pre-conference service at the Dorset Road Methodist Church. Demonstrators were issued with admission tickets forged by Pat Pottle and Terry Chandler's Stanhope Press (which that year was also responsible for the Merlin Press's facsimile edition of the Chartist *Red Republican* and *Friend of the People*). Terry thought it a good idea to print more tickets than had been asked for and Nicolas was among those he let have one. So it was that Nicolas initiated cries of "Hypocrite!" too early while George Brown, the deputy prime minister, was speaking and when Harold Wilson mounted the pulpit to read the second lesson "pandemonium broke loose." Nicolas and Jim Radford were charged with indecent behaviour in church under the Ecclesiastical Courts Jurisdiction Act, 1866, and each sentenced to two months in Brixton. Nothing was to give Nicolas more satisfaction than to read in Wilson's memoirs the admission that this was "one of the most unpleasant experiences of my premiership."[13]

In 1968 he became chief sub-editor of the *Times Literary Supplement* (*TLS*), under the admired editorship of Arthur Crook, who made a series of impressive appointments. This was a job for which Nicolas was ideally suited and which he relished, regaling friends with entertaining anecdotes of life at the *TLS*—such as the peculiarities of another staff member, Martin Amis—and slipping in short pieces on the Situationists and B. Traven. As the historian of the *TLS* recounts:

> James Morris wrote to ask if there was anarchist on the paper, because on a proof he had received he had found the name "Kropotkin" added to a list of people he had mentioned in a review. It transpired that Walter was in the habit of dropping anarchists' names into reviews that he subbed, not changing the author's meaning—where the reviewer wrote, for instance, "unlike Tolstoy" he would simply add "or Kropotkin"...[14]

He did not, however, approve of the *TLS*'s changing from anonymous to signed reviews and so moved to the Rationalist Press Association (RPA), first as editor of the *New Humanist*, from 1975 to 1985, and then as Director of the RPA until his retirement at the end of 1999. Work at the RPA enabled him to be paid for propagating the dual cause of atheism and rationalism—together with anarchism, the passions of his intellectual life—and this in part by writing letters to the press. This latter was the capacity in which Nicolas was known to the wider public. It was estimated in 1994 that he had written 14,000 letters to newspapers and periodicals with a success rate of some 2,000 published (or one or two a week).[15] These appeared not only under his own name but under a variety of pseudonyms: Arthur Freeman, Anna Freeman, Mary Lewis, Jean Raison, and others. ("MH" in *Freedom* was originally the abbreviation for the collaborative "Many Hands," but later used by Nicolas exclusively.) This enormous body of letters, frequently correcting trivial errors, gave the impression of a pernickety and pedantic obsessive; and on retiring as editor of the *Spectator*, Charles Moore included Nicolas in the select group of bores whom he certainly would not miss. The astringency of his extensive book reviewing, from *Freedom* to the *London Review of Books*, contributed to an erroneous public persona of a desiccated and negative crank. The man in reality was the exact reverse: warm, generous, humorous, loved by children, a wonderful friend.

In 1969 Colin Ward turned over the whole of *Anarchy*, no. 100, to *About Anarchism*. *Blasphemy: Ancient and Modern* (1990) and *Humanism: What's in the Word* (1997) are both small books of ninety-six pages, but *About Anarchism* was Nicolas's most sustained and equally successful anarchist publication. It appeared the same year as a separate pamphlet and went through two further editions before he withdrew it from circulation pending a personal revision that never materialized. (The new edition of 2002 could only be published after his death.) *About Anarchism* has been translated into many other languages, including Russian, Serbo-Croat, Greek, Turkish, Chinese, and Japanese, and apparently its popularity led some anarchist parents to name their boys "Nicolas." And, for example, it was reading *About Anarchism*, along with Wilde's *The Soul of Man under Socialism* and the events of May 1968 in Paris, which was responsible for Peter Marshall becoming an anarchist. In the 1960s alone Nicolas had had several contracts from commercial publishers, advances were paid, but the books were never written—even though his young family could have done with the money—and the advances were refunded. It was a mystery to admirers such as myself why he did not produce the books that his great gifts and immense energy amply equipped him to do. The explanation seems to lie in his perfectionism: he completed innumerable articles to his personal satisfaction yet he was unable to do this at book length. The contract which resulted in *Anarchy in Action* was passed on from Nicolas to Colin Ward, but Colin here—and even more in other books—incorporated and built on existing work; and Paul Goodman, Alex Comfort, and George Woodcock were obvious exemplars of those who were highly successful in recycling already published material. This was the other puzzle. Nicolas published a vast amount of journalism, much of it first rate (as I trust the present selection as well as *The Anarchist Past* make entirely clear), but he never collected any of it in permanent form. I found it particularly odd that Freedom Press failed to enable him to do this and he agreed that he believed the best of his work deserved to appear as one (or more) of their volumes. The problem here seems to have been his incompatibility with Vernon Richards, who until his retirement in 1995 was responsible for selecting the Freedom Press titles and went so far as to call Nicolas in the columns of *Freedom* an "academic snob" (yet despite his entirely proper high intellectual standards nobody could have been less of a snob of whatever kind).[16]

During the first half of the 1970s Nicolas was drawn into working on Wynford Hicks's attractive papers, *Inside Story* and *Wildcat*, and collaboration was something he particularly enjoyed and was good at, for he was a social and sociable person. It was in 1983 that he first came into contact with the German anarchist historian Heiner Becker, and by the end of the decade such was their rapport that all Nicolas's scholarly output on anarchist and historical subjects was in effect jointly written with Heiner. When Peter Marshall and myself withdrew (presciently, as matters worked out) from involvement in Freedom Press's projected new quarterly publication, Heiner stepped in, conceived *Raven*, and in association with Nicolas brought out a run of seven outstanding issues (1987–89).

In 1974 Nicolas had been diagnosed as having testicular cancer. One testicle was extracted, he was treated with radiotherapy, and for a while all seemed fine. Then he began to have problems with his digestive system, he constantly vomited and his weight plummeted from twelve to eight stone. It was eventually realized that excessive doses of radiation had damaged the adjoining area of his body. A considerable length of intestine was removed and he began to recover his health. In 1983, however, it became apparent that his spine and the upper muscles of his thighs had also been affected and progressive disablement set in. As he announced in a letter to the *Guardian*:

> . . . I contracted cancer in my thirties, began to suffer from the long-term side-effects of radiotherapy in my forties, and am now suffering from progressive paralysis and other complications in my fifties. . .[17]

First he had to use crutches, but by 1997 this formerly fit and very vigorous man was confined to a wheelchair. When asked in 1994 why he did not sue the NHS, he retorted:

> Why should I? It was just bloody bad luck. I'm not complaining. I have only got praise for the people working in hospitals and the social services, even though they are all exhausted and the hospitals are filthy. If I sued the NHS for negligence and won, it would mean there was less money for other people.[18]

Ruth and Nicolas had divorced in 1982. I vividly recall meeting him in the British Museum Reading Room and (though he was later to deny this) his saying, as we were leaving, in Great Russell Street that the decree nisi had just come through and he would never make the mistake of getting married again. Yet, as in other cases where he made an impulsive dogmatic pronouncement (such as writing for the *Guardian* no more after its publication of the executioner's account of the hanging of Derek Bentley), he could be flexible and had the good sense and great fortune to marry Christine Morris (*née* Barnett), like Ruth Oppenheim a secular Jew, in 1987. Their way of life was to live during the week in the flat on the top storey of 88 Islington High Street above the RPA offices, where Christine also worked for five years, and to spend weekends at her house in Leighton Buzzard. At the end of 1999 Nicolas retired, Christine took redundancy from Relate and they withdrew to live full-time in Leighton Buzzard, from where Nicolas would be able to take the train to St Pancras and work in the new British Library. At just this time, though, the cancer returned; squamous cell carcinoma was diagnosed and at the beginning of 2000 pronounced terminal. With the fortitude that had characterized his entire life he ended it on March 7.

For many years I jested that I would never publish a book on anarchism since I could not face the prospect of Nicolas's savaging it in a review. When I eventually assembled the collection that appeared in 1989 as *For Anarchism* I sent my draft introduction for his comments and corrections—he was an old friend whose opinion I esteemed—and I was surprised when he requested that his name should not be included in the acknowledgments. His review in *Freedom* was dismissive, particularly of the introduction, and relations between us were cool for several years. What made it all the more galling is that I have come largely to concur with his criticisms. One of the most excoriating reviews I have ever read was Nicolas's demolition in *Peace News* of Richard Taylor's first, co-authored book on the nuclear disarmament movement, *The Protest Makers* (1980) and I was very uneasy when bringing it to Dick's attention. In contrast he praised *Against the Bomb* (1988) as excellent and the best history of the subject and, knowing that Dick was a friend and colleague, repeated this judgment to me over the years. Richard Taylor now tells me that he considers Nicolas's criticisms of *The Protest Makers* were entirely justified—although admitting to a "feeling of near panic, or desolation" at the time—while generously praising him as "one of the most interesting left intellectuals of the second half of the twentieth century in Britain." Scarcely surprisingly, I braced myself for the worst when Freedom Press brought out my editions of the anarchist writings of Alex Comfort and Herbert Read; but in a joint notice Nicolas, while lambasting Read and continuing to esteem Comfort, pronounced my introductions as "models of their kind—well informed, well researched, well written and well worth reading."[19] This was praise indeed! My contributions to *Herbert Read Reassessed*, another volume I edited, were also commended by Nicolas. When I rang to thank him for writing such nice things he responded tartly: "There is no need to thank me. I merely said what I think."

The present volume is intended as a tribute to a much loved, but sometimes irritating, friend. He is greatly missed: no more has there been the unmistakable large and sprawling hand on envelopes (latterly usually containing his unexpurgated copy for the "posh" papers, as he called them) or his rich, warm voice on the telephone. Someone who knew a good deal about our relationship commiserated by saying "he was like a brother to you—a difficult brother." I just hope that Nicolas would approve of this introduction and my choice of contents, as well as the extensive editing, and give his book—together with the preceding *The Anarchist Past*—a good review.

Notes
   [1] What, remarkably, I never knew until a belatedly careful reading of Nicolas's "The Spies for Peace and After" was that Paul, while still an Oxford student, had been sentenced to three months' imprisonment in 1958 for his part in describing the Signals Intelligence system in *Isis*.
   [2] See, for example, *Freedom*, November 10, 1962, and July 11, 1964. For Karl Walter's obituary: *Freedom*, November 13, 1965
   [3] W. Grey Walter, "The Development and Significance of Cybernetics," *Anarchy* 25 (March 1963). There is an obituary by "AF" [i.e. Nicolas Walter] in *Freedom*, May 28, 1977; see also *The Times*, May 9, 1977.
   [4] *New Statesman*, September 6, 1958. See also *The Times*, September 2 and 3, 1958; and Richard Clements, "S. K. Ratcliffe," *Ethical Record*, October 1968.
   [5] For Bill Beck's obituary: *The Times*, October 27, 1997.
   [6] *Encounter* 49 (October 1957). See also *London Magazine* 5 (12), (December 1958), for a letter attacking an article on Aldous Huxley by Colin Wilson.
   [7] Richard Boston, "Conversations about Anarchism," *Anarchy* 85 (March 1968), 75.

[8] *Manchester Guardian*, November 5, 1956 (reprinted in *Guardian*, May 4, 1996).

[9] This description of Comfort, omitted from *Non-violent Resistance*, appears in "Disobedience and the New Pacifism," *Anarchy* 14 (April 1962): 112.

[10] Peter Hennessy, *The Secret State: Whitehall and the Cold War* (London: Allen Lane The Penguin Press, 2002), 101 *et seq.*, 169.

[11] ". . . there are things which I have done in the general anti-war movement, which I suppose one could say are the sort of things which I've done as an anarchist. One thing was being involved in the Spies for Peace. . . . information fell into the hands of people in the Committee of 100, of whom I was one. And we published it, secretly, we didn't want to get caught' (Boston, "Conversations about Anarchism," 68). See also the cryptic clue inserted in April 1963 into *Non-violent Resistance*, as well as its 1979 postscript (see pp. 20, 51 below).

[12] *Independent*, March 13, 2000.

[13] Harold Wilson, *The Labour Government, 1964–1970: A Personal Record* (London: Weidenfeld and Nicolson and Michael Joseph, 1971), 288.

[14] Derwent May, *Critical Times: The History of the "Times Literary Supplement"* (London: HarperCollins, 2001), 356. See also May, 421–22, and Richard Boston's obituary of Crook, *Guardian*, July 21, 2005.

[15] Hunter Davies, "O Come All Ye Faithless," *Independent*, December 20, 1994. See also *Observer*, May 11, 1980, and *The Times*, December 22, 1981.

[16] "Anarchist Fundamentalists?," *Freedom*, December 1, 1990.

[17] *Guardian*, September 16, 1993.

[18] Davies, "Oh Come All Ye Faithless."

[19] *Freedom*, July 23, 1994, and reprinted in *Raven* 28 (Winter 1994).

1
THIRTY YEARS' WAR: SOME AUTOBIOGRAPHY

My first acquaintance with anarchists began exactly thirty years ago, during the double crisis of Suez and Hungary in October and November 1956. (At the age of twenty-one, I had just left home and begun my last year at university.) The simultaneous attacks by Britain and France on Egypt and by Soviet Russia on Hungary, which started the general process known as the New Left, also started my personal journey from conventional politics towards anarchism. I took part in some of the demonstrations against the Suez War, and when a letter I wrote about them was published in *The Guardian* (on Guy Fawkes Day), I was sent a friendly note from *Freedom* with some recent issues of the paper—an easy and effective way of making new contacts. This was my first introduction to the anarchist movement as a living phenomenon.

I was a fairly typical middle-class recruit to the movement during the late 1950s. I had been brought up (by my mother) as a rather orthodox liberal socialist with strong anti-religious, anti-militarist and anti-statist tendencies, but no systematic ideology or practical experience. In spite of—or because of—an excellent education in history and politics, I knew virtually nothing about anarchism, and virtually everything I did know about it was wrong. I had a grandfather who had once been an active anarchist (Karl Walter, who wrote in *Freedom* and many other papers and was a British delegate to the International Anarchist Congress in Amsterdam in 1907) and a father who often called himself an anarchist (Grey Walter, the neurologist), but I was no more influenced by them than by having a grandmother who had become a Quaker and was an active pacifist or a stepfather who had been an active Communist and was still a Marxist. It took me a couple of years' absorption of libertarian literature, involvement in left-wing politics, and resumption of family relationships to make the necessary connections and work out my own position.

I found (and find) most current libertarian writing rather unconvincing; but I remember being impressed by Alan Lovell in *New Left Review*, Chris Farley in *Peace News*, and Colin Ward in *Freedom*. I felt (and feel) much more strongly pushed in a libertarian direction by my personal experience; I was active in the old New Left and the old nuclear disarmament movement, reading papers and books, going to meetings (especially in the Partisan) and on demonstrations (from the Aldermaston March onwards), and discussing politics with everyone I knew. At the end of 1958 I was finally brought into direct contact with anarchists through my father and grandfather, the latter introducing me to Lilian Wolfe. At last the pieces fell into place, and I began to think of myself as an anarchist.

During 1959, I began to visit the Freedom Bookshop regularly and attend London Anarchist Group meetings, to make friends (and enemies) among the anarchists, and to write in anarchist papers—starting with Victor Mayes's *University Libertarian* (whose last two issues I helped my grandfather to produce during 1960), but concentrating on the publications of the Freedom Press—using my own name or initials and also an expanding series of pseudonyms. I have now written in *Freedom* for more than twenty-seven years, working first with Vero Richards and the old editorial group, and then with the protean editorial collective, and becoming more closely involved since 1980. I wrote in *Anarchy* for more than thirteen years, working first with Colin Ward and then with that even more protean editorial collective until 1974. I have also written in many other anarchist papers, producing hundreds of articles altogether, as well as various leaflets, pamphlets and books (which is what I am concentrating on now). All this time, I have earned my living in demanding editorial jobs, so I have been reluctant to spend too much time on extra editorial work, but I have now been drawn into several editorial collectives from time to time (*Freedom* and *Anarchy*, *Resistance* and *Solidarity*, *Inside Story* and *Wildcat*).

At the same time, I have written hundreds of articles in other papers—liberal and socialist, pacifist and libertarian—and I must have sent several thousand letters to the press over a period of more than thirty years. I have remained active in left-wing politics—especially in the nuclear disarmament movement (being a founding member of the Committee of 100 in 1960 and the London Committee of 100 in 1962, of the Spies for Peace in 1963, and of Peace Anonymous in 1983 and Summit 84 in 1984) and in the wider anti-war movement (involvement with the Vietnam Action Group got me two months' in prison for my part in the Brighton Church Demonstration of 1966). I have taken part in socialist activity (even working briefly for the Labour Party during the unilateralist phase of 1960–61) and in liberal campaigns (free-thought and civil liberties, capital punishment and prison reform, abortion and euthanasia, obscenity and blasphemy, official secrets and homelessness). I have joined all sorts of demonstrations, and been arrested and imprisoned. I have spoken at all sorts of meetings, and on radio and television. Somehow I have managed to enjoy a busy private life (both my children are strong libertarians), to grow ill and old, then to get better and feel young again.

The Freedom Press has been one of the few fixed points in the revolving world of politics during my adult life, and indeed during my whole life. In fact, I even feel that I can divide the past half-century into five periods which apply equally to my own experience, to the work of the Freedom Press, and to the wider left—a decade of war and despair, a decade of austerity and struggle, a decade of affluence and hope, a decade of confusion and contradiction, and a decade of disillusion and decay. During my own activity in the last three of these decades, I have found that the Freedom Press, with its periodicals and other publications, and the Freedom Bookshop have represented a rare example of persistence and consistency.

Of course, the Freedom Press has frequently been criticized during its second fifty years, just as it was during its first fifty years—but generally for the wrong reasons. Militant anarchists have accused it of being quietist, philosophical anarchists of being adventurist, dogmatic anarchists of being opportunist, pragmatic anarchists of being sectarian, and so on. I have been critical myself, but for different reasons. At times when I have been involved in particular activities, I have found it badly informed, out of touch, and too willing to rely on other papers; and at all times I have found much of the material badly thought out and badly written up. But the quick answer to such criticisms is the old anarchist imperative—if you think something should be done, do it yourself—and this is what I have tried to do.

Anyway, against all such criticisms must be put the facts that for nearly all the past hundred years and for all the past fifty years there has always been at least one regular forum in this country for expressing libertarian opinions and reporting libertarian activities, and that the people producing it have always tried both to give a clear voice to a broad central interpretation of anarchism and to give a fair hearing to all other varieties of anarchism. At most times at least some members of the group have been personally involved in the events they describe and discuss; this has been healthy. At some times the whole group—or at any rate its dominant members—have been particularly committed to various activities or attitudes; this has not been healthy. Contrary to repeated criticisms that it stands too far outside events, its strength is precisely its independence from any single group or aspect of the anarchist movement. This is one reason why it is so irritating but at the same time so important, and also why it has survived when other papers and publishers have not done so.

I wrote for other anarchist papers and publishers before the Freedom Press, I have done so on and off for nearly thirty years, and I shall go on doing so. But I have written far more here than anywhere else, and I shall go on doing so. The reason is not sectarianism or traditionalism, or even personal or political loyalty, but the old virtues of persistence and consistency. The Freedom Press has been working for anarchism longer and better than anyone or anything else, and is still doing the same job after a century. It deserves its success and survival, and therefore gets my support and co-operation.

So where do I stand after what seems like a thirty years' war? I have become increasingly committed to mainstream anarchism, because it combines my original liberalism and socialism and reconciles the contradiction between individuality and solidarity. But I still consider that, while anarchism may be the truth, it is not the whole truth, and no particular variety of it can claim to be nothing but the truth. We must recognize the value of different roads to freedom and also of differing paths in our own road. We must remember that the end does not justify the means, but that means are ends. We must learn to get on with each other, or we shall never get on at all. What matters in the end is not the anarchist movement, but anarchist movement. This is the direction I have been taking all my life, and I hope to go on doing so for the rest of it. It has been hard work, but also good fun, and even if it hasn't done much for the world, it has done a lot for me. So I thank Freedom Press for everything it has given to and taken from me. On to the second century.

Originally published in the Freedom *Centenary Edition, October 1986.*

2
AN AUTOBIOGRAPHICAL AND TEXTUAL NOTE

MY ESSAY ON NON-VIOLENCE, *NON-VIOLENT RESISTANCE: MEN AGAINST WAR*, arose not from theoretical speculation but from practical consider-ations. It was written for an occasion—or rather, a series of occasions—connected with critical periods in the history of the Committee of 100.

When the Committee of 100 was formed, in autumn 1960, I had been involved on the edge of the New Left for four years, of the nuclear disarmament movement for two and a half years, and of the anarchist movement for a year. Like so many other people, I was pushed out of conventional politics by the double stimulus of Hungary and Suez in 1956. I went to meetings and on marches, I listened and talked in places like the Partisan coffee house, I wrote in and helped to produce papers. But none of this was enough. Like so many other people again, I found the *Evening Standard* report on September 23, 1960, that Bertrand Russell and Michael Scott were organizing mass civil disobedience against nuclear weapons to be the answer to my hopes. I wrote to several papers defending them against the universal barrage of criticism, and on October 4, I had my first letter printed in *The Times*. An unexpected result was that I was invited to join the Committee of 100, as one of the unknown people brought in to make up the magic number when the supply of well-known people ran out. I was never at all important in the Committee of 100, but it was very important to me.

I attended the inaugural meeting of the Committee of 100 on October 22, 1960, and remained a member until June 1961, when I resigned because of disagreement with its rhetoric and tactics, which worried me from the beginning. But it was the best thing there was, and I continued to go to its public meetings and to go on its demon-strations, so that by the end of 1961 I had been arrested half-a-dozen times. Then I made my contribution to the propaganda, associated with the Committee's short but significant impact on British politics. I had written about it in *Freedom* and the *London Letter*, and on October 6, 1961, I wrote my first article for *Peace News,* criticizing the over-optimistic reaction to the great Trafalgar Square sit-down of September 17—a criticism which was vindicated by the debacle of the multiple demonstrations of December 9. This was when I began writing the first versions of this essay.

The monthly *Anarchy*, edited by Colin Ward and published by the Freedom Press, began publication in March 1961. In view of the impact of the Committee of 100 during the next few months, Colin decided to devote two special issues to direct action and disobedience, and in December he asked me to write a long article on each subject, empha-sizing the historical and ideological background of the Committee of 100. Meanwhile the bi-monthly *New Left Review*, which had emerged from the *Universities and Left Review* and the *New Reasoner* at the be-ginning of 1960, was suffering a painful transition from the old to the new New Left, from ex-Stalinists to neo-Trotskyists. At the end of 1961, the former group had dissolved but the latter group had not yet crystallized, and a transitional group led by Raphael Samuel was work-ing on a double issue of the paper. In November, Raphael asked me to write a long article on the Committee of 100, emphasizing its historical and ideological background.

So I began preparing all this material at once, trying to address an-archists and other libertarians on one side and Marxists and other so-cialists on the other. I found little literature on the subject which was both accessible and acceptable, so I started from scratch. I talked to a few people with direct knowledge, such as Michael Randle and April Carter in the Committee of 100, Hugh and Eileen Brock at *Peace News,* Vernon Richards and Colin Ward at *Freedom*, and I also read a great many books, pamphlets and papers in the British Museum.

The *NLR* article was meant to be urgent, so I did it first; but under Raphael's pressure I had to do it over and over again, and it appeared last. I wrote a first draft in December 1961, a second draft just be-fore Christmas, and a third draft in January 1962; this was drastically abridged in February, and I read proofs in March. Meanwhile, I did the two *Anarchy* articles. The direct action one was finished at the beginning of February and the disobedience one at the beginning of March; there were no more drafts and no proofs, and each appeared within a month, with few changes and some errors.

"Direct Action and the New Pacifism" was published in *Anarchy* 13 at the beginning of March, and "Disobedience and the New Pacifism"

in *Anarchy* 14 at the beginning of April 1962. The articles more generally welcomed by both anarchists and pacifists, and had some influence
in drawing libertarians and unilateralists together; they also won me
the friendship of Colin MacInnes and Alex Comfort. But they were
ignored elsewhere.

"Damned Fools in Utopia" was published in *New Left Review* 13–
14 at the beginning of April 1962. (The title expressed two ideas. One
was the belief—which I still hold—that the Bomb will one day cause
a situation like that which prompted Lord Melbourne's remark about
Catholic Emancipation in 1830: "What all the wise men promised has
not happened, and what all the damned fools said would happen has
come to pass"; the other was the belief—which I also still hold—that
it is more realistic to pursue utopia than what Gustav Landauer called
"topia.") The article was generally disliked by socialists, the politest
comment coming in *NLR* 15 (May–June 1962), when Mervyn Jones
said that it "compels both respect and irritation in the highest degree,
which was no doubt its purpose" (my favorite description of my writing for twenty years!). But it won praise from John Freeman in the
New Statesman on April 13, and it also led to my first broadcast. Tony
Whitby asked me to provide one minute of voice-over for film of the
Wethersfield demonstration in a BBC Gallery programme about the
nuclear disarmament movement; it was broadcast on April 12, and my
little speech was published in *Peace News* on April 20. A few weeks later,
Alastair Hetherington asked me to write an article on the Committee of
100 for *The Guardian*, which was published on June 22, 1962.

Meanwhile, the Committee of 100 had expanded and exploded
in all directions, the original Committee being superseded by a dozen
regional Committees. I attended the inaugural meeting of the London
Committee of 100 on April 1, 1962, and remained a member until
summer 1965, when I resigned for much the same reasons as before.
During its first year I was more active in the movement than at any
other time, and I met my wife and most of the people who have been
our friends ever since. When the Committee began to disintegrate after the Cuba Crisis of October 1962, we were involved in the developments that led to the Spies for Peace but at the same time my articles
were resurrected.

During the long winter of 1962–3, many attempts were made
to work out the theory of what had been done in practice during the
previous year or two. Private and public meetings were held all over
the country to discuss various aspects of non-violence in the context
of the achievements of the Committee of 100. The Committee itself,

which already had several specialized sub-committees (Legal, Welfare, Industrial, International), established the Schools for Non-violence for those with experience of recent activity to talk to each other and to newcomers. One London group involved in the Schools for Non-violence, which was based at Ann Davidson's house in Hampstead and was called Nonviolence 63, decided to produce some publications on the subject. Finding that *Anarchy* 13 was already out of print, Ann and Dennis Gould suggested reprinting my two *Anarchy* articles together as a pamphlet; I suggested that I should rewrite them as a single essay, and this was agreed in March 1963.

As I said in the preface, "I have tried to put the two articles together into a single account, and I have also removed some dead wood, corrected some mistakes, and added some now material I have found during the last year." I incorporated material that had previously appeared in *Freedom*, the *London Letter*, *Peace News* and *New Left Review*. I also inserted a surreptitious reference to the Spies for Peace:

> In the past we had to decide not to become war criminals. Today we have to decide to become peace criminals, or else become war criminals by default. We have to be prisoners of our own side (like the Good Soldier Schweik), and spies against our own side (like Our Man in Havana).

No one noticed.

I rewrote the essay in March, and Ann and Dennis got it printed by the Goodwin Press in April. I had wanted to call it *Men against War*, but Dennis wanted to call it *Non-violent Resistance*; so we compromised and called it *Non-violent Resistance: Men against War*. The little pamphlet, which had forty pages and cost 1s 6d (7½p), was meant to be ready for the Aldermaston March on April 12, but because of production difficulties I saw proofs on April 8; the 2,000 copies were printed the following week and published on April 19. Perhaps this was just as well, since the march was of course dominated by the Spies for Peace pamphlet and demonstration. Anyway my effort fell almost dead-born from the press. It was ignored in most places, unfavorably reviewed in a few places, and it received one very strong protest. Stuart Morris, the veteran secretary of the Peace Pledge Union, wrote on me on May 6, 1963, complaining about my references to the PPU. I promised him that I would take his criticism into account if the pamphlet were ever reprinted; I am glad to be able to do so at last, after sixteen years, and in a PPU publication—not that he would have liked the result!

Stuart said that I made the following mistakes.
1. I was wrong to say that "the unfortunate result of the formation of the Peace Pledge Union was to drive the religious pacifists and the political anti-militarists apart"; he said the PPU was not "predominantly religious" and included both kinds of war resisters.
2. I was wrong to say that in the Second World War "thousands of men broke their pledge"; he gave no alternative figure.
3. I was wrong to say that in the Second World War the PPU "was reduced to publishing vague propaganda and totting up the numbers of COs in the registrations"; he said that it opposed conscription, helped COs in many ways, campaigned against particular war policies, and indeed protested so strongly against the war in general that it was prosecuted for a poster in 1940.

My replies are as follows, based partly on my reading of Sybil Morrison's official history of the PPU, *I Renounce War* (1962):

1. Most non-religious war resisters found the PPU to be predominantly religious in tone, an impression confirmed by the book. Of course there were many non-religious members, but the leadership was always largely Christian and even clerical. Even so, I may have been unfair.
2. The book says that more than 100,000 men signed the peace pledge by 1939 but Dick Sheppard rightly said that 50 percent of them would change their minds if war came. No actual figure is given, but it seems clear that thousands of men did break their pledges. I don't think I was unfair.
3. The book shows that, although the PPU did what it could, this amounted to little more than vague propaganda and practical work for COs. It is significant that the 1940 prosecution led to the offending poster being withdrawn and those responsible agreeing to be bound over—whereas Trotskyists and anarchists prosecuted for similar offences persisted in their war resistance until they were imprisoned. I don't think I was unfair.

Non-violent Resistance: Men against War soon went out of print, as had *Anarchy* 13 and as did *Anarchy* 14 and *NLR* 13–14. In 1964, I gave several talks on "dogmatic" and "pragmatic" non-violence, and I began to turn them into an article for *Anarchy* to be called "Beyond Non-violence," but I abandoned it because the issue seemed to be moribund. In 1965, when my wife and I finally left the Committee of 100, we expressed our view of the experience in a polemic with Diana Shelley—see "The Committee of 100: Ends and Means." In 1966, I took part in my last illegal demonstration, and in 1967 I spent two months in prison as a result. In 1969, after the nuclear disarmament movement had been supplanted by the student movement and after the "events" of 1968, I wrote my essay "About Anarchism"—first published as *Anarchy* 100 (June 1969), immediately republished as a pamphlet, and frequently reprinted and translated since then—in which I gave my last thoughts on non-violence and the Committee of 100.

I wouldn't want to reprint this essay myself, but I wouldn't want to revise or repudiate it. I agree with what I said, though not always with the way I said it. I still prefer resistance to non-resistance and non-violent resistance to violent resistance, but I am even more pessimistic than I was in 1961–3. I still think that the pacifists are the best people in the anti-war movement, but I am even more convinced that neither dogmatic nor pragmatic non-violence will succeed, and that war will come. Even so, it was—and is—worth trying, and I am glad I tried it. I hope my ideas are wrong, but I know my actions were right.

Originally published in Studies in Nonviolence 5 *(April 1979).*

eason

33 Shop Street
Galway

PRODUCT		QTY	EURO	VAT
09-06-11 17:53 SALE	6 9440			15

SPECIAL ORDER TITL   1   22.35 1

TOTAL	1	22.35
CASH		50.00
TOTAL TENDERED		50.00
CHANGE		27.65

Tax Summary	Goods	Tax
1=VAT 0.00	22.35	0.00

VAT Reg No.: IE8T49114D

Thank you for shopping with us today.

Eason - worth another look

www.easons.com

| 08-06-11 17:53 SALE S 9440 | 15 | | |
| PRODUCT | QTY | EURO | VAT |

| SPECIAL ORDER TITL | 1 | 22.35 | 1 |

TOTAL	1	22.35
CASH		50.00
TOTAL TENDERED		50.00
CHANGE		27.65

| Tax Summary | Goods | Tax |
| 1=VAT 0.00 | 22.35 | 0.00 |

3
DAMNED FOOLS IN UTOPIA

ADVOCATES OF UNILATERAL NUCLEAR DISARMAMENT LABOR UNDER TWO contradictory but complementary disadvantages—what they want is almost unattainable, and what they fear is almost unimaginable.

The hopes of idealistic unilateralists and multilateralists are that the balance of terror will be lightened either by one side after the other or by both sides at once. But every realistic unilateralist or multilateralist knows the far more probable future—that the balance will become heavier and heavier until the scales break under the strain, and the present nuclear stalemate will suddenly become mutual checkmate. On the other hand, even the most bitterly realistic unilateralist cannot accept the approaching death of mankind as a fact to live with—like the corpse in Ionesco's play, it would grow until there was no room for anything else. We talk glibly enough about the risk of a nuclear holocaust, but we get up each morning without expecting to find the mushroom cloud at the bottom of the garden. Perhaps we don't really see how we can get rid of the Bomb, but we don't really see how they could drop it either. So we try to avert the unimaginable by pursuing the unattainable.

This helps to explain the curious unreality of the whole business. "No Taxation without Representation!," "Home Rule for Ireland!," "Votes for Women!," "Not a Penny off the Pay; Not a Second on the Day!," even "Workers of the World Unite!"—these are slogans with definite meanings. *Ban the Bomb!* is a very different matter. The demands of most protest movements would bring immediate benefits to specific groups of people. Again, nuclear disarmament is a very different matter. No one who thinks that "Ban the Bomb!" is enough; but no two people seem to agree on anything more. The only thing we can all see is unilateral nuclear disarmament, somewhere on the horizon. This is our utopia, like the Kingdom of Heaven, or the Rule of the Saints, or the

Dictatorship of the Proletariat. We will work out everything else when we get there. The odd thing is that there are so many of us. The unilateralist movement is unique in the history of political dissent outside the class-struggle: it is a utopian movement with mass support.

One of the most interesting results is that attention has been drawn away from the movement's actual proposals towards its methods. Its history will be told—if there is time to tell it—not in terms of the shift from Little Englander isolationism to positive neutralism or of the particular disarmament plans that have been put forward, but in terms of the deepening conflict between persuasion and resistance, between the techniques of orthodox demonstration and agitation and of unorthodox direct action and civil disobedience. This history is indeed already being laid down in an acceptable fossilized form, as vague memories harden into convenient myths. Ask anyone when the unilateralist movement began, and who began it. Ask for the dates of the first examples of civil disobedience and direct action against the Bomb, of the first Aldermaston demonstration and the first London sit-down. In almost every case the reply will be connected to some big name or other, to the adherence of a reputable person or body to an otherwise disreputable movement. For although unilateralism is a utopian cause, there is a sort of conspiracy to avoid admitting this openly, to pretend it is in some way practicable within the present environment and is therefore "respectable"—and in particular to suck it into the official labor movement, pouring it into the mould of traditional "Labourism," or (more plausibly) to suck it into the unofficial labor movement, pouring it this time into the mould of the traditional class struggle. The tendency is always to assimilate it or to explain it in conventional terms.

But the fact is that the unilateralist movement is essentially pacifist and anarchist, and was begun by people normally regarded as cranks. This isn't just a tidbit of useless information—it is a point of fundamental significance. The full flower of British unilateralism has only been visible for four or five years; its roots, which go back half a century, lie in the underground world of personal and political extremism. It will be known by its fruits, but it can only be understood by its roots. After Catholic Emancipation 130 years ago, Lord Melbourne is said to have remarked: "What all the wise men promised has not happened, and what all the damned fools said would happen has come to pass." It would be hard to think of a better comment on the story of unilateralism in this country.

Take the genealogy of the Committee of 100, for example. Its dominant parent—which it absorbed last July—was the Direct Action

Committee against Nuclear War, which derived from the Non-Violent Resistance Group, which was formed under the name "Operation Gandhi" by some members of the Non-Violent Commission of the Peace Pledge Union, which soon after its formation absorbed the No More War Movement, which derived from the No Conscription Fellowship, which was the organization of extremist conscientious objectors during the First World War. Even the almost painfully respectable Campaign for Nuclear Disarmament, which was the other parent of the Committee of 100, derives from the National Council for the Abolition of Nuclear Weapon Tests, which was formed by some pacifists in the offices of the National Peace Council. Or take the activities of the Committee of 100. During 1961 it was responsible for six major sit-downs in the Metropolitan Police District, each involving between 500 and 5,000 people. Then was the first London sit-down the one led by Bertrand Russell and Michael Scott on February 18, 1961? No, you may say if you know a thing or two, it was the one that followed the launching meeting of CND on February 17, 1958; and you may add that this was the beginning of the real unilateralist movement. But you will be wrong. The first London sit-down was more than ten years ago, on January 11, 1952, when eleven pacifists in Operation Gandhi sat down outside the War Office and were fined 30s (£1.50) apiece; the unilateralist movement had been going for years when CND stepped in to take it over, and it was always a crank movement.

And it still is. When the Committee of 100 turns from civil disobedience in urban canters to direct action against military bases in the countryside, its crankiness is revealed, and its big names and much of its mass support fade away of their own accord. In fact, you will find that nearly all the people in the Committee who do the hard work (and get the long prison sentences) are obscure pacifists or anarchists or both. This is not a coincidence—the Committee of 100 is basically a crank organisation dressed up in respectable clothes, and when it reverts to its basic activity its clothes are quickly discarded. The same would probably be true of CND if its leaders weren't so determined to be respectable and so frightened of taking their clothes off. The real achievement of the Committee of 100 is that it has managed to enjoy the support of so many ordinary people for its extraordinary measures. They don't usually go out into the streets and break the law on purpose in protest against the Warfare State; but illegal demonstrations of completely altruistic and almost completely non-violent passive resistance have abruptly become a commonplace of British politics, and have even been taken as a model in Germany, Scandinavia and North America.

Not that the idea is new—what *is* new is the scale of the thing. Socrates and Jesus, Fox and Bunyan, Thoreau and Tolstoy all preached passive resistance, but they were individualists, and their passive resistance was inner-directed, bearing witness rather than making propaganda. Gandhi and his successors have organized mass passive resistance, but they have opposed racial and national oppression rather than the military policies of democratic states; and the same is true of the outbreaks of passive resistance to the Nazis in occupied Europe. The Chartists, Suffragettes and Hunger Marchers often staged mass illegal demonstrations, but they were seldom non-violent and never altruistic. Only the Bomb seems to have been able to bring the Indian ideas of *ahimsa* and *satyagraha* home to us, to replace Eichmann's *Befehl ist Befehl* with Luther's *Hier stehe ich*, to stimulate mass other-directed passive resistance.

The achievement of the Committee of 100 is all the more remarkable when it is considered in the light of earlier attempts at illegal action against the Bomb. That first London sit-down involved eleven people, the one outside Mildenhall US base in July 1952 involved only two. Other pioneer demonstrations by the Operation Gandhi Non-Violent Resistance Group—such as those at Aldermaston in April 1952, at Porton in March 1953, at Harwell in April 1953, and at Woolwich in July 1954—were attended by a few dozen pacifists at a time and were quickly forgotten. The fact that almost everyone puts the first Aldermaston demonstration six years late shows how ineffective the real first one was.

Passive resistance was put on the political map by the Direct Action Committee (DAC), which was formed in November 1957, and its brave demonstrations at Aldermaston in September 1958, at North Pickenham in December 1958, at Harrington in January 1960, at Finningley in July 1960, and at the Holy Loch in May 1961—together with those at Foulness in April and May 1960 (organized by the Southend CND)—have become a vital part of the unilateralist mythology. We should also remember the attempts to enter the Sahara test-area in December 1959 and January 1960, the CND demonstration at Selby in July 1959, the invasion of the lost village of Imber in January 1961, and guerrilla activity like that of the Polaris Action *francs-tireurs* during last spring and summer. Nor should we forget that the first Aldermaston march in April 1958 was originally organized by a sub-committee of DAC as a direct action demonstration, but was more or less taken over by CND, along with Gerald Holtom's nuclear disarmament symbol. The CND leadership borrowed a radical technique without intending to use it radically; after 1958 they therefore turned the march back to front, so that it became a march *from* Aldermaston instead of *to* Aldermaston, almost a symbol of the retreat from direct action to a conventional demonstration—but the rank and file remained radical, which was why they flocked so rapidly to the banner of the Committee of 100 when it was raised during 1961.

But there were never more than about a hundred people taking part in any illegal unilateralist demonstration before the formation of the Committee of 100 in October 1960; after three years it seemed that DAC had made no real impact at all, while CND had reached the stage that it often couldn't count its own numbers. But of course the direct action sit-downs were only the top of the DAC iceberg, just as the more spectacular marches were only the top of the CND iceberg. The much more important activity has been going on all the time beneath the surface, as CND built up the mass support and the structure of local organizations, and DAC got inactive law-abiding people used to the ideas of doing things themselves and even of breaking the law together for conscience's sake—and as left-wing periodicals tried to knock the unilateralist case into a plausible shape and kept the discussion going. *Enfin* Schoenman *vint*, and mass civil disobedience became the most prominent technique and the Committee of 100 the most prominent organization in the movement.

But civil disobedience is not direct action. Here we come up against the difficulty that in this context "direct action" must be interpreted rather metaphorically. The idea comes from syndicalist doctrine, where it involves a general stay-in strike and decentralized do-it-yourself revolution, as opposed to the more familiar *coup d'état* carried out by an elite. In theory, unilateralist direct action involves an analogous pre-emptive strike against war and decentralized do-it-yourself disarmament, as opposed in this instance to disarmament carried out by a Labour Party converted by the CND pressure group. But in practice it has involved something altogether different, so that none of the "direct action" demonstrations I have mentioned actually qualifies as genuine direct action at all. Let's face facts. A non-violent blockage by a few devoted cranks of a single entrance to a single military base, which is tolerated by the authorities for a few hours and then cleared and punished by small fines or prison sentences, cannot even begin to constitute a real threat to the Warfare State—though no doubt it counts as conduct prejudicial to good order and discipline. The nearest approach to genuine direct action came in the first demonstration at North Pickenham, and the result was sadly significant: the demonstrators were attacked, not only by servicemen and police, but also by the civilian laborers working on the site.

We have now managed to raise a few hundred or even thousand people instead of a few dozen or even scores; but we should recognize just how narrow our limits still are, whether the voluntary limits we impose on ourselves by the discipline of non-violence, or the involuntary limits imposed on us by the enormous power of the State and the dead weight of the acquiescent or indifferent majority. Many people have been converted by the cranks, but many more haven't even been stirred, and the State stands firmly in our way quite confident of their support. We march or sit in splendid but rather terrifying isolation.

After all, unilateralist demonstrations have been designed as a form of "propaganda by deed." But they aren't very effective deeds; nor are they very effective propaganda, if by propaganda we mean something more than preaching to the converted and encouraging each other. How many working-class people have left their jobs in, or even gone on token strike against, armament production? How many middle-class people have committed themselves in their private and professional lives, not just in opinion and occasional demonstration? How many decent-minded scientists and technologists and technicians work on defence? How many people realize that we are already involved in the next war before it comes, just as the Germans were already involved in the Nazi regime before it was established? How many people see that war—all war—is mass murder?

The fact is that the members and supporters of the Committee of 100 are still cranks, and their disturbing ideas and actions are written off by most people just as briefly as most of us would have written off the first London sit-down ten years ago. We have earned the name of crank by calling pacifists and anarchists cranks in the past. We should come to terms with this difficulty instead of trying to pretend it isn't really there. Too many people who support the Committee, like too many of those who supported DAC, suffer from a delusion of grandeur, what might be called the sickness of political onanism—the tendency to believe in one's own propaganda. The Committee of 100 is the best unilateralist body we have, but after all the CND marches and all the DAC sit-downs—and, more important, after all the grinding educational work of both organizations—the people who came forward to help the Committee were still largely the same young *déracinés*, middle-class intellectuals and bohemians who had dominated the unilateralist movement all along, and frighteningly few of those who didn't come forward were even sympathetic. We may be a happy few, but we are still only a few.

This wouldn't necessarily matter, but here our non-violence has its own disadvantages. The immediate one is that as soon as we meet the slightest physical resistance we are powerless. If we ever did manage to get inside a military base by surprise, we would be checked by the first man who stood in our way. Or would we? How deep does our non-violence really go? How far is it merely symbolic of our impotence, a sublimation of our frustration by the infinite violence before us? How non-violent would we be if it seemed that violence might get us further than non-violence? Is our non-violence really what Gandhi called "the non-violence of the weak?" Whatever the answer is, it is worth remembering that the successful use of non-violence depends on the non-use of violence that is kept in the background—on the existence, that is, of potential power that could give victory anyway, of an overwhelming physical or moral superiority on the side of the non-violent demonstrators. Gandhi won not just because he was non-violent, but because he was supported by the mass of the Indian people and because the British *raj* had a guilty conscience. Things are different now—Nehru sends Russell his congratulations, but another tale is told by Kashmir, Hyderabad and Goa. Gandhi was in opposition; Nehru is in office. God is always on the side of the big battalions, even if they hold their fire. And although the Committee of 100 can muster bigger battalions than any of its predecessors in illegal activity, they are not big enough by a long, long way.

So the Committee of 100 belongs not to the tradition of majority revolution but to the tradition of minority dissent. Because its carrot is out of reach and its stick is out of sight, it can scarcely shift the mule of public opinion an inch. Because it doesn't appeal to religion or descend to intrigue or resort to violence, all it can do is sit, in Colin Ward's phrase, "as a symbolic gesture of its own impotence." We have the initiative, but what can we do with it?

The Committee certainly can't afford to try and seize power by direct action; on the other hand, it can't afford to wait for opinion to swing round in its favor—this would amount to sheer *attentisme*, the primrose path trodden by every minority that lives by faith alone, imagines it has willed the means when it has only willed the end, and wastes its time waiting for Lefty or Godot. The balance of terror keeps us on the brink of destruction, but it hasn't created anything like a revolutionary situation.

This is where people start asking what we should do, what the Committee should become. I think this quite the wrong approach. We should be asking what we *are* doing, what the Committee is *now*, particularly when so many sections of the left are taking a not entirely unselfish interest in its future. Communists and orthodox socialists see it as an unfortunate deviation which should be straightened out; pacifists and unorthodox socialists see it as an eccentric *avant-garde* which should be properly organized and disciplined; right-wing pacifists and left-wing liberals are disturbed by its militancy, and project their unconscious approval on to the irrelevant civil liberties issue; anarchists and syndicalists see it as an imperfect model of anarcho-syndicalist action which should be made more consistent and self-conscious; even people who are very close to or actually in the Committee are none too sure what it is. Advice comes from all sides, detailed programs from several. No one is indifferent. The Committee of 100, it seems, is important a year and a half after it was formed; sometimes it looks rather like Little Red Riding Hood.

But, as Thurber pointed out, it is not so easy to fool little girls nowadays as it used to be. Siren voices call, but unilateralists have learnt from other unlucky people to stop up their ears. Two main temptations are proffered to them. First there is the straightforward demand that they should enter (or re-enter) the official labor movement by working through the Labour Party; this follows the old doctrine that there is no salvation outside the Church. *Tribune* and the *New Statesman* and most of the Labour Left take this line, deploring our disillusion with parliamentary democracy and begging us to return to "political action." It is an oddly narrow view of political action that excludes mass demonstrations of passive resistance (and tries hard to ignore them when they occur), but never mind—the point is taken. The simple answer is that we don't trust the Labour Party—how many times have even the best of them silently swallowed their consciences for every time they have noisily followed them? No realistic unilateralist was surprised when the Scarborough vote was reversed at Blackpool, or expected conventional trade- union action to be any more successful than unconventional direct action. We remember the variously gruesome fates of Keir Hardie and Ramsay MacDonald and George Lansbury and Aneurin Bevan, and have no illusions about the chances of the Labour Party ever going genuinely unilateralist, of a Labour government ever taking Britain out of the Cold War. We cannot forget who began making the British Bomb. We cannot forget the behavior of almost all social democrats in every national war. We have become too familiar with the asymptotic curve of parliamentary socialism, which starts at right angles to the Establishment but flattens out as it approaches power until in the end it runs parallel to its old enemy. No, we aren't interested in the Labour Party, thank you very much.

Nor are we attracted by the Communist Party or the Socialist Labour League or the Socialist Party of Great Britain or even the Independent Labour Party. But there is the second and much subtler temptation before us: the demand that the Committee of 100 should take part in conventional politics on its own account, as part of a wider independent mass movement on the left, to include CND and the New Left and dissident socialists and pacifists in general, with a platform of unilateralism, neutralism, anti-colonialism and so on. As put forward by Edward Thompson and John Saville in *Peace News* last October, the first step in such a movement would be unilateralist intervention at a by-election on such a scale that Thompson sums it up in one word—BANG. Yes, it would be rather good fun, but say the result was bad. What word would sum it up then? Or say the result was good—say an independent unilateralist candidate was returned to the Commons. What then? Would we put up more? Would they apply for the Labour whip? Aren't there dozens of unilateralists in Parliament already? What good have they been able to do? And what if the Labour Party proscribed the unilateralist movement? What would the Labour Left do then—form a new ILP, or scuttle back into the fold? I can see a lot of unilateralists contracting a nasty case of Labourism, and pouring all their energy into a futile parliamentary campaign.

The real question is: Does the Committee of 100 belong to the official labour movement? And the answer is surely: No. Both the temptations before it would make it go where it wouldn't fit. Isn't the distinction between the Committee and CND precisely that CND, at least as far as the intentions of its leaders go, *does* belong to the official labor movement? Anyone in the Committee who wants to work along conventional political lines as well can easily do so by following the "Fabian" pattern of CND; and in fact there is a considerable overlap in the membership and support of the two organizations, and more liaison between them than is realized. But it was precisely because so many of the CND rank and file were impatient of their leaders' moderation that the Committee of 100 was so suddenly successful. If the Committee doesn't belong to the official labor movement, where does it belong? It does to some extent belong to the *unofficial* labor movement, which has remained immune to Marx's "incurable disease of parliamentary cretinism." Hence the formation of its industrial sub-committee last October and the loose alliance with the rather conspiratorial syndicalist movement. There is a similar alliance with the anti-racialist movement; Operation Gandhi itself organized a demonstration at South Africa House back in September 1952, and mass passive resistance was after all developed in the struggle of coloured people against their white oppressors. It is possible to see a valid extension of the direct action technique into areas like housing, poor relief, traffic, subtopia, bureaucracy—wherever it seems appropriate. But what cannot be valid is any pretence that the Committee is in some way part of the socialist movement or can be properly discussed in terms of socialist thought. Socialists must stop being either patronizing or possessive about unilateralists.

The Committee of 100 should really be seen as a unique organization representing the political "abstentionism" mentioned in the editorial of *NLR* 6, which remarked in passing that "anarchism and libertarianism has been a most fertile element in the Campaign": it had already born fruit. The formation of the Committee of 100 in the very month of the Scarborough vote was a deliberate rejection of conventional unorthodoxy in general, of the Labour Left in particular. It is true that many sitters (as well as marchers) remain in the Labour Left, but they aren't at home there. They are really what Don Arnott has called "refugees" and Jay Blumler has called "*emigrés*" from conventional politics; they are cranks. We find ourselves perched on the horns of Weber's imaginary dilemma, torn between the "ethic of responsibility" and the "ethic of ultimate ends." But we have come to see that the worship of responsibility leads straight to profound irresponsibility in a nuclear age, that only the constant memory of ultimate ends can ensure truly responsible action. Means *are* ends, in practice.

The trouble is that far too few people on the left understood that the unilateralist movement, as the editorial of *NLR* 8 put it, "eludes all the fixed categories of 'politics'"; and far too many try to explain the Committee of 100 with the old formulas when the old formulas aren't valid any more, if they ever were. If I may postulate a political equivalent of thermodynamics, its first law is that political energy cannot be created or destroyed, that no political change occurs in isolation; and its second law is that every political system tends to run down, for political entropy is just as real as physical entropy, though even more indefinable (see Zamyatin's essay "On Literature, Revolution and Entropy," 1924). Thus once you start protesting against the Bomb rather than against class oppression or personal violence, you find yourself opposing all war and the whole Warfare State. And when socialists start opposing war as such and pacifists start opposing the State as such, their separate paths lead directly to non-violent anarchism, and energy—in the form of numbers, money, effort, time, sacrifice and trust—begins to flow rapidly away from the socialist and pacifist movements into the new unilateralist movement. This is exactly what has happened. Of course it would be just as absurd to define the Committee of 100 in old-fashioned anarchist terms, but it is no coincidence that a lot of things about the Committee that have thrilled or mystified socialists and pacifists are quite familiar to anarchists.

The conventional wisdom defines democracy in terms of the stock notions of representation, delegation, elections, officers, discipline and so on. The Committee of 100 has thrown all this out as so much dirty bathwater and kept the baby—democracy defined in terms of face-to-face liberty, equality and fraternity. With this in mind, turn to what *Peace News* said after the Trafalgar Square sit-down last September when it called for "a new basis to society and government" as the only framework in which unilateralism could be effective. Then remember Alan Lovell telling his interviewers in *NLR* 8 about his discovery that "the whole question of non-violent civil disobedience is very closely tied up with decentralization" and about his conception of "a kind of gradual revolution" in which "you take direct action, yet you never actually capture power or anything like that," and commenting that his argument "involves a whole different kind of politics." There is also the editorial of *NLR* 6, remarking that the anarchist case "is weak largely because it has not been put." And there is John Morris claiming that "these concepts of direct democracy are new to modern political thought."

These are put forward as new ideas. But are Winstanley, Rousseau, Godwin, Fourier, Owen, Proudhon, Bakunin, Morris, Kropotkin, Cole and all the rest really nothing more than names? Has the anarchist stream in socialist and pacifist thought really been driven so far underground? In fact, "formal" anarchists have been playing a private game with the New Left and the new pacifist movement, finding in their articles and discussions dozens of ideas straight out of anarchism, which have been dressed up as new departures in socialism and/or pacifism. Not that this is any compliment for the anarchists. On the contrary, it shows up their failure to break through the thought-barrier surrounding them. But it also shows up the disastrous failure of so many socialists and pacifists to follow the logic of their ideas and actions through to inconvenient conclusions. We are all so helplessly imprisoned by our own orthodoxies that this is not surprising, but it is still regrettable. Nothing is quite as barren as sectarianism, especially when everything is in what Captain Boyle would call a "state of chassis." It is pure sectarianism that leads people to tell the Committee of 100 its own business; I think the Committee would be killed stone dead if it tried to act out of character by following the advice of people whose interests aren't really the same as its own; I think the Committee has its own function and should stick to it.

What I have been leading up to is the insistence that the unilateralist movement and particularly the Committee of 100 must be discussed in its own terms. The criterion of discussion is not what you or I think the Committee should do in the future but what it has done already and is doing now. It is in a way an existentialist organisation, drawing life from what it does. Its detailed relationship with, say, CND and the New Left is irrelevant, and will certainly be much healthier if it remains as informal as possible so people can wander in and out when and where they like. It has plenty of work in its own job, which as *Peace News* said is "building a resistance movement which will enable us to achieve 'the revolution.'"

Of course, this isn't the old cataclysmic revolution, but the Committee with its sinister name is a revolutionary organization. How the Committee will succeed, if it does succeed, we can't tell. Didn't Marx and Bakunin agree it was wicked to think about the future? But right now the Committee leads the *maquis* of the British section of the third force in the Cold War. It is the spearhead of the *minorité consciente* of modern mass society. René Cutforth wondered whether the Aldermaston Marchers weren't "the only people left alive in Britain"; the sitters are just a bit more alive—and mad, of course. It would be reasonable to label them "infantile leftists," as Kingsley Martin does, if only the adult rightists hadn't got us into such a bloody horrible mess. In the Country of the Blind, and all that. The unilateralist movement is at the head of the "permanent protest," in which there is no success or failure, no distinction between ends and means, no hope or despair, no gain or loss—"but today the struggle." The State is not abolished: it is whittled away. Or, as Gandhi put it, "a society organized and run on the basis of complete non-violence would be the purest anarchy."

In practice this means that discussion of the Committee's future should centre on tactics rather than strategy, on its day-to-day contact with the authorities and the public—the danger of the middle-class image; the danger of relapsing into obstructionism, even nihilism; the danger of seeing arrest and imprisonment as the individual goal, the numbers taking part and getting arrested as the collective goal; the danger of the personality cult and of the leaders becoming a sort of stage army as they pass through the courts and jails over and over again; the danger of too much or too little organization or bureaucracy or unanimity; the danger of self-escalation, of building belief on hope and hope on belief until the whole edifice collapses. Above all, I am convinced we should resist any idea of take-over bids by or for the Committee, of getting mixed up in conventional politics in any way. Our strength is drawn from our unwavering uncompromising independence, our personal and political autonomy—let's keep it that way. Our only chance is to confront people with the Bomb in the way we have chosen. This is the central issue, the only justification for the Committee's existence.

But I must admit that I feel deeply pessimistic about the outcome. I think our utopia will never come, will always be nowhere, until the awful consummation of the world. I think the "damned fools" will be right, as they usually are, and the real damned fools will go and drop their damned bomb on each other's damned topias. I think this is the way the world will end, with a bang and a whimper of *I told you so*. And my only brief consolation will be that I joined the right damned fools in utopia.

Originally published in New Left Review *13–14 (January–April 1962).*

4
NON-VIOLENT RESISTANCE: MEN AGAINST WAR

WE KNOW FROM ARISTOTLE'S *POLITICS*, WRITTEN IN THE FIRST DAWN OF Western political thought, that "man is by nature a political animal." That is, men want to rule and to be ruled. They are *authoritarian*, obsessed with power and obedience and slavery and inequality and competition and pain and hatred. But, as Oscar Wilde said in *The Soul of Man under Socialism* (1891), "wherever there is a man who exercises authority, there is a man who resists authority." For men also want to rebel. They are *libertarian*, obsessed with freedom and disobedience and liberty and equality and fraternity and pleasure and love. The motto of the ruler is *Befehl ist Befehl*. The motto of the rebel is *Non serviam*.

The myths of Prometheus and Lucifer, of the revolt of the small against the great, are some of the oldest and finest of all. Adam's first action (even before he "knew" Eve) was to disobey his creator. Nor is mythological disobedience mere nihilism. Prometheus brought fire to the earth, Lucifer brought light; Adam ate the fruit of the tree of knowledge of good and evil, and he did not die, as God had threatened, but his eyes were opened. "Disobedience, in the eyes of anyone who has read history," said Wilde, is man's original virtue. It is through disobedience that progress has been made, through disobedience and through rebellion.

DISOBEDIENCE

According to *The Communist Manifesto* (1848), "the history of all hitherto existing society is the history of class struggles." That is, haves try to remain haves and have-nots try to become haves. But there are two factors that confuse the simple issue of revolution. One is that many have-nots accept inequality, and many haves accept equality. The great majority of men are willing slaves—they must be, or they wouldn't be slaves. The great majority of revolutionary leaders, on the other hand, begin with all sorts of advantages of birth, wealth, education, or luck. Marx and Engels, Bakunin and Kropotkin, nearly all such men were haves who turned their coats. (Prometheus and Lucifer were not men— one was a Titan, and the other was an Angel.)

The other confusing factor is that the revolt against a present inequality usually intends not so much to destroy it as to replace it by a future inequality based on a different principle—to expropriate the expropriators—and even without this intention the result is usually the same. Every revolution is "betrayed," even if it has no Eighteenth Brumaire, simply because power tends to corrupt and absolute power corrupts absolutely. The Commonwealth of 1649 is followed by the Protectorate of 1653, the Declaration of Rights by the Reign of Terror, the February Revolution by the October Revolution, the new dawn by the new darkness at noon. The classless society never comes, the State never withers away. "Revolution is the most authoritarian thing imaginable," said Engels.

Gustav Landauer, the German anarcho-socialist, developed a remarkable theory of revolution in his book *The Revolution* (1907), which has unfortunately never been translated into English. The core of his theory is as follows:

> Revolution concerns every aspect of human life—not just the State, the class structure, industry and commerce, arts and letters, education and learning, but a combination of all these social factors which is at a given moment in a state of relative stability. This general combination of social factors in a state of relative stability I will call the *topia*.
>
> The topia is the source of wealth as well as hunger, of housing as well as homelessness. The topia rules all the details of human existence. It fights wars abroad, it exports and imports goods, it opens and closes frontiers. The topia encourages intelligence as well as stupidity, good behavior as well as bad, happiness as well as unhappiness, satisfaction as well as dissatisfaction. The strong hand of the topia is felt even where it does not belong, in the private life of the individual and the family . . .
>
> The relative stability of the topia gradually changes until it reaches a point of delicate equilibrium. This change in the stability of the topia is caused by the *utopia*. The utopia belongs by nature not so much to social as to personal life. It is the combination of individual efforts and wishes which usually exist singly and separately, but which in a moment of crisis and under the influence of intoxicating enthusiasm can unite and organize themselves into a whole, into a form

of social life, with the purpose of creating a perfect topia which will have no unpleasant or unjust factors at all. But the utopia leads to a new topia, which is essentially different from the old topia, but is still a topia.

From this, Landauer derived the "first law of revolution," which is that "every topia is followed by a topia, which is followed by a utopia, and so on," and he went on to define revolution: Revolution is the period between the end of the old topia and the beginning of the new topia. It is therefore the path from one topia to the next, from one relative stability to another, through chaos and revolt, individualism, heroism and bestiality, the loneliness of the great and the total disappearance of the atom in the mass.

It is hardly surprising to learn that Landauer was killed during the collapse of the Bavarian Soviet Republic in 1919, when a utopia turned back into a topia.

A similar idea was developed by the Russian writer Yevgeni Zamyatin, the author of the anti-Bolshevik novel *We*. In 1925 he confessed that he was no longer a Bolshevik, and a few months before he had written a remarkable essay "On Literature, Revolution and Entropy" (1924):

> Revolution is everywhere and in all things; it is infinite, there is no final revolution, no end to the sequence of integers. Social revolution is only one in the infinite sequence of integers. The law of revolution is not a social law, it is immeasurably greater—it is a cosmic, universal law, such as the law of the conservation of energy and the law of the loss of energy, or entropy . . . Red, fiery, death-dealing is the law of revolution; but that death is the birth of a new life, of a new star. And cold-blue as ice, as the icy interplanetary infinities, is the law of entropy. The flame turns from a fiery red to an even, warm pink, no longer death-dealing but comfort-producing. The sun ages and becomes a planet suitable for highways, shops, beds, prostitutes, prisons—that is a law. And in order to make the planet young again, we must set it on fire, we must thrust it off the smooth highway of evolution—that too is a law.

But infinite revolution needs an infinite number of revolutionaries:

> Explosions are not comfortable things. That is why the exploders, the heretics, are quite rightly annihilated by fire, by axes, and by words. Heretics are harmful to everybody today, to every evolution, to the difficult, slow, useful—so very useful—constructive process of coral

reef building. Imprudently and foolishly they leap into today from tomorrow. They are romantics . . . It is right and proper that heretical literature, literature that is damaging to dogma, should have its head cut off—such literature is harmful. But harmful literature is more useful than useful literature, because it militates against calcification, sclerosis, encrustation, moss, peace. It is ridiculous and utopian . . . Ideas which feed on minced meat lose their teeth just as civilized men do. Heretics are necessary to health. If there are no heretics, they have to be invented.

This is what Alex Comfort meant when he turned Marx on his head: "The war is not between classes . . . The war for freedom is a war against society . . . Revolution is not a single act, it is an unending process based upon individual disobedience." This is what Max Stirner meant when in *The Ego and His Own* (1845) he distinguished between revolution and insurrection: "Revolution aims at new arrangements— insurrection aims not at any new arrangements *of* ourselves but at arrangements *by* ourselves." And this is what Albert Camus meant when in *The Rebel* (1951) he distinguished between revolution and rebellion: "The claim of rebellion is unity, the claim of revolution is totality . . . One is creative, the other is nihilist . . . Instead of killing and dying to create what we are not, we should live and let live to create what we are."

The revolutionary goal is liberty, equality, and fraternity, but the revolutionary way leads straight to slavery, inequality, and misery. The idea of libertarian revolution—of rebellion or insurrection—is that there is no distinction between ends and means, because *means are ends.* Revolution simply overturns the State, rebellion and insurrection overthrow it. The libertarian revolution is permanent protest, permanent disobedience, refusing assent to superiors without demanding it from inferiors, the utopia without any topia.

This idea of revolution lies at the centre of what Comfort in his "Art and Social Responsibility" (1942) called the "ideology of romanticism." This ideology is based on the conviction "that the common enemy of man is death, that the common tie of man is victimhood, and that anyone who in attempting to escape the realization of that victimhood in himself increases its incidence upon others, is a traitor to humanity and an ally of death." Thus

the romantic has only two basic certainties—the certainty of irresoluble conflict which cannot be won but must be continued, and the certainty that there exists between all human beings who are involved in this conflict an indefeasible responsibility to one another. The

romantic has two enemies, death, and the obedient who by conformity to power and irresponsibility ally themselves with death.

In his lecture on "Politics as a Vocation" (1918), the German sociologist Max Weber distinguished between the "ethic of ultimate ends"
and the "ethic of responsibility." I would deny this distinction. I would
say that the way and the goal are one—that "he who would do good to
another," in Blake's words, "must do it in minute particular"—and that
there is no one more irresponsible than the so-called "responsible" people
who have the Bomb, and no one more responsible than the so-called "irresponsible" people who resist the Bomb in the name of ultimate ends. I
would go back to what Comfort said in *The Pattern of the Future* (1949):

> Responsibility to our fellow men as individuals transcends all other—
> to local groups, to nations, to political parties. All these subsidiary
> allegiances, which are so numerous, are substitutes for human beings
> . . . For us as individuals, the only immediate defence against official
> delinquency lies in our own action. The concentration camps and the
> atom bombs are the fantasies of psychopaths. They become realities
> when other individuals are ready to acquiesce in them, to guard them,
> to make them, and to use them . . .
>
> There is no tyranny which is independent of its public. There
> is no delinquent policy in any contemporary culture which could be
> carried out in the face of sufficiently widespread public resistance . . .
> There is one revolution we can all produce at once, in the privacy of
> our own homes. We may not be able to prevent atrocities by other
> people, but we can at least decline to commit them ourselves . . . this
> revolution is something no party or government is going to do for you.
> You have to do it yourself, beginning tomorrow.

This takes us straight back to Henry David Thoreau, the American
writer. Thoreau was so unpolitical that he preferred to live completely
alone, but he had nothing to learn about the realities of politics. He
refused to pay his poll tax to a State which was maintaining slavery and
was fighting a war of conquest, and he was imprisoned in the town jail
at Concord, Massachusetts, for his pains. His reflections on that experience, which he put into a lecture called *Resistance to Civil Government*
(1848)—though it is usually known as *The Duty of Civil Disobedience*—
are a classic text of libertarian revolution:

> It is not a man's duty as a matter of course to devote himself to the
> eradication of any, even the most enormous wrong; he may still

properly have other concerns to engage him. But it is his duty at least to wash his hands of it, and if he gives it no thought longer not to give it practically his support. If I devote myself to other pursuits and contemplations, I must first see at least that I do not pursue them sitting upon another man's shoulders . . . What I have done is to see, at any rate, that I do not lend myself to the wrong which I condemn.

Yes, says the conventional dissenter, but why break the law? Why not get it changed?

> Unjust laws exist: shall we be content to obey them or shall we endeavour to amend them and obey them until we have succeeded, or shall we transgress them at once? . . . Under a government which imprisons any unjustly the true place for a just man is also a prison . . . As for adopting the ways which the State has provided for remedying the evil, I know not of such ways. They take too much time, and a man's life will be gone. I have other affairs to attend to. I came into this world not chiefly to make this a good place to live in, but to live in it, be it good or bad. A man has not everything to do, but something.

Thoreau wasn't an anarchist. He agreed with Jefferson's motto, "That government is best which governs least," and with its corollary, "That government is best which governs not at all." But he added: "To speak practically and as a citizen, unlike those who call themselves no-government men, I ask for not at once no government but at once a better government." Nevertheless, the implications of his deeds and his words alike are purely anarchic, and no anarchist would deny his judgment of his self-righteous, law-abiding fellow-citizens:

> I think we should be men first, and subjects afterward . . . I quarrel not with far-off foes, but with those who near at home co-operate with and do the bidding of those far away and without whom the latter would be harmless . . . There are thousands who are *in opinion* opposed to slavery and to the war, who yet in effect do nothing to put an end to them . . . They hesitate, and they regret, and sometimes they petition, but they do nothing in earnest and with effect. They will wait, well disposed, for others to remedy the evil, that they may no longer have it to regret. At most, they give only a cheap vote and a feeble countenance and god-speed to the right as it goes by them. There are 999 patrons of virtue to one virtuous man . . . Even voting for the right is *doing* nothing for it. It is only expressing to men feebly your desire that it should prevail . . . How can a man be satisfied to entertain an

opinion merely, and enjoy *it*? . . . Cast your whole vote, not a strip of paper merely, but your whole influence. A minority is powerless while it conforms to the majority; it is not even a minority then; but it is irresistible when it clogs by its whole weight.

And anyone who has spent only a few hours in jail after a unilateralist demonstration will recognize Thoreau's reaction to his single night inside:

> I saw that if there was a wall of stone between me and my townsmen, there was a still more difficult one to climb or break through before they could get to be as free as me . . . I saw that the State was half-witted, that it was as timid as a lone woman with her silver spoons, and that it did not know its friends from its foes, and I lost all my remaining respect for it, and pitied it . . . I saw more distinctly the State in which I lived. I saw to what extent the people among whom I lived could be trusted as good neighbours and friends—that their friendship was for summer weather only, that they did not greatly propose to do right . . . I think sometimes, "Why, these people mean well, they are only ignorant, they would do better if they knew how—why give your neighbours this pain to treat you as they are not inclined to?" But I think again, "This is no reason why I should do as they do, or permit others to suffer much greater pain of a different kind."

It is easy to think of Thoreau's disobedience as inner-directed, as a form of conscientious objection; but he certainly thought of it as other -directed, as a form of propaganda by deed. Remember that he read his lecture to the very fellow citizens he despised. He was an individualist and a transcendentalist first and a man of action afterwards, but all the same he wanted to improve society, and he did what he could. More, he called for other people to follow his example. "Any man more right than his neighbours constitutes a majority of one," he declared; and "if one honest man in this State of Massachusetts, ceasing to hold slaves, were actually to withdraw from this co-partnership and be locked up in the county jail therefore, it would be the abolition of slavery in America." And Thoreau was one of the few people who spoke out for John Brown when he withdrew from the co-partnership and defied the State of Virginia at Harper's Ferry in October 1859, and was hanged therefore—John Brown, whose body lies a-mouldering in the grave, but his soul goes marching on, and the abolition of slavery in America came in less than three years.

It may seem surprising that a gentle person such as Thoreau should support a violent person such as John Brown. Not so, as you can see in Thoreau's own words:

If the alternative is to keep all just men in prison, or give up war and slavery, the State will not hesitate which to choose. If a thousand men were not to pay their tax-bills this year, that would not be a violent and bloody measure, as it would be to pay them and enable the State to commit violence and shed innocent blood. This is in fact the definition of a peaceful revolution, if any such is possible. If the tax-gatherer or any other public officer asks me, as one has done, "But what shall I do?" my answer is, "If you really wish to do anything, resign your office." When the subject has refused allegiance, and the officer has resigned his office, then the revolution is accomplished. But even suppose blood should flow. Is there not a sort of blood shed when the conscience is wounded? Through this wound a man's real manhood and immortality flow out, and he bleeds to an everlasting death. I see this blood flowing now.

The same sort of attitude may be found in another gentle person, the English novelist E. M. Forster, who coined the motto *Only Connect*. Just before the last war, he wrote an essay called "What I Believe" (1939). "I do not believe in Belief," he began. "I have, however, to live in an Age of Faith," he went on, "and I have to keep my end up in it. Where do I start? With personal relationships."

And he went on to make his confession:

I hate the idea of causes, but if I had to choose between betraying my country and betraying my friend, I hope I should have the guts to betray my country . . . Probably one will not be asked to make such an agonizing choice. Still, there lies at the back of every creed something terrible and hard, for which the worshipper may one day be required to suffer, and there is even a terror and hardness in this creed of personal relationships, urbane and mild though it sounds. Love and loyalty to an individual can run counter to the claims of a State. When they do—down with the State, say I, which means that the State would down me.

Forster isn't an anarchist either, though his creed of "personal relationships" is no distance at all from Kropotkin's principle of "mutual aid." He expresses some support for democracy ("two cheers for democracy: one because it admits variety and two because it permits criticism") and some for aristocracy:

Not an aristocracy of power, based upon rank and influence, but an aristocracy of the sensitive, the considerate and the plucky . . . They represent the true human tradition, the one permanent victory of our queer race over cruelty and chaos . . . an invincible army, yet not a victorious one . . . All words that describe them are false, and all attempts to organize them fail . . . The Saviour of the future—if he ever comes—will not preach a new Gospel. He will merely utilize my aristocracy, he will make effective the good will and the good temper which are already existing. In other words he will introduce a new technique.

And this leads on to what Herbert Read said towards the end of the last war, in *The Politics of the Unpolitical* (1943):

> The world is waiting for a new faith—especially the youth of the world is waiting for a new faith. The old institutions, the old parties, are dead at the roots: they receive no refreshment. The young men and women stand apart, indifferent, inactive. But do not let us mistake their indifference for apathy, their inactivity for laziness. Intellectually, they are very wide awake. But they have rejected our abstract slogans and the hollow institutions in which old men gibber about freedom, democracy and culture. They don't want freedom if it means the freedom to exploit their fellow-men: they don't want democracy if it means the ridiculous bagmen of Westminster: they don't want culture if it means the intellectual dope of our academies and universities . . . They want a world that is morally clean and socially just, naturally productive and aesthetically beautiful. And they know they won't get it from any of the existing parties, from any of the existing political systems. They hate fascism, they recoil from communism, and they despise democracy. They are groping towards a new faith, a new order, a new world. They are not a party and never will be a party: they have no name and will perhaps never have a name. But they will act, and onto the ruins of war they will cast the tarnished baubles and stale furnishings of those parliaments which brought death and despair to two successive generations of young men.

Towards the end of the last war, too, Alex Comfort wrote its obituary in "The End of a War" (1944):

> This war has not been unique. Its lesson is identical with the lesson of every previous war. The record of it is the record of the incredible, somnambulant heroism of the people of both sides, and the corruption and duplicity of their governments. The outcome of it has been the same outcome as in every previous war—the peoples have lost it . . . Yet the war has been unique in one respect. It has shown as never

before that society is the enemy of man—not one economic form of society, capitalist or socialist, but all irresponsible society—and that in peace as in war *the only final safeguard of freedom is the ultimate willingness of the individual to disobey* . . .

Barbarian society is rooted today in obedience, conformity, conscription, and the stage has been reached at which, in order to live, you have to be an enemy of society . . . The choice is not between socialism and fascism but between life and obedience. Every atrocity of the war was the direct consequence of somebody obeying when he should have thought. We have to learn the lesson of resistance, evasion, disappearance, which the occupation taught the people of France . . . I hope so to instruct my sons that they will give the recruiting agent the one reply he merits—a good eyeful of spit . . . War is a two-headed penny, and the only way to treat it is to sling it back at those who offer it to you . . . It will be a new just cause next time, and when they begin to say, "Look, injustice!" you must reply, "Whom do you want me to kill?" . . .

You can abolish firing-squads only by refusing to serve in them, by ramming the rifle down the throat of the man who offers it to you if you wish—not by forming a firing-squad to execute all other firing-squads. We cannot salvage society by obeying it: we cannot defend the bad against the worse . . . Armed revolution can succeed, but armed revolution, being based on power, has never succeeded in producing anything but tyranny . . .

The *maquis* of the war may allow themselves to be reabsorbed into the structure of citizenship. We will be the *maquis* of the peace . . . Up till now, it has been an article of pride among English politicians that the public would shove its head into any old noose they might show it—unflinching, steadfast patriotism, unshakable morale—obedience and an absence of direct action. *We are going to alter that* . . . When enough people respond to the invitation to die not with a salute but with a smack in the mouth, and the mention of war empties the factories and fills the streets, we may be able to talk about freedom.

This must be our aim. We must be revolutionaries, but we must remember what Bart de Ligt said in 1937: "The more violence, the less revolution." We must be agitators, and remember what Oscar Wilde said in 1891:

> Agitators are a set of interfering, meddling people, who come down to some perfectly contented class of the community and sow the seeds of discontent among them. That is the reason why agitators are so absolutely necessary. Without them, in our incomplete state, there would be no advance towards civilization.

And we must be utopians and remember what Wilde said again:

> A map of the world that does not include Utopia is not worth even glancing at, for it leaves out the one country at which Humanity is always landing. And when Humanity lands there it looks out and, seeing a better country, sets sail. Progress is the realization of Utopias.

But how?

ANTI-MILITARISM

There are two obvious ways of rebelling against war—a mutiny by those who fight, or a strike by those whose work supports those who fight.

In fact mutineers have usually protested against their low standard of living rather than against their low way of life, against those who give them their orders to kill rather than against the orders themselves. Mutiny is anyway a rebellion of armed men, and armed men don't disarm themselves (see John Arden's *Serjeant Musgrave's Dance*). A soldier, said Swift, is "a yahoo hired to kill," and once he has let himself be hired (or conscripted) to kill it is hard for him to stop killing and start being a man again. If he does, he immediately ceases to be a soldier, and his protest is no longer mutiny. True, soldiers are often the most resolute of pacifists, *after* they get out of uniform. "If my soldiers learnt to think," said Frederick the Great, "not one would remain in the ranks." But soldiers are carefully taught *not* to think, and a soldier who begins to think is on the way to discharge. Mutiny only works when it involves thousands of men, as it did in Russia, Germany and France at the end of the First World War; and then it is often the beginning of civil war.

But the mutiny of the soldier is an interesting model of disobedience, just as the discipline of the soldier is an interesting model of obedience. A soldier is an ordinary citizen, only more so. This point was well understood by Thoreau:

> A common and natural result of an undue respect for law is that you may see a file of soldiers, colonel, captain, corporal, privates, powder-monkeys and all, marching in admirable order over hill and dale to the wars, against their wills, ay against their common sense and consciences, which makes it very steep marching indeed, and produces a palpitation of the heart. They have no doubt that it is a damnable business in which they are concerned; they are all peaceably inclined. Now what are they—men at all? or small moveable forts and magazines at the service of some unscrupulous man in power? . . . The

mass of men serve the State thus, not as men mainly, but as machines, with their bodies. They are the standing army, and the militia, gaolers, constables, etc. In most cases there is no free exercise whatever of the judgment or of the moral sense; but they put themselves on a level with wood and earth and stones; and wooden men canperhaps be manufactured that will serve the purpose as well. Such command no more respect than men of straw or a lump of dirt. They have the same sort of worth only as horses or dogs. Yet such as these even are commonly esteemed good citizens.

A strike against war seems more feasible than a mutiny. The working classes aren't committed to war or subjected to military discipline, and they have a long tradition of strike action against their superiors. But the hard fact is that the left—socialist, communist, and anarchist—has a shocking war record. People who are quite willing to strike against their employers for higher pay are less willing to strike against their rulers for peace. Most wartime strikes have been intended not to stop the war but to stop rulers and employers using the war as an excuse to increase discipline or decrease wages. Even when a strike is against a war, it is almost always against that particular war, not against *all* war; and even when it really *is* against all war, it is almost always against *national* war and not against *civil* war as well (or vice versa). But war is only a name for organized mass violence, and a vertical war between social classes is just as much a war as a horizontal war between national states. Nevertheless, left-wing disapproval of horizontal war is usually in direct proportion to approval of vertical war. The man who won't fight the enemy abroad will fight the enemy at home. When it comes to the point the left will fight as willingly as the right, and as often as not they fight on the same side. Even people who oppose the use of violence in theory resort to the use of violence in practice, and no one who accepts the use of violence really rejects war. "All men desire peace," said Thomas à Kempis, "but very few desire those things which make for peace."

The strongest opponents of war on the left used to be the anti-militarists who, before 1914, were close to (or the same as) the anarchists and anarcho-syndicalists as well as the extreme socialists. The proclaimed weapon of the anti-militarists was the general strike against war, but in the event this proved to be as much of a myth as the general strike described by Georges Sorel—except that Sorel *meant* his to be mythical. Not only moderate leaders like Bebel, Jaurès and Keir Hardie, but even the really determined anti-militarists deceived themselves as well as their followers, and were genuinely surprised when the labor movement first let the First World War begin *and then joined it*. Only a few hard-headed realists such as Gustav Landauer and Tom Keell realized the true weakness of left-wing anti-militarism, and no one imagined that formerly passionate anti-militarists such as Gustave Hervé and Benito Mussolini would actually *lead* the labor movement into the war effort.

In fact anti-militarists have had little *anti-militarist* influence on the official or unofficial labor movement, whatever other influence they have had, and the little influence they have melts away to nothing when the political temperature rises and *la patrie est en danger*. Consider Keir Hardie and George Lansbury and Aneurin Bevan in this country alone. For all the fine talk at peacetime conferences and all the big demonstrations at times of crisis, most social democrats become social patriots when the blast of war blows in their ears, and even the few who refuse to take up oars with the rest also refuse to rock the boat. "The lads who have gone forth by sea and land to fight their country's battles," said Keir Hardie a few days after the beginning of the First World War, "must not be disheartened by any discordant note at home." And while Bevan opposed the conduct of the Second World War, he never opposed the war itself.

Among socialists, only the Marxists stood firm in 1870, and even Marx thought Bismarck was fighting a "defensive" war. Only the extreme Marxists and some other left-wing socialists stood firm again in 1914; and of course the Marxists began fighting furiously four years later. In 1939, only a very few very extreme socialists still stood firm, and the Marxists made themselves thoroughly ridiculous. The anarchist record is better, but many sincere and loyal comrades followed Kropotkin in 1914 and Rudolf Rocker in 1939 when on two separate occasions the best-known anarchist leader split the anarchist movement by supporting a world war.

But even if all the anarchists and anarcho-syndicalists and left-wing socialists *had* stood firmly by their anti-militarist convictions, war would still have come in 1870 and 1914 and 1939. For militarism is stronger than anti-militarism, nationalism is stronger than internationalism, conformism is stronger than non-conformism, obedience is stronger than disobedience—and never more so than at the end of a war crisis. A general strike against war before the State has contracted the war fever is difficult enough; a general strike against war *after* the State has succumbed is almost impossible. If the left is reluctant to challenge the State when the circumstances are all favorable, how much more reluctant will it be when the circumstances are all completely unfavorable? Once the State is down with the fever, it is *already too late* to protest or demonstrate or strike, because the fever is so infectious that the people catch it before anyone realizes what has happened; and when war breaks out at last, it comes as a relief, like vomiting after nausea.

The problem is one of timing. Randolph Bourne, the American liberal pragmatist whose observation of the First World War drove him to anarchist pacifism, poverty, disease and death, pointed out in his brilliant unfinished essay on *The State* (1918) that "it is States which make war on each other, and not peoples"; but "the moment war is declared, the mass of the people, through some spiritual alchemy, become convinced that they have willed and executed the deed themselves"—with the result that "the slack is taken up, the cross-currents fade out, the nation moves lumberingly and slowly, but with ever-accelerated speed and integration, towards the great end," towards "that peacefulness of being at war" (a phrase he took from L. P. Jacks, the English Unitarian). Bourne didn't belong to the labor movement, but he had far more insight into the relationship of war with society and the State than the anti-militarists who did:

> *War is the health of the State.* It automatically sets in motion throughout society those irresistible forces for uniformity, for passionate co-operation with the Government in coercing into obedience the minority groups and individuals which lack the larger herd sense.

For war isn't just against foreigners:

> The pursuit of enemies within outweighs in psychic attractiveness the assault on the enemy without. The whole terrific force of the State is brought to bear against the heretics.

Of course, "the ideal of perfect loyalty, perfect uniformity, is never really attained"; but "the nation in wartime attains a uniformity of feeling, a hierarchy of values culminating at the undisputed apex of the State ideal, which could not possibly be produced through any other agency than war," and "a people at war have become in the most literal sense obedient, respectful, trustful children again." Nor are the working classes immune to "this regression to infantile attitudes" and "into the military enterprise they go, not with those hurrahs of the significant classes whose instincts war so powerfully feeds, but with the same apathy with which they enter and continue in the industrial enterprise." People whose highest ambition is to capture the State for themselves can't really be expected to destroy it in its hour of need.

Few of us can sneer at this, or evade Auden's description of the *Unknown Citizen*: *When there was peace, he was for peace. When there was war he went.*

We are all for peace now. How many of us would still be for peace if war came? But the question has become academic. We'll all go together when we go, next time. The choice has been forced back so that we have to make it now, *before* war comes. In the past we had to decide not to become war criminals. Today we have to decide to become peace criminals, or else become war criminals by default. We have to be prisoners of our own side (like the Good Soldier Schweik), and spies against our own side (like Our Man in Havana). Those who were anti-militarists once have to go further now, and become pacifists.

PACIFISM

Thou shalt not kill was a religious command, and pacifism began as a religious or quasi-religious doctrine. A condemnation of individual retaliation appears in most "higher" religions and philosophies—non-resistance in Christianity, non-violence in Indian religion, non-assertion in Chinese Taoism, non-injury in Socratic philosophy. The power of apparent weakness over apparent strength, of right over might, of life over death, is illustrated in every mythology—David and Goliath or Daniel in the Lions' Den, Rama and Ravan or Gautama and Mara, the Battle of Marathon or the Battle of Britain, Horatius on the Bridge or a schoolboy's voice saying *Play up, play up and play the game,* Jack the Giant-Killer or Thurber's Termite.

The difference is that Jesus and Gautama and Lao-tzu and Socrates made non-retaliation a moral command rather than just the moral to a story. But it was only *individual* non-retaliation—the State still had to punish offenders at home and fight enemies abroad. And there were personal inconsistencies—Jesus would not resist evil, but he drove the moneychangers from the Temple by force; Socrates would not fight the Athenian State which condemned him, but he fought in the Athenian army; Marcus Aurelius as a philosopher was a pious Stoic, but as a Roman Emperor he was a persecutor of Christians and a campaigner against barbarians; Ashoka was converted to Buddhism and renounced war, but he kept his conquests and ruled India as firmly as before.

The contradiction between the known wrongness and the continued practice of violence is usually rationalized by the assertion that life in this world is either evil or illusory; so that either you have to do bad things for good reasons, or else it doesn't really matter what you do anyway. Followers of non-violent systems in theory tend in practice to make life tolerable by treating their more difficult beliefs as counsels of perfection, or to withdraw from life into asceticism or quietism or complete indifferentism. These tendencies are of course greatly reinforced if a religion or philosophy is established by the State. "Every Church," said Tolstoy, "excludes the doctrine of Christ." This point was not quite understood by Thoreau. He wondered why the State did not "cherish its wise minority," and asked "Why does it always crucify Christ, and excommunicate Copernicus and Luther, and pronounce Washington and Franklin rebels?" The "no-government men" could have told him that.

The story of pacifism is in fact the story of the way saints and heretics defended the doctrine of Christ against the Church. The early Christians, who were themselves saints and heretics, took non-resistance seriously. It is well-known that many of them refused to sacrifice to the Roman gods and were therefore martyred; it is less well-known that many of them similarly refused to bear arms in the Roman legions and were therefore martyred as well. Roland Bainton states in his book on *Christian Attitudes toward War and Peace* (1960) that "the early Church was pacifist to the time of Constantine." But this naturally changed at the beginning of the fourth century, when Christianity was made the state religion of the Roman Empire—when, said the Spanish humanist, Luis Vives, "Constantine entered the house of Christ with the Devil at his side." This was when Aristotle's revolting doctrine of the "just war" was developed into a Christian doctrine, though to see it at its best you must read Augustine or Aquinas. The Czech theologian Petr Chelcicky wrote a book called *The Net of Faith* (1443), based on an allegorical interpretation of a biblical text (Luke 5: 4–7), which described how the net of faith had been strong enough to hold little fish like the early Christians, but was broken by big fish like Constantine, so that nearly all the fish got away.

But not quite all. The stream of pacifist (and anarchist) thought runs underground in Christian history, but never disappears altogether. The doctrine of non-resistance, which was specifically taught in the Sermon on the Mount (Matthew 5: 38–48 and Luke 6: 27–35), was held by early heretical sects such as the Montanists and Marcionists, and by later ones such as the Albigenses and Waldenses. Sixteenth-century humanists such as Erasmus and Vives condemned war in near-pacifist terms. But modern pacifism began in what George Huntston Williams calls *The Radical Reformation* (1962). The followers of Wyclif in England (called Lollards) and of Hus in Bohemia (called Hussites) tended towards anarcho-pacifism whenever it became clear that the Kingdom of Heaven was *not* of this world.

When the extreme Hussites (Taborites) were routed in 1434 by the moderate Hussites (Calixtines) after twenty years of bitter war, the surviving Taborites formed the new sect of Bohemian Brethren (the *Unitas Fratrum*, or *Jednota Ceskych Bratri*). The Bohemian Brethren were inspired by Chelcicky, himself an admirer of Wyclif and Hus, and they influenced the extremists in the Protestant Reformation during the sixteenth century. *The Net of Faith* was first printed in 1521, the year of the Diet of Worms. The "anabaptists" (i.e. extreme radical Protestants) were famous for their violence—at Mühlhausen in 1525, for instance, or at Münster in 1534—but they should have been famous for their non-violence. The Czech Bohemian Brethren and Moravian Brethren, the Dutch Mennonites and Collegiants, the German Hutterites and Schwenkfelders, and the English Brownists and Baptists were only a few of the unknown number of anabaptist sects who turned towards anarcho-pacifism during the sixteenth and seventeenth centuries. The Schleitheim Confession of the Swiss Anabaptists, which was drawn up in 1527, stated that no Christian could take part in government or war.

But of all the "peace sects," the best-known is the Society of Friends, which has been chiefly responsible for keeping Christian pacifism alive for the last three hundred years. There have been plenty of later sects— the French Camisards, the Russian Molokans and Dukhobors, the Anglo-American Shakers, Christadelphians, Seventh-Day Adventists and Jehovah's Witnesses—but the Quakers have had by far the most influence; possibly because they have taken the maximum part in conventional life with the minimum compromise of their unconventional principles, and because they have been so much more tolerant than most other extremist sects. The "inner light" is after all a more peaceful basis for truth than the text of the Bible.

The "peace testimony" of the Friends appeared unmistakably in George Fox's brave reply to Cromwell's Army Commissioners in 1651, and again in James Naylor's last words in 1660; and it was formally stated for the first time in the official declaration of the Society in January, 1661:

> We certainly know and do testify to the world that the spirit of Christ, which leads us into all truth, will never move us to fight and war against any man with outward weapons, neither for the Kingdom of Christ nor for the kingdoms of this world . . . When we have been wronged we have not sought to revenge ourselves. Never shall we lift

> up hand against any that thus use us, but desire the Lord may have
> mercy upon them, that they may consider what they have done.

This is a perfect formulation of the classic doctrine of non-resistance. It is also a close repetition of the views of Gerrard Winstanley, the
leader of the Diggers of 1649, who held virtually non-religious versions
of the religious doctrines of the inner light and of non-violence; how
many disappointed Diggers became Quakers during the 1650s?

But the remarkable thing about the pacifism of the Quakers is that
they never wavered from their first position. Penn's "Holy Experiment"
of Pennsylvania was the nearest thing to a non-violent state in history,
from its foundation in 1682 to the fall of the Quaker regime of 1756.
Robert Barclay said in his *Apologia* (1676): "It is not lawful for Christians
to resist evil or to war or fight in any cause." Jonathan Dymond said in
his *Essay on War* (1829): "Either we must refuse to fight or we must
abandon Christianity." This is still the Quaker view today. When A. C. F.
Beales began writing his *History of Peace* (1931), he was "surprised to
find that every single idea current today about peace and war was being
preached by organized bodies over a century ago, and that the worldwide
ramifications of the present-day peace movement can be traced back in
unbroken continuity to a handful of forgotten Quakers in England and
America at the close of the Napoleonic Wars."

The Quakers have taken a leading part in both official and unofficial peace movements. It was Quaker initiative that led to the formation
of the British Peace Society in 1816 and of the National Peace Council
in 1905, and the Quakers have always been active in war relief work
(which won them the Nobel Peace Prize in 1947). More important, it
was at the same time Quakers who bore the brunt of resistance to the
Militia Acts between 1757 and 1860, both by public protest and by personal refusal, and who led the conscientious objectors in the First World
War. So they worked against war in the abstract and tried to wreck it in
concrete terms as well.

The point is that the Quakers haven't really practised the doctrine
of non-resistance at all. Fox told Cromwell in 1654: "My weapons are
not carnal but spiritual." They were effective weapons for all that. ("The
armed prophet triumphs," said Machiavelli, "the unarmed prophet
perishes." Fox's soul goes marching on—but where is Cromwell's?)
Quakers have constantly protested against social injustices and have
frequently taken action against them. Elizabeth Fry's work for prisoners and Joseph Rowntree's work for the poor are hardly examples of
"non-resistance." Quakers led the campaign not only to improve the

conditions of slaves but to abolish slavery altogether, right from the early protest of the German Friends in Pennsylvania in 1688 to the formation of the Society for the Abolition of the Slave Trade in 1787, and on to the end.

In fact, one of the interesting things about the history of modern dissent is the close connection between professed non-resistance to evil and sustained resistance to racial oppression. William Lloyd Garrison, the Abolitionist leader in the United States, wasn't a Quaker because he wasn't a Christian at all, but he was a non-resistant (what we would call a pacifist) like most of his colleagues Ballou, Musser, and Whittier. Garrison actually symbolizes this curious connection, for he was not only the founder of the New England and American Anti-Slavery Societies and the editor of the Abolitionist paper, the *Liberator*, but also the founder of the New England Non-Resistance Society and the editor of the pacifist paper, the *Non-Resistor*.

The Boston Peace Convention of 1838, where the Non-Resistance Society was formed, deserves a detailed examination to itself. It passed a resolution that "no man, no government, has a right to take the life of man, on any pretext, according to the gospel of Christ," and it issued a *Declaration of Sentiments*, including the following:

> We cannot acknowledge allegiance to any human government . . . Our country is the world, our countrymen are all mankind [this was the motto of the *Liberator*, and had been said by Diogenes two thousand years earlier] . . . We repudiate all human politics, worldly honours and stations of authority . . . We cordially adopt the non-resistance principle.

Here is pure Christian anarcho-pacifism, derived straight from sixteenth- century anabaptism—no wonder it excited Tolstoy so much. But these gentle, unwarlike, unworldly cranks were right in the front of the battle against slavery, and Garrison was notorious for his violent language about the American slave-owners. Non-resistance indeed!

The fact is that non-resistance in theory only means non-resistance in practice when it remains silent. The mere declaration of conscientious objection to violence is a form of resistance, since it implies non-co-operation with the State's key functions of punishment and war. The State can tolerate the abolition of slavery, but not of violence as well. When Jesus abrogated the talion law of Jewish and Roman law, he was unknowingly challenging his State. When Dymond said in 1826, "Now is the time for anti-slavery exertion; the time will come for anti-war exertion," he was knowingly challenging his State—and ours. As Bourne said in 1918, "We cannot crusade against war without crusading implicitly against the State." Pacifism is ultimately anarchism, just as anarchism is ultimately pacifism.

It is because most pacifists never realize this that they are constantly surprised by the hostility they provoke. Most pacifists are really sentimentalists—hoping to get rid of war without changing anything else, so you can hurt people as long as you don't actually kill them. It was because the greatest of all pacifists—Tolstoy—saw through this sentimentalism that he became an anarchist as well as a pacifist. (He never called himself an anarchist, since he used the word to describe those who relied on violence, but his bitter condemnation of the State makes him one of the greatest of all anarchists too.) His remark that "the most frightful robber-band is not as frightful as the State," is simply an echo from Augustine's *City of God* without Augustine's pious reservation: "Without justice, what are States but great robber-bands?" And because Tolstoy utterly denied the justice of the State's power, he had to proclaim the duty of "non-resistance" (that is, non-violent resistance) to the State's demands. It is ironical that he derived the right of resistance to the State from the same source that Augustine derived the right of oppression by the State—God. "The clear and simple question is this," he said in his *Letter to the Russian Conscientious Objectors* (1909): "Which law do you consider to be binding for yourself—the law of God, which is your conscience; or the law of man, which is the State?" The answer is in no doubt. "Do not resist evil," he said in his *Letter to a Hindu* (1908), "but do not participate in evil either." The doctrine is still non-resistance, but the implication is total resistance. He had already said in his *Letter to the Swedish Peace Party* (1899): "Those in power neither can nor will abolish their armies." And the solution? "The people must take the matter into their hands." How?

This is where religious pacifism and political anti-militarism came to the same conclusion, for what Tolstoy was advocating was in fact a non-violent general strike against war—individual civil disobedience on such a scale that it becomes mass direct action, the revolutionary technique proposed by the proto-anarchists (such as Winstanley and Godwin) and the later peaceful anarchists (such as Proudhon and Tucker), an anarchist insurrection without the violence that disfigures the proposals of Bakunin and Kropotkin. But how can such a non-violent strike, such an anarchist insurrection be organized? Here the pacifists proved to suffer from the same false optimism as the anti-militarists, for when the First World War came their non-violent strike turned out to be just as mythical as the industrial strike; and they were reduced to individual conscientious objection.

CONSCIENTIOUS OBJECTION

It is often thought that military conscription was unknown in this country until the First World War, but there were the press-gangs in the seventeenth and eighteenth centuries and the Militia Acts in the eighteenth and nineteenth centuries, and the Quakers had resisted both of these without fail. But conscription in its modern form didn't appear on the horizon until the weakness of the British Army was revealed by the Boer War (the first serious war for half a century). The formation of the National Service League in 1902 began a long campaign for compulsory military service, against strong opposition from pacifists and patriots alike. Even when the First World War came, the Government delayed as long as possible, in the hope that Alfred Leete's picture of Kitchener saying *Your Country Needs You* would be enough. But within the first year of the war the failure of voluntary recruiting led to national registration (of all men and women between 15 and 75), which showed that two million men of military age had decided not to fight for their King and Country. After this, the process was fairly rapid, with "attestation" in October 1915, conscription for single men in January and for married men in May 1916, and further extensions in March and May 1917 and again in January and April 1918. Conscription didn't come to an end until August 1921.

Nothing is more instructive than the way the leaders of the official labor movement rejected every stage in this process before it happened and then accepted it, condemning the principle of conscription each time they collaborated with it. In exactly the same way they managed, between the World Wars, to oppose pacifism and unilateral disarmament on one hand and conscription and rearmament on the other, and once again they accepted the fact of conscription when it returned in April 1939. After the last war, of course, it was the Labour Party which extended conscription in peacetime in 1947 and also decided to make and test the British Bomb.

In exactly the same way, the official peace movement (the conference and arbitration people), which had been trying to build igloos in the desert for a century, collapsed as ignominiously as the Second International in 1914, and offered even less resistance in 1939. On both occasions the only people who stood firmly and bravely against all war were the extreme pacifists and the extreme anti-militarists (both socialists and anarchists). Here we come to the crucial problem, which consists of two questions—*Who are the real war resisters?* and *How can the war resisters really resist war?*

The answer to the first question was given in the First World War, when both the labor movement and the peace movement failed to resist, and when the people who formed the No Conscription Fellowship (NCF) in November 1914 and began going to jail in January 1916 turned out to be mostly members of the Society of Friends and the Independent Labour Party. Real pacifism and real anti-militarism were in fact the same thing, since they pursued the same end by the same means. Religious people had to have political feelings to make the public protest, and political people had to have religious feelings to take the punishment.

Remember what the punishment was, and how unpleasant it was to be a "conchie" in the First World War. It is estimated that 6,000 men went to prison, and the common sentence was two years; worse, you could be rearrested immediately after release if they wanted to play cat-and-mouse with you (just like the suffragettes). More than 650 people were imprisoned twice, and three were actually put inside six times in succession. Arthur Creech Jones, later a Labour Colonial Secretary, got six months, twelve months, two years, and two years again; Fenner Brockway, founder of the NCF and later of the Movement for Colonial Freedom, got six months, twelve months, and two years. (Note how they are both strong anti-racialists as well as anti-militarists.) At least 34 men were taken over to France in May 1916 and sentenced to be shot, though Asquith stopped any of the sentences being carried out; and more than twice that number died as a direct result of the brutal treatment they received in custody.

It is a valid criticism of individual war resistance to point out that it is ineffective, but no one can deny that it demanded great courage and determination. The obvious corollary is that this courage and determination should somehow be organized effectively, and the obvious hope after the First World War was that this would happen. But that hope was false.

The NCF was dissolved in November 1919, though it was revived in February 1921 as the No More War Movement. In February 1937 this was absorbed by the Peace Pledge Union (PPU), which had been formed after Dick Sheppard's famous letter of October 1934. (It is odd how Arthur Ponsonby's similar declaration of December 1927 has been forgotten, while the Peace Pledge has become part of the national memory, along with the irrelevant Peace Ballot of 1934–35 and the unimportant Oxford Union resolution of February 1933.) The unfortunate result of the formation of the PPU was to drive the religious pacifists and the political anti-militarists apart; and the alliance between them couldn't be restored by the War Resisters' International (formed in Holland in 1921), because its British section was the predominantly religious PPU.

It is true that the PPU kept the faith alive and gathered well over 100,000 pledges by 1939; but it was passivist as well as pacifist, and when the war against Fascism began and thousands of men broke their pledges, it was reduced to publishing vague propaganda and totting up the numbers of COs in the registrations (seldom more than two percent and often less than one percent). So after 1945 the situation was far more hopeless than it had been before 1914, because the war resisters had failed miserably twice; and far more urgent too, because the Bomb meant the next war really would be the war to end war, and everything else with it. The first question had been answered, but there was still no answer to the second question—*How can war resisters really resist war?* Perhaps it was just because everything looked so hopeless and so urgent that an answer came at last.

NON-VIOLENT RESISTANCE

The point was that you must not only *renounce* war, and not only *resist* war, you must also *replace* war. William James gave a lecture a few months before he died on "The Moral Equivalent of War" (1910). He put himself "in the anti-militarist party," but he declared that "a permanently successful peace-economy cannot be a simple pleasure-economy," and insisted that "we must make new energies and hardihoods continue the manliness to which the military mind so faithfully clings." For "martial virtues must be the enduring element" in a peaceful society, and anti-militarism must develop its own form of militancy. Like many other people before and since, he was sure that "the martial type of character can be bred without war," and he called for an "army against nature" to replace the armies against fellowmen. (This idea of a peace army is the basis of Pierre Ceresole's Service Civile Internationale, whose British section is the International Voluntary Service.)

Ten years after the First World War, Walter Lippmann wrote an article on "The Political Equivalent of War" (1928), in which he pointed out that it is not sufficient to propose an equivalent for the military virtues. It is even more important to work out an equivalent for the military methods and objectives. War is after all "one of the ways by which great human decisions are made," so "the abolition of war depends primarily upon inventing and organizing other ways of deciding those issues which hitherto have been decided by war." Political anti-militarists have often assumed that these issues could be decided by another form of war—violent revolution—and religious pacifists have often assumed that they could be eliminated altogether by non-war—mutual reconciliation. Lippmann would have none of this: "Any real programme of peace must rest on the premise that there will be causes of dispute so long as we can foresee, and that those disputes have to be decided, and that a way of deciding them must be found which is not war."

The problem is that we must replace war *before* we resist it, and resist it *before* we renounce it. If we put our priorities the other way round, we end as sentimental pacifists again. Our war resistance must itself be both a moral and a political equivalent to war. The irony is that a solution has been there all the time. The Kantian antinomy between violent resistance and non-resistance is only superficially insoluble, and submits quite readily to Hegelian dialectic. The thesis is violent resistance; the antithesis is its opposite, non-resistance (properly, non-violent non-resistance); and the synthesis is non-violent resistance (or passive resistance). But what sort of synthesis is this in practice? Lassalle said "passive resistance is the resistance that doesn't resist." Is this true?

The trouble is that passive, or non-violent, resistance is usually thought of as an inner-directed and ineffective technique, a way of bearing witness rather than of resisting evil or producing good; and both the idea and the history of other-directed and effective non-violent resistance have been forced underground by the human obsession with violence. A clear and unprejudiced study of non-violence in theory and practice is long overdue. In fact the idea that non-violent resistance might work runs under the surface of western political thought without ever quite disappearing. Etienne de La Boétie, the French humanist, wrote an *Essay on Willing Slavery* (1546) against tyrants and the subjects who maintain them, in which he suggested that "if nothing be given them, if they be not obeyed, without fighting, without striking a blow, they remain naked, disarmed, and are nothing." And his advice to those who groan under a despot follows logically enough: "Resolve not to obey, and you are free. I do not advise you to shake or overturn him. Forbear only to support him, and you will see him, like a great colossus from which the base is taken away, fall with his own weight and be broken in pieces."

Godwin's theory of resistance was similar to La Boétie's: "When such a crisis has arrived, not a sword will need to be drawn, not a finger to be lifted up in purposes of violence." And Shelley put Godwin's theory into verse, in his *Masque of Anarchy* (1819):

> Stand ye calm and resolute,
> Like a forest close and mute,
> With folded arms and looks which are
> Weapons in unvanquished war.

And this is closely echoed in the French syndicalist song:

> Ce n'est pas à coup de mitraille
> Que la capital tu vaincras;
> Non, car pour gagner la bataille
> Tu n'auras qu'à croiser les bras.

"You have only to fold your arms." Before the rise of syndicalism, the Belgian anarchist Anselme Bellegarrigue developed a "theory of calm," which he propounded during the turbulent days of the French Second Republic. "You thought until today that there were tyrants?" he asked: "Well, you were mistaken—there are only slaves. Where no one obeys, no one commands."

He called for a non-violent revolution, to be brought about "by the sole strength of right, the force of inertia, the refusal to co-operate." Bellegarrigue had visited the United States. Had he met Thoreau?

At least it is clear that the syndicalist theory of resistance by mass non-violent direct action had already been fully elaborated a hundred years ago. But mass resistance of this kind isn't just another clever idea which hadn't been tried history is full of examples.

The most obvious method is the mass exodus, such as that of the Israelites from Egypt in the Book of Exodus, that of the Roman plebeians from the city of Rome in 494 BC (according to Livy), that of the Barbarians who roamed over Europe during the Dark Ages looking for somewhere to live, that of the Puritans who left England and the Huguenots who left France in the seventeenth century, that of the Jews who left the Russian Empire in the nineteenth century and Nazi Germany in the 1930s and 1940s, that of all the refugees from Fascist and Communist countries since the 1920s.

Or there is the boycott, used by the American colonies against British goods before 1776, by the Persians against a government tobacco tax in 1891, by the Chinese against British, American and Japanese goods in the early years of this century, by several countries against South African goods today, and—in a different sense—by the negroes who organized the bus boycotts in Montgomery in 1955 and Johannesburg in 1957.

Then there is the political strike, such as the first Petersburg strike in 1905, the Swedish and Norwegian strikes against war between the two countries in the same year, the Spanish and Argentine strikes against their countries' entry into the First World War, the German strike against the Kapp *putsch* in 1920, and dozens of minor examples every year—in fact most strikes are examples of a familiar form of non-violent resistance. The syndicalist general strike and the pacifist general strike are both ideas derived from the ordinary industrial strike, which is after all the basis of the strength of the labor movement.

There is also the technique of non-co-operation, as used by the Greek women in Aristophanes' *Lysistrata*, by the Dutch against Alva in 1567–72 (see the film *La Kermesse Héroïque*), by the Hungarians against the Austrians in 1861–67 (consider how their leader Ferenc Deák is much less famous that Lajos Kossuth, because he was much less romantic—and much more successful), by the Irish against the English in 1879–82 (until Parnell made the Kilmainham Treaty with Gladstone), by the German sailors against their own admirals in 1918, and by the Germans in the Ruhr against the French in 1923–5. When this technique is used against an individual it is called "sending to Coventry"; the people mentioned above sent their oppressors to Coventry.

General resistance to oppression is often non-violent, not because of principle but because violence is for some reason unnecessary or useless. This sort of resistance without violence was used by the Jews against Roman governors in the first century AD, by the English against James II in 1686–8, by the German Catholics and Socialists against Bismarck in 1873–83, by the English Nonconformists against the Education Act of 1902 and the English trade unionists against the Trade Disputes Act of 1906, by the Finns against the Russian introduction of conscription in 1902, by the Koreans against the Japanese and the Egyptians against the British in 1919, by the Samoans against the New Zealanders in 1920–36, by the Norwegians and Danes against the Nazis in 1940–43, and by the Poles and Hungarians against the Russians in 1956.

All these examples of resistance were non-violent, at least for a time, but mass non-violence is usually just as much of a second-best as individual non-violence. But a double change is possible. The non-violent action can be chosen deliberately because it is expected to work better than violent action, and it can be turned into direct action. Whenever we feel that pacifism must stop being passivism and become activism, that it must somehow take the initiative and find a way between grandiose

plans for general strikes which never have any reality and private protests which never have any effect, that it must become concrete instead
of abstract—when in fact we decide that what we want is not so much a
negative programme of non-resistance or non-violent passive resistance
as a positive programme of non-violent active resistance, not so much a
static peace without life as a dynamic war without death—then our only
possible way out of the dark wood is by mass non-violent direct action.

The point about mass non-violent direct action is that it absorbs all
kinds of non-violent resistance. The distinction between civil disobedience and direct action becomes meaningless. Thoreau's refusal to pay his
poll tax was civil disobedience, less important in itself than as a gesture;
his help for a negro slave on the run to Canada was direct action, equally
important both in itself and as a gesture. But if thousands of people
refuse taxes or help slaves, there is a difference. Mass non-violent direct
action is clearly the only way the war-resisters can really resist war, as
Alex Comfort saw so clearly at the end of the last war, in his pamphlet
on *Peace and Disobedience* (1946):

> Objection is not enough. The objector, particularly the religious objec-
> tor, is politically irrelevant because he is chiefly interested in safeguard-
> ing his own conscientious objection to one aspect of state irresponsibil-
> ity. You do not want objection, you want resistance, ready to adopt every
> means short of violence to destroy and render useless the whole mech-
> anism of conscription. It is not enough to secure the immunity and
> support of religious believers and a politically conscious minority. The
> opposition of the ordinary man to military service must be canalized.

But *how is* this canalization to be organized? An answer was given
more than half a century ago, not by a war resister at all, but by the man
who was leading resistance to racial oppression in South Africa, an obscure Gujarati lawyer called Mohandas Karamchand Gandhi.

"SATYAGRAHA"

Gandhi came to South Africa at the age of twenty-three with a brief
from a Muslim firm in his home town of Porbandar. He got the case
settled within a few months, but he decided to stay in South Africa to
organize Indian resistance to the colour bar. That was in 1894. He became the trusted leader of the Indian community, but there was nothing
remarkable about his career. What happened—and what made Gandhi

so important in the history of non-violence—was that he became a "charismatic leader" (the phrase used by Max Weber for a person who seems to have superhuman qualities and exerts inexplicable influence over both followers and opponents) and invented "*satyagraha.*"

The significant date for the birth of *satyagraha* is September 11, 1906, when Gandhi administered an oath of passive resistance against Transvaal's "Black Bill" to 3,000 Indians in the Imperial Theatre at Johannesburg. The two great operations of 1907–09 and 1913–14 that followed this made both Gandhi and his technique of *satyagraha* famous. Soon after he returned to India in 1915, he began using *satyagraha* against the British *raj* and against local injustices of all kinds. There were local operations at Viramgam (1915), Champaran (1917), Ahmedabad (1918), Kheda (1918), Kaira (1918), Kotgarh (1921), Borsad (1923), Vaikam (1924–25), Nagpur (1927), Bardoli (1927–28), and in the Native States (1938–39); and there were three pairs of national operations, in 1919 and 1920–22, in 1930–31 and 1931–32, and in 1940–41 and 1942. In the end, as everyone knows, the British Labour Party granted (granted!) independence to India after partition (1947); and then, as everyone also knows, Gandhi was shot a few months later by a Hindu fanatic called Vinayak Godse (1948)—killed by his own like Socrates and Jesus.

Gandhi said, "Let no one say he is a follower of Gandhi," but thousands do. His mysterious *charisma* lives on. Like Albert Schweitzer, he has become what Colin MacInnes calls a "liberal saint," and his name is constantly invoked by people for whom his work means nothing. The Indian Government and the Congress Party claim him; but if he has a successor, it is not Jawaharlal Nehru, the *kaisar* of a new *raj*, but Vinoba Bhave, the leader of the agrarian *Bhoodan* movement since 1951. But there are true Gandhians outside India—Albert Luthuli in South Africa, Kenneth Kaunda in Rhodesia, Martin Luther King in the United States, Danilo Dolci in Sicily, and Michael Scott in this country—people who are more interested in Gandhi's message than his name, who have adopted *satyagraha* because they find it the only valid form of political resistance in the shadow of the concentration camp and the firing squad and the Bomb.

But what is *satyagraha*? It is a Gujarati word coined by Gandhi to replace the traditional term "passive resistance," which he disliked because it was in a foreign language and didn't mean exactly what he meant. Satyagraha is usually translated as "soul-force," but the more literal translation is "holding on to truth" (we should imagine a French or German Gandhi coining a word like *vériténitude* or *wahrhaltung*). For

Gandhi, the goal was truth, the old Indian idea of *satya*; and the way was non-violence, the old Indian idea of *ahimsa*. But in the Indian *dharma*, as in the analogous Chinese *tao*, the way and the goal are one—so non-violence *is* truth, and the practice of *ahimsa* is *satyagraha*.

This sort of reasoning can of course lead to meaningless and even dangerous metaphysical statements (such as the one that since non-violence is truth, violence is untruth and so doesn't exist); but it also leads to a healthy refusal to make any convenient distinction between ends and means. "We do not know our goal," said Gandhi: "It will be determined not by our definitions but by our acts." Or again, "If one takes care of the means, the end will take care of itself." Compare St Paul: "Faith without works is dead." All this is a refreshing change from traditional political thought, for most western philosophers have tended to believe that if one takes care of the ends, the means will take care of themselves. This line of reasoning leads to Auschwitz and Hiroshima. Gandhi was sometimes guilty of humbug, but it was verbal rather than murderous.

There has been rather a lot of fruitless discussion of the exact meaning of *satyagraha*. We are told that it isn't the same as passive resistance, which has been given another new name—*duragraha*—and is thought of as stubborn resistance which negatively avoids violence for tactical reasons, rather than as resistance which is positively non-violent for ethical reasons, as *satyagraha* is. *Duragraha* is just a subtle method of coercion, but *satyagraha*, according to Gandhi, "is never a method of coercion, it is one of conversion," because "the idea underlying *satyagraha* is to convert the wrongdoer, to awaken the sense of injustice in him." This is done by drawing the opponent's violence onto oneself by some form of non-violent direct action, causing suffering in oneself rather than in the opponent. "Without suffering it is impossible to obtain freedom," said Gandhi, for only suffering "opens the inner understanding in man." The object of *satyagraha* is in fact to make a partial (or, if necessary, a total) sacrifice of oneself, to become a martyr in the literal sense of a witness to the truth.

But Gandhi saw more in this than individual conscientious objection: "Non-violence in its dynamic condition means conscious suffering. It means pitting one's whole soul against the will of the tyrant."

Here perhaps is the dynamic war without violence that we needed, a moral and political equivalent of war, and at the same time a real way of resisting war itself.

It is important to remember that *satyagraha* was not meant to be a second best. Gandhi always reserved particular scorn for what he called the "non-violence of the weak" (such as that of the prewar and postwar appeasers of aggression and oppression), and called for the "non-violence of the strong." He was above all an Indian patriot. "I am not pleading for India to practise non-violence because she is weak," he said: "I want her to practise non-violence conscious of her strength and power." He was no weakling, in any sense. "Where there is only a choice between cowardice and violence," he said, "I would advise violence." But this wasn't the choice: "I believe that non-violence is infinitely superior to violence." This is significantly close to what Garrison the non-resistor said just before the beginning of the American Civil War: "Rather than see men wearing their chains in a cowardly and servile spirit, I would as an advocate of peace much rather see them breaking the head of the tyrant with their chains."

It is typical of Gandhi that, though his first principle was non-violence, he raised Indian ambulance units to serve in the British Army for the Boer War, the Zulu rising of 1906, and the First World War; and in 1918 he even began a recruiting campaign in India. He said that after independence he "would not hesitate to advise those who would bear arms to do so and fight for their country." What would he have said about Kashmir, Hyderabad, Goa, Ladakh? Who knows? He also seems to have thought that violent resistance against hopeless odds and a ruthless enemy (such as the Warsaw Ghetto rising in 1943) almost qualified as a form of *satyagraha*.

But of course Gandhi's usual advice was to resist evil without any violence at all. He did not hesitate to advise the Chinese, the Abyssinians, the Spanish Republicans, the Czechs, the Austrians, the Poles, the Jews, the British, and anyone else who was attacked, to offer *satyagraha*. For even unarmed men have the strength of right and of numbers. ("Ye are many, they are few.") Even a few weak men can use the non-violence of the strong if they rely on their own consciences. ("The strongest man is the one who is most alone.") This is the reverse of "peace at any price"— it is peace at *my* price. It is saying to the aggressor: "You can come and take my country and my home and my possessions, and you can hurt and even kill me and my friends, but I shall resist you to the end and accept my suffering, and I shall never accept your authority. You may prevail for a time, but I or my successors shall win in the end." This is not mere passive resistance, for *satyagraha*, as Gandhi said, "is much more active than violent resistance." This is not "willing slavery," but willing suffering.

And yet, in the face of all the evidence, Gandhi denied any coercive intentions. In fact, he was much given to chivalrous gestures (calling off the 1914 operation when a white rail strike began, not taking advantage of the removal of a police cordon at Vaikam in 1924) and to over-chival-rous compromises (with Smuts in 1908, and with Lord Irwin in 1931). Richard Gregg, in *The Power of Non-Violence* (1934), is sure that 'non-violent resistance is a pressure different in kind from that of coercion', and this is the orthodox view of most Gandhians. But Joan Bondurant, in her *Conquest of Violence* (1958), admitted that "throughout Gandhi's experiments with *satyagraha* there appears to be an element of coercion," albeit "coercion whose sting is drawn." And Clarence Case unhesitat-ingly defined *satyagraha* in the title of his *Non-Violent Coercion* (1923).

The truth is surely that there are two sides to coercion, and while a *satyagrahi* may be sincerely innocent of any wish to coerce, the person at the receiving end of his *satyagraha* may feel very decidedly coerced. Some people have even called *satyagraha* "moral blackmail," and I think there is something in this. Whatever Gandhi felt about what he was doing during his half-century career of resistance, there was no doubt in the minds of his South African, British and Indian opponents about what was happening to them. Satyagraha was "nothing but the applica-tion of force under another form," complained Lord Irwin, the Viceroy who had to deal with the great Salt March of 1930 (and who, as Lord Halifax, became Foreign Secretary in time for Munich). In the end, the precise amount of coercion in *satyagraha*, and even the precise definition of *satyagraha* itself, are rather academic points. The important point is whether *satyagraha* works, how it works, and what we can learn from it. If we can't convert an opponent, it is clearly better to coerce him gently rather than roughly. For, as Gandhi said, "You can wake a man only if he is really asleep; no effort that you make will produce any effect upon him if he is merely pretending sleep."

Satyagraha is "not a subject for research," Gandhi told Joan Bon-durant (when she was carrying out research into *satyagraha*): "You must experience it." No doubt, but first you must observe it in action; and an interesting thing about Gandhi's action is that it failed in direct propor-tion to the size of his objectives. The Viramgam tariff barrier and the Champaran indigo racket and the Kaira forced-labor custom and the Vaikam road ban were all broken, but were the Indians in South Africa freed? Were even the Indians in India freed? Gandhi acknowledged that he was "a determined opponent of modern civilization," and he insisted that independence meant more than "a transference of power from white bureaucrats to brown bureaucrats." But *swaraj*, which meant personal self rule before it came to mean Indian Home Rule, has in fact brought little more than government by Indians instead of Englishmen, and has hastened the irresistible advance of modern civilization throughout the sub-continent. Who uses a hand spinning-wheel if he can use a spinning-machine? Who wears home-spun *khadi?* Would Gandhi be found among the Gandhians any more?

The fact is that Gandhi won the little battles and lost the big ones. No doubt the little battles might have been lost as well if he hadn't been there, and the big defeats might have been much bigger (though Subhas Bose wasn't the only one who said Gandhi made things worse, not better); but his victories were still minor ones. Nor were they bloodless. The Amritsar Massacre at the Jallianwalla Bagh on April 13, 1919 was a direct result of Gandhi's campaign, and he himself admitted a "Himalayan miscalculation" and he wasn't able to do very much to stop the frightful communal riots after partition, though he did what he could. Gandhi always succeeded most when he attempted least. His ideal was reconciliation, but the only people he reconciled were those who accepted his terms in the first place. The Boers just stepped back to gain time and strength for a bigger jump, and the English just lost their tempers with the inscrutable orientals who kept outwitting them. Gandhi didn't win his enemies over like a modern Christ (did Christ, for that matter?); he threw them neatly over his shoulder like a modern Jack the Giant-Killer using judo. The important thing about Gandhi isn't so much what he tried to do as what he did.

We should remember this when we use his ideas. He linked many things to *satyagraha* which aren't essential to it. His religious ideas (non-possession, non-acquisition, chastity, fasting, vegetarianism, teetotalism) and his economic ideas (self-sufficiency, "bread-labor," agrarianism) don't necessarily have anything to do with post-Gandhian non-violence. Remember what Gandhi said about himself: "It is profitless to speculate whether Tolstoy in my place would have acted differently from me." He wasn't Tolstoy; we aren't Gandhi. Everyone has a unique background and personality. Gandhi came from the puritanical Vaishnava sect and the respectable Modh Bania sub-caste, and he had a profound sense of sin (or obsessive guilt complex, as the case may be). We don't have to share his background and personality to qualify for non-violent action. Don't worry that he said *satyagraha* is "impossible without a living faith in God"; he also said that "God is conscience, he is even the atheism of the atheist." When he talked about the *ramaraj* (the kingdom of God), he meant not a Hindu theocracy but a society based on *sarvodaya* (the good of all). It doesn't matter that he said "it takes a fairly strenuous course of training to attain to a mental state of non-violence," when we now know that untrained people can be completely non-violent, and that the best course of training for non-violent action is in fact experience of non-violent action. When Gandhi rejected *bhakti* and *jñana* for *karma,* he was only saying that love and knowledge aren't enough, that action is necessary too. When we are horrified by his plan for a sort of revised seventh age of man—sans meat, sans drink, sans sex, sans everything—we should remember that he followed the traditional yearning for *moksha* (release from existence, the same as *nirvana*). We can just as reasonably base our non-violence on a love for life as on a wish for death. We can profit from what he did without agreeing with what he thought.

What we should do—what he would have wanted us to do—is to take from him what we can, without being false to ourselves. "A tiny grain of true non-violence acts in a silent, subtle, unseen way," he said, "and leavens the whole society." Our task is to sow it, and this is what the new pacifists have tried to do.

THE NEW PACIFISM

The new pacifism isn't really all that new. From the old pacifists comes the refusal to fight; from the old anti-militarists comes the determination to resist war; and from Gandhi comes the idea of mass non-violent action. There are other borrowings. From the socialists comes the optimistic view of the future; from the liberals comes the idealistic view of the present; from the anarchists comes the disrespect for authority. But the new pacifists are selective. They reject the sentimentality of the old pacifists, the vagueness of the old anti-militarists, the priggishness of Gandhi, the rigidity of the socialists, the respectability of the liberals, the intolerance of the anarchists.

The basis of the new pacifism is unilateralism, the demand that this country should offer a sort of national *satyagraha* to the world, that whoever presses the button it isn't us. "Someone has to arise in England with the living faith to say that England, whatever happens, shall not use arms," said Gandhi just before the last war. But "that will be a miracle." Miracle or not, that is what we are trying to say. Unilateral disarmament—that is our utopia. Mass non-violent action—that is our myth. Every active ideology depends on a utopia and a myth, a vision of the world to come and a way to get there. "Man is a teleological animal," said Adler, and our *telos* or goal isn't so much the ultimate utopia as the immediate myth. The utopia is static, the myth is dynamic. It's having a myth that keeps us going.

It is important to remember what Sorel said about myths in his *Reflections on Violence* (1906):

> Men who are participating in a great social movement always picture
> their coming action as a battle in which their cause is certain to tri-
> umph. These constructions, whose knowledge is so important, I pro-
> pose to call myths . . . Myths are not descriptions of things but expres-
> sions of a determination to act . . . A myth cannot be refuted, since it is
> at bottom identical with the convictions of a group . . . The myth must
> be judged as a method of acting on the present; any attempt to discuss
> how far it can be taken literally as future history is senseless . . . for
> there is no process by which the future can be predicted scientifically.

The unilateralist utopia and myth can be compared to others. The
Christian utopia is the Kingdom of Heaven, and the myth is the Last
Judgment. The Liberal utopia is parliamentary democracy, and the
myth is the general election. The socialist (that is, communist) utopia is
the classless society, and the myth is the authoritarian revolution based
on the proletarian rising. The anarchist utopia is the free society, and the
myth is the libertarian revolution based on mass non-co-operation. The
syndicalist utopia is anarcho-socialist, and the syndicalist myth is the
general strike (the myth Sorel was interested in).

Now the pacifist utopia is world peace—but the pacifist myth?
Paradoxically, the fatal defect of the old pacifists was that they had no
myth. But they borrowed a myth from Tolstoy and the political anti-
militarists and the anarcho-syndicalists and the anarcho-pacifists—the
myth of the general strike, minus its violence. This myth was elaborated between the wars by politically conscious pacifists, such as the
Dutch anarcho-pacifist Bart de Ligt, who wrote *The Conquest of Violence*
(1937), one of the few texts of non-violence by a non-Gandhian. (Bart
de Ligt also wrote a much longer book called *Creative Peace*, which for
some reason has never been translated into English.) There is an interesting appendix to *The Conquest of Violence*, which consists of the plan
for "Mobilization against All War" put by de Ligt to the 1934 conference of the War Resisters' International. This plan was an ambitious and
detailed version of the non-violent general strike, but the point is that it
had nothing to do with reality.

The task of the new pacifists has been to make the myth real. And
yet the new pacifism grew straight from the old. The British unilateralist movement was begun not by the British Peace Committee or
the Campaign for Nuclear Disarmament, but by orthodox pacifists.
Unilateralism came to life in this country when Harold Steele, an old
member of the No Conscription Fellowship, proposed to enter the
British nuclear test area at Christmas Island early in 1957. The CND

leaders like to take a lot of credit for their success during the last five years, but this was made possible only because the ground had been prepared for so long.

The beginning of postwar pacifist unilateralism was right back in 1949, when some members of the PPU formed a Non-Violent Commission; and in 1951 some members of the NVC formed "Operation Gandhi" following a walk-in on the German Iron Curtain and a pair of sit-downs at the Trawsfynydd camp in Wales earlier in the year. It was "Operation Gandhi" that carried out the first London sit-down, which was not the one led by Bertrand Russell and Michael Scott on February 18, 1961, or the spontaneous one after the launching meeting of CND on February 17, 1958, but was the one by seven men and four women outside the War Office on January 11, 1952. "Operation Gandhi"— which became the Non-Violent Resistance Group—was responsible for many more pioneering demonstrations which have passed into undeserved oblivion. Who now remembers the actions at Aldermaston (yes, Aldermaston) in April 1952, at Mildenhall in July 1952, at South Africa House in September 1952, at Porton in March 1953, at Harwell in April 1953, and at Woolwich in July 1954? Who, for that matter, remembers any unilateralist action before the march to Aldermaston at Easter 1958?

The turning-point in the public attitude to unilateralist demonstrations came at the time of Suez (when the Labour Party discouraged "unconstitutional" obstruction of the attack on Egypt), Hungary (when hundreds of Communist activists found themselves in the political wilderness), and the first British nuclear tests (when the Labour Left began to consider a unilateralist campaign)—that is, at the end of 1956 and the beginning of 1957. The Japanese non-violent demonstration at the Tachinawa base near Sunigawa in October 1956 may have had some impact too. Anyway, the British unilateralist movement was properly organized during 1957. The National Council for the Abolition of Nuclear Weapon Tests was formed in February; the Emergency Committee for Direct Action against Nuclear War was formed to support Harold Steele in April; the H-Bomb Campaign Committee was formed by the Victory for Socialism and Movement for Colonial Freedom groups in August; and the Direct Action Committee against Nuclear War (DAC) was formed to take over from the Non-Violent Resistance Group in November.

At the same time, Albert Schweitzer condemned nuclear tests, Bertrand Russell organized the first Pugwash Conference, and Stephen King-Hall broke through his "thought-barrier" and became converted to the idea of non-violent resistance. Since 1957, unilateralism has never been absent from British thought and British politics. But right from the start it took two forms, orthodox and unorthodox, conventional and unconventional, constitutional and unconstitutional, and was advanced by two kinds of organization—the pressure group, planning demonstrations and marches and meetings, and the revolutionary cell, planning "direct action." The chief unilateralist pressure group for five years has been the Campaign for Nuclear Disarmament, which was developed from the National Council for the Abolition of Nuclear Weapon Tests in January 1958; the chief unilateralist "direct action" groups have been the DAC, and the Committee of 100 (which was invented in May 1960 and formed in October 1960, and which absorbed the DAC in July 1961).

It is not yet possible to write the history of CND. It has never been a pacifist or anarchist body, at least in intention. It has always been a body bringing pressure to bear on the British Government and the Labour Party, at least in intention. It has often seemed to fall into a sentimentalism as dangerous as the old pacifist sentimentalism—so that by getting rid of the British Bomb without changing anything else, we can kill people as long as we don't kill too many at once, and we can let other countries kill as many as they like as long as we don't. This rather opportunist impression was reinforced by the new policy statement, *Steps towards Peace*, which was issued last November.

But CND has nevertheless served a most useful purpose—for pacifism, despite itself, because it has built up mass opposition not only to the Bomb but to all bombs and all war; and for anarchism too, even more despite itself, because it has built up mass opposition not only to the Warfare State that makes and might use the Bomb but to the whole social system that maintains the Warfare State. The rank and file of CND, especially among the young, has always been more radical and militant than the leadership; so what began as a campaign to make the Labour Party (and/or the British government) promise to ban the Bomb, became an unwilling apprenticeship for non-violent revolution. The part played by the New Left in the early part of this process was decisive.

But the real vanguard of the British unilateralist movement was the DAC, whose important contribution to the new pacifism was that it put illegal non-violent action on the political map in this country. The Aldermaston march was invented by DAC as a direct action operation, and the first Aldermaston march was planned by a DAC sub-committee. After 1958 the Aldermaston march was taken over by CND, along with

Gerald Holtom's "nuclear disarmament" symbol (which was designed for the 1958 march and later became the universal unilateralist badge). CND significantly turned the Aldermaston march back to front, so that it became a pilgrimage *from* instead of *to* the research establishment—as if to symbolize the retreat of the conventional unilateralists from unorthodox direct action back to orthodox action (or inaction)—and assumed the trappings of an annual spring festival, ending with a bump at a dull meeting in central London.

Not that DAC was deflected from its chosen course. There was the almost forgotten sit-in at Aldermaston in September 1958, and then the famous sit-downs at North Pickenham in December 1958 and at Harrington in January 1960; these were followed by actions at Foulness in April and May 1960 (organized by an *ad hoc* committee with DAC and CND members), at Finningley in July 1960 (organized by the Northern DAC), and at the Holy Loch in May 1961, and have rightly become a vital part of the unilateralist mythology. We should also remember the attempts to enter the French nuclear test area in the Sahara at the end of 1959 and the beginning of 1960, the CND demonstration at Selby in July 1959, the invasion of the lost village of Imber in January 1961, the guerrilla activities of Polaris action in the spring and summer of 1961, and the Voice of Nuclear Disarmament.

There was never non-violent action like this before in Britain. The Chartists, Suffragettes and Hunger Marchers organized all sorts of spectacular demonstrations, and the Aldermaston march was getting bigger every year, but the DAC was doing something quite different— getting ordinary people used to the idea of not only thinking for themselves and speaking for themselves, but taking action for themselves and inviting punishment for themselves as well. In 1917 the leaders of the Champaran indigo-workers said to Gandhi: The idea of accommodating oneself to imprisonment is a novel thing for us. We will try to assimilate it.

This is what we might well have said forty years later to Michael Scott (who had taken part in *satyagraha* in South Africa during the 1940s) and to Michael Randle and Pat Arrowsmith and April Carter; and they did their best for three years to show us how.

Their methods weren't strictly Gandhian. Gandhi's favorite techniques were the boycott and strike (*hartal*), the fast unto death (*prayopaveshana*), and civil disobedience (*ajnabhanga*), all traditional Indian forms of non-violent resistance. But he rejected the equally traditional technique of the sit-down (*dharna*), calling it barbaric and comparing it with violent sabotage—though his followers often used the sit-down technique, notably in Calcutta in 1922 and in Bombay in 1930. It is ironical that, under the influence of industrial techniques in the West, the sit-down has in fact become the favorite method of the new pacifists, whether it is used for "direct action" (against military sites or other centres of power) or for "civil disobedience" (at significant places in large towns). There are other points of difference with Gandhi. The new pacifists have little training or discipline, and in most cases little love for their opponents. More important, they have had little chance for direct action, or for mass action.

A demonstration doesn't become direct action just because someone says it does. "Wishful thinking," as Peter Cadogan remarks, "has nothing to do with the case." The idea of direct action comes of course from syndicalist doctrine, where it involves a general stay-in strike and a decentralized do-it-yourself revolution, as opposed to the more familiar *coup d'état* carried out by an elitist party at the head of a mass rising. In theory, unilateralist direct action involves an analogous pre-emptive strike against war and decentralized do-it-yourself disarmament, as opposed in this instance to disarmament carried out by a Labour Party converted by the CND pressure group. In practice, unilateralist direct action involves nothing of the kind, and should be interpreted metaphorically rather than literally. It is a myth, an expression of a determination to act, not a description of a thing.

The truth is that the so-called "direct action" demonstrations by the radical unilateralists were really what April Carter in her *Direct Action* (1962) calls "symbolic action"—that is, they went further than "constitutional action" but they didn't go as far as genuine "direct action." Despite all their preparatory work, the DAC was never able to involve the people who make the weapons and build the sites; and when it came nearest to direct action—at North Pickenham—the demonstrators were attacked not only by the servicemen and the police but also by the civilian laborers working on the site. The DAC demonstrations were really propaganda by deed; but they weren't very effective deeds, nor were they very effective propaganda either.

For in just the same way, the demonstrations by the radical unilateralists were "group action"—that is, they went further than individual action, but they didn't go as far as genuine mass action. It is sad but true that there were less than fifty arrests at North Pickenham, less than ninety at Harrington, less than forty at Foulness, and less than thirty at Finningley. Thousands of people would march from Aldermaston to London, but barely a hundred would sit down at a missile base. Part of the trouble may have been that DAC was forced to choose unfavorable times of year and inaccessible corners of the countryside, and part may have been that its members seemed to be rather self-righteous about their message and their methods. Whatever it was that stopped them breaking through the deed barrier, the fact remains that their courageous work was no real threat to the Warfare State—though it was certainly conduct prejudicial to good order and Cold War discipline. Each of their demonstrations illustrated Colin Ward's remark that "the middle-class sits in puddles as a symbolic gesture of its own impotence," and his conclusion that the unilateralist task is "part of a larger task: that of turning the mass society into a mass of societies."

But the first task was to lay the foundations of a movement for mass non-violent resistance. It would be disastrous for the radical unilateralists to calculate their success entirely in terms of the names or the numbers of people who come to or get arrested at illegal demonstrations— we must indeed get beyond counting arses—but names and numbers are significant all the same. It was Ralph Schoenman's recognition of this point that created the Committee of 100. It is not yet possible to write the history of the Committee of 100 either, but it is possible to give an outline of its first two years. It was formed in October 1960 as an act of dissatisfaction with both the moderate compromising CND and the puritanical DAC, and as a gesture of no confidence in orthodox political action—this was after all the month of the unilateralist vote by the annual conference of the Labour Party at Scarborough.

The Committee began as a group of well-known people (with enough unknown people to make up the magic number), which would give authority to demonstrations of increasingly massive civil disobedience. In 1961 the Committee rose. The two formal sit-downs in central London (February 18 and April 29), the four Embassy sit-downs (American, April 3 and September 6; Russian, August 31 and October 21), and the dramatic weekend of mass resistance (Holy Loch on September 16, Trafalgar Square on September 17)—this seemed to be the beginning of a real threat to the Warfare State. But the next weekend of mass resistance (December 9, at Wethersfield, Ruislip, Oxford, Bristol, Cardiff, Manchester and York) proved to be not the end of the beginning but the beginning of the end. In 1962 the Committee fell.

It would be premature to say what went wrong with the Committee of 100. There have been invisible public factors and invidious private factors at work. There has been a tragic waste of energy, trust, and cash. The Committee has not failed—it has disappeared, and been replaced by something else with the same name. All that can be usefully done is to say what has happened. The Wethersfield demonstration in December 1961 was the greatest blow by the Committee at the State; and the Wethersfield trial in February 1962 was the greatest blow by the State at the Committee. In September they arrested the wrong people, but in December they arrested the right people. Before Wethersfield the initiative was in our hands; after Wethersfield it was in theirs. The Committee of 100 never recovered from the Trial of the Six. I still think we were right to go to Wethersfield in December, and I still think we were wrong not to go back to Wethersfield in February. This was our greatest test, and we failed.

In the spring of 1962, the Regional Committees became autonomous, a London Committee was formed, and the National Committee became a co-ordinating body. But this decentralization turned out to be the beginning of a ritualized disintegration, not only of the original Committee into the Regional Committees, but of each Committee into its natural parts. The national office became a tomb, and the national meetings became factious and factitious debates. The same fate later overtook the London office and the London meetings. In the meantime the well-known people who had been members and supporters of the Committee one by one withdrew their membership and sometimes even their support.

The same story was told by the demonstrations in 1962. The two "public assemblies" in central London (March 24 and September 23), the two American Embassy sit-downs (April 26 and July 9), the two "national demonstrations" (Holy Loch on June 9, Greenham Common on June 23)—this seemed to be the end of any real threat to the Warfare State. At the same time the ambitious and enthusiastic Industrial and International Sub-Committees of the Committee of 100 only achieved one real success, the brilliant joint operation at Moscow in July. The terrible weakness of the Committee of 100—and the whole British unilateralist movement—was cruelly revealed last October. On October 20, there was a direct action demonstration at Honington (organized by the East Anglia Committee of 100), which was interesting and imaginative, but still involved only about 200 people. Then on October 23, the Cuban crisis broke, and there was virtually no resistance to the Warfare State at all—no real strikes and no real sit-downs, no barricades and no sabotage, whether violent or non-violent. We lay down and waited to die; the two who went to Ireland were the sensible ones. Since Cuba we have had no doubt about our strength—it is nil. We have been forced to retire to the hills, to fight not as soldiers in the open but as guerrillas in hiding.

But we aren't dead yet, and while there is life there is hope. Gandhi said: "A non-violent revolution is not a programme of 'seizure of power;' it is a programme of transformation of relationships." Landauer said:

> The State is not something which can be destroyed by a revolution. The State is a condition, a certain relationship between people, a way of human behaviour; and we destroy it when we contract different relationships and behave in a different way.

Whatever our own doubts about the effects of our resistance, our rulers seem to have none. They drag us about, and throw us into puddles and fountains, and fine us, and imprison us, and fear us. They beat up Adam Roberts in a police station; they try to deport Ralph Schoenman; they give George Clark nine months; they give the Six twelve or eighteen months; they give Des Lock fifteen (or nine) months; they silence our witnesses and open our letters and tap our telephones. They will hammer us if we undermine them, just as they hammered three anarchists in 1945, and hammered pacifists and anti-militarists in 1939 and 1915, and are hammering the servicemen who have withdrawn their allegiance from the Warfare State. And let us remember these men: Jon Tremain and Brian Magee and Michael McKenna and Edward Parker and Kevin Baxter and Keith Manning and Francis Smith are the vanguard today.

"Freedom—is it a crime?" demanded Herbert Read at the time of the Anarchist Trial. If, like him, you define freedom as "the will to be responsible for one's self," then *of course freedom is a crime*, because it replaces the law of man with the law of God, conscience, principle, decency, inner light, truth, responsibility, humanity, or what you will. The freedom to take direct action, to do it yourself, is both a political and a criminal offence. Even the most pitiful protest against war is resistance to the Warfare State. Any man's death diminishes me, and any man's rebellion strengthens me. We shall go on making our point until it is taken. We are a few, but a happy few. We are in debt, but not in despair. We make mistakes, but people who don't make mistakes don't make anything. We are not grown up, but we never stop growing. We are one-eyed, but we are living in the Country of the Blind. We are neurotics who defy our political parents; but they are psychotics building worlds of fantasy that will collapse around themselves—and us. We are amateur incendiaries, but they are professional pyromaniacs. We are living in a world where faith is always misplaced and hope is always betrayed, and somehow we contrive to keep faith and hope alive; we try to keep charity alive too, though it is difficult.

Instead of playing Greeks and Trojans or Montagues and Capulets, we play Troilus and Cressida or Romeo and Juliet. We are radioactive atoms trying to build up a critical mass and start off a chain reaction. The story isn't over yet. The Committee of 100 is dead: long live the Committee of 100. There is something there, created yesterday and creating tomorrow—but today the struggle. And the struggle is Alex Comfort's struggle: Man against Obedience, Man against Death. If we cannot win the second battle, we can at least win the first. We refuse to be the men of war, we are the men against war. *Non serviamus*—we shall not be slaves.

Originally published as a pamphlet by Nonviolence 63 (London, 1963) [revision of "Direct Action and the New Pacifism," Anarchy 13 (March 1962), and "Disobedience and the New Pacifism," Anarchy 14 (April 1962)].

5
THE COMMITTEE OF 100: ENDS AND MEANS

NEITHER I NOR ANY OTHER MEMBER OF ANY COMMITTEE OF 100 can say what the policy of the Committee of 100 is, because the Committee has no official policy and no power to enforce one if it had. We all make up our minds in our own way, and one of the few things we agree about is precisely that there are few things we agree about. But we are united by the two fundamentals which brought us together in the first place—unilateral nuclear disarmament as the end, and mass non-violent action as the means.

It is true that many Committee people have always wanted a proper policy statement, and there is a sub-committee working on yet another draft for the National Committee; but the National Committee has no more authority over the Regional Committees than they have over their own members, so the best we shall ever see is probably some sort of personal manifesto. This situation is implicit in the very structure of the Committee of 100—the National Committee is simply a co-ordinating group of members from the thirteen Regional Committees, and each of these autonomous Regional Committees and each of the various autonomous sub-committees is simply a co-operating group of autonomous individuals. We are learning how to build chains of communication instead of command and how to keep ideas and information moving without profit or punishment. We can do this because we are not afraid to disagree with one another and because we agree about the basic ends and means.

Our end is familiar now. Most people who support the Committee of 100 also support the Campaign for Nuclear Disarmament, because the two wings of the unilateralist movement have no quarrel about ends, and in general we accept the decisions of CND annual conferences. We want Britain to ban the Bomb and leave NATO, to disengage from the

Cold War and adopt positive neutralism, to reject colonialism abroad and racialism at home. Many of us go further than this. Because of our sympathy with friends in America we favor American as well as British unilateralism, and because of our left-wing political affiliations we favor radical or revolutionary solutions to the problems of our own society.

But very few of us are Communists or fellow travellers or even "Trotskyists," and we condemn the nuclear policy of the Russian Government just as vigorously as that of our own. A small and decreasing number of us are adventurers who come for excitement and find enlightenment instead. A small but increasing number are anarchists who have taught us that war is the health of the State and the State is the disease of society. A larger number—including the best of us—are pacifists who have taught us how to protest and resist. Some of us are religious and some of us aren't, and no one cares who are which. The great majority of us are socialists with libertarian and syndicalist tendencies who have been driven into the Committee of 100 by a growing impatience with conventional political methods, though many of us still give grudging support to the Labour Party as well as CND. Lastly, we are patriots who wish our country would help to make the world a better place.

Our unconventional political methods derive from the belief that we must say "No" to the Bomb in deeds as well as words and to the smallest violence as well as the greatest, and that we must force people to hear us even if they hurt us too. Whether ours is the non-violence of the weak or of the strong, we must take non-violent action against this thing or take no action at all. We only do together what conscientious objectors have always done alone, but we won't wait until the Third World War begins. I am not a pacifist, but my conscience objects now, and I must obey my conscience even if I disobey the State. Everyone blames war criminals like Eichmann who don't break the law—we are peace criminals. Everyone says something should be done—we say do it yourself. The politicians say: If you want peace, prepare for war. We say: If you want peace, prepare for peace. They say the end justifies the means—we say means are ends.

Our means still seem unfamiliar, in spite of the long illegal tradition of the Levellers, Radicals, Chartists, Suffragettes, and hunger marchers, in spite of the long non-violent tradition of Winstanley, Fox, Godwin, Thoreau, and Tolstoy, and in spite of the work of Gandhi who united these two traditions. For ten years before the emergence of the Committee of 100, small groups of unilateralists were pioneering civil disobedience "sit-downs" at town centres and direct action "sit-downs" at military sites. The people in these groups were dismissed as harmless cranks, but during the last few months the same people in the Committee of 100 have taken the Bomb to the highest court in the land, and have forced our rulers to use the Public Order Act and the Official Secrets Act against us, though we have caused no disorder except in the minds of our fellow countrymen and have betrayed no secrets except those hidden from them. Does a free society put harmless cranks in prison? Perhaps we aren't harmless; perhaps our society isn't free.

The most important activity of the Committee of 100 is the organization of illegal demonstrations against the Bomb (though there are several sub-committees doing other work, especially industrial agitation). A Committee demonstration is a form of propaganda by deed, an opportunity for mass protests, a rehearsal for mass resistance, and a dramatic symbol of what we are talking about. When the servants of the State defended Wethersfield against us with all their military paraphernalia, and when one of them was forced by one of us to admit in public that he would press the button, we made our point—that the obverse of the Welfare State is the Warfare State, that Auschwitz is being budded here in England's green and pleasant land.

We shall go on making our point until you take it. We are a few, but a happy few; we are in debt, but not in despair. We make mistakes, but people who don't make mistakes don't make anything. Our programme is full—there are direct action demonstrations against two nuclear bases this month, in September there will be the biggest demonstration of civil disobedience London has ever seen, and this will be followed by more direct action. We are radioactive atoms trying to build a critical mass and start a political chain reaction. I am glad to be one of these atoms. When I think of the people I love and the fate being prepared for them, I know what I must do. What about you—would you press the button?

Originally published in The Guardian, *June 22, 1962.*

6
THE COMMITTEE OF 100 AND ANARCHISM
(WITH RUTH WALTER)

IN HER ARTICLE ON "ANARCHISTS AND THE COMMITTEE OF 100" (*Anarchy* 50), Diana Shelley came to the right conclusion—that the process was one of "exodus" rather than "influx," and that "many more anarchists came out of the Committee of 100 than ever went into it"—but in doing so she gave a false impression of the early period of the Committee which should be corrected before it becomes generally accepted.

To begin at the beginning, Diana Shelley is wrong about the origins of the Committee. It isn't true that "the Committee of 100 began as a purely breakaway movement from CND, and arose from a disagreement over tactics rather than aims." This was the attitude of some members, especially among the "names," but not of the Committee as such. It is true that "the whole image was far removed from that of the Direct Action Committee," but no further than it was from that of CND. It is true that "it looked at one point in 1960 as if CND might be persuaded to advocate and organize civil disobedience," but this never happened, and that was exactly why the Committee of 100 appealed both to CND supporters who weren't happy with constitutional methods and to DAC supporters who weren't happy with small numbers, as well as to unilateralists (like ourselves) who weren't happy with either CND or DAC.

The point of the Committee of 100 was that it was meant to be a new departure, but if anything it was a breakaway movement from DAC rather than from CND, and it always owed more to DAC than to CND. Its first Secretary came from DAC; its first two full-time workers were the Chairman and Secretary of DAC; it was joined by all but two of the members of DAC before its first demonstration in February 1961; between 40 and 50 percent of the members of its Working Group during the first six months came from DAC; in March 1961 there was even some fear that it might be dominated by DAC; and in June 1961, after the first Holy Loch demonstration, it absorbed DAC.

The Committee's President, Bertrand Russell, and its Vice-President, Michael Scott, personified on one hand the double origin of the new organization—with, however, a clear bias towards DAC—and on the other hand the moderation of its well-known members. It is important to realize that most of the "names" in the Committee always lagged behind the rank and file—hence the "hardly revolutionary" tone of the Russell-Scott manifesto *Act or Perish*, and the "respectable" image of the early Committee demonstrations, which concealed a revolutionary and hardly respectable purpose—and that the Committee of 100 began in effect as a "front" organization. The "names" gave authority to a program which might otherwise have been as timid as that of CND or as unpopular as that of DAC.

Incidentally, Ralph Schoenman can't be taken as one of the "exceptions" to the "liberal" approach of the Committee—he was after all the main driving force behind the formation of the Committee and behind its activity during its first year, and the approach of his *Peace News* articles (February 17 and August 25, 1961) would have been shared by most of its members throughout that time. Nor can he be so easily distinguished from the "formal" anarchists, for he called himself an anarchist, and his general ideas were close to those of the other anarchists—"formal" and otherwise—in the Committee at that time.

Secondly, Diana Shelley is wrong about the attitude of the anarchist movement during the early period of the Committee of 100. It is true that "the editorials in *Freedom* were hardly a reflection of the feeling in and around the Committee," but for one thing they weren't intended to be, and for another they weren't always a reflection of the feeling in and around the anarchist movement either. It isn't true that the attitude to the Committee of the editors of *Freedom* "began as an aloof one." They always supported the Committee of 100—as they had previously supported the DAC—and they printed plenty of contributions showing that many anarchists were deeply committed to it. During 1960, before the Committee had been formed, *Freedom* published several articles and letters suggesting that the next step for the unilateralist movement should be something more than had yet been attempted by either CND or DAC:

> Constitutional protest is ultimately useless, since it can be ignored
> . . . and unconstitutional protest based on civil disobedience is almost
> as useless, so long as the disobedience is too damned civil for words.

Bearing witness is not enough. Nor is it enough to muster as many people as watched the Cup Final or filed past Princess Margaret's wedding bouquet, if all they are going to do is to wave banners or listen to speeches. Sooner or later a great many laws must be broken by a great many people if anything radical is to be done on this island. [June 4]

It is better to march against bombs than to talk or write against them, but it won't in itself get rid of bombs. The only way to do that is to go and pull the bloody things to bits or bury them . . . If only a march would just once turn into a mob and break into the Aldermaston establishment or the House of Commons, the marchers might realise their potentiality. For ultimately it is as futile to wave banners or to sit in the mud as it is to fight windmills with a lance . . . Civil disobedience and passive resistance and hunger-strikes and marches and processions and so on are all very well. But in the end disobedience is nothing unless it is extremely uncivil. What are we waiting for? [September 3]

The answer to that last question was, apparently, the Committee of 100, which was formed in the following month. The editors of *Freedom* welcomed its appearance: "A movement of civil disobedience will probably not succeed in removing the threat of nuclear weapons. But it may well do something to shake enough people in this country and the world into a new way of thinking." [November 5].

During 1961, when the Committee was riding high, they published many articles and letters about it. They printed *Act or Perish*, although it was "hardly revolutionary" (January 21). Before the Committee's first demonstration, they advised the readers of *Freedom* to "sit down—without illusions," and added that "anarchists are very much in favour of movements which are prepared to engage in acts of civil disobedience" (February 18). The main front-page article in the Aldermaston issue of *Freedom* that year was an account of the Committee of 100 by one of its anarchist members (April 1). *Freedom* always devoted considerable space to favorable reports of the big Committee demonstrations (March 4, May 7, September 23, December 16), just as they had done for the DAC (January 17, 1959, and January 9, 1960). The editors of *Freedom* declared their support and solidarity when George Clark was imprisoned and Ralph Schoenman threatened with deportation (November 18), and again when the Six were imprisoned (February 24, 1962).

It is true that "*Freedom* argued strongly against the . . . belief in the value of being jailed" and was "unconvinced of the worth of the sit-down as a tactic," but many members and supporters of the Committee felt the same. It is not quite true that "the only well-known anarchists who were originally members of the Committee faded from it just at the time when the action envisaged turned in more anarchistic directions." Alex Comfort said at the first meeting of the Committee that he wouldn't take part in its demonstrations, although he supported them (and remained a member until he had to accept a binding-over order in September 1961), and at the same meeting he advocated the "other activities in the movement" which he then turned to instead to be in good time for the Committee's first demonstration. As for Herbert Read, he never tried to exert a specifically anarchist influence on the Committee, and always saw his part in it as that of a "name" giving authority to and sometimes taking part in large-scale set pieces of straightforward civil disobedience (as on February 18 and September 17, 1961).

Thirdly, Diana Shelley is wrong about the attitude of the Committee of 100 during its early period. It isn't true that "the Committee of 100 evolved into a decisive and influential experiment in libertarian action," or that "during the first year of its existence . . . the Committee took several steps in the direction of an anarchist position." The Committee *began* as an organization for libertarian action, and its position never changed. John Morris's article in *Peace News* (October 6, 1961) gave a false impression of the early Committee meetings; the "series of clear, simple decisions, usually almost unanimous," existed only in his imagination—in fact, the decisions of the Committee then, as since, were usually confused, complex, and far from unanimous, especially when there was a wide choice of projects. What happened after the first demonstration on February 18, was typical.

On March 12 there were fifteen resolutions on future action, of which only two minor ones got a two-thirds majority; on May 7 there were seven resolutions on future action, of which none got a two-thirds majority; on May 27 there were nine resolutions on future action, of which only one got a two-thirds majority (this was for the September weekend of mass resistance against Polaris). Things were the same at the beginning as they were one or two years later.

It may be true that the Committee's "instinctive rejection of the apparatus of indirect democracy" and the "concepts of direct democracy" which it adopted instead seemed to John Morris—and even perhaps to "most supporters"—to be "new to modern political thought," but he was wrong, for they were nothing of the kind. Nor, however, were they the result of any "anarchist principle of autonomous decentralization"— at first they were the only way of organizing civil disobedience demonstrations, and later they were the only way of keeping the movement going. Supporters were allowed to demonstrate as they wished, and Regional Committees were allowed to set themselves up as they wished, not only because of principle, but also because they were going to do what they wanted anyway. The Committee always realized that it couldn't hope to control its supporters on demonstrations, and the marshalling system was always felt to be unsatisfactory. In the same way, the Committee always realized that it couldn't hope to control its supporters between demonstrations either, and the growth of the regional and local organization was a result of this; during September 1961, the Working Group decided that "Committees should be formed as they crop up" (September 25), and the Committee noted that "Committees of 100 are already being formed throughout the country whether we like it or not" (September 30).

It isn't true that "in terms of action, too, there was a move further away from conventional demonstrating towards a more anarchist approach." As we have shown, the Committee always owed more to the DAC than to CND, and this can be seen in its discussions as well as its personnel. During the first few months of its life, the Committee considered demonstrating at "a rocket base," Fylingdales, Woolwich, Aldermaston, Foulness, Holy Loch, Porton, and Imber, as well as in London. It went on demonstrating in London for so long not because it was "moderate" rather than "radical," or "conventional" rather than "anarchist," but because it was practical. After the first demonstration on February 18 the Working Group decided

> that, while the Committee should not confine its activities to London, the next two or three demonstrations might have to be in the London area because of the importance of ensuring really large numbers. That direct action against nuclear bases and installations was necessary, but as such demonstrations were likely to involve smaller numbers their timing would have to be carefully planned so that they could not be written off as defeats for the Committee [March 10].

Thus the decision to stay in London was tactical, not ideological, a matter of timing, not principle. The Committee always wanted to get on with direct action, but not until the right moment, and when at last it did so—on May 27—this was not a move towards an anarchist approach, but a decision that the right moment had come.

So it isn't true that the idea of combining the direct action of the DAC with the numbers of "mass civil disobedience" came after the

Trafalgar Square demonstration on September 17, 1961. This idea was one of the fundamentals of the Committee, it was the constant preoccupation of the Committee, and it was put into practice by the Committee on the day before the Trafalgar Square demonstration. It is true that "the Wethersfield demonstration was radical, when compared with the Committee's previous activities," but it wasn't as radical as all that. There was no "disregard for property, involved in climbing fences and walking on"—on the contrary, the Committee specifically asked demonstrators not to climb fences or damage property in any way. It was not the first time the Committee had challenged "a law with more serious penalties than that of obstruction"—there had always been the common laws of conspiracy and of incitement (for which George Clark had got nine months), and in September there had also been the Justices of the Peace Act and the Public Order Act (both carrying a maximum penalty of six months). Nor was Wethersfield the first time the Committee had attempted "the real physical obstruction of the State's weapons of war as opposed to symbolic obstruction outside the ministries which ostensibly controlled the weapons"—it had organized a demonstration at the Holy Loch on September 16 and 17 when there were at least four times as many demonstrators as at the DAC demonstration there four months earlier, and at least twice as many as at the Wethersfield demonstration three months later.

The Wethersfield demonstration was a failure not only because many of the people who had made the Trafalgar Square demonstration a success were not prepared to go to a nuclear base, but also because many demonstrators went to Ruislip instead (thus one of us went to Wethersfield, and the other to Ruislip); and the Committee's mistake was not so much that it decided to go to Wethersfield as that it decided to go to Ruislip on the same day. Many of the people who had made the Trafalgar Square demonstration a success were quite prepared to go to a nuclear base, but they took the easier choice and went to the demonstration nearer London. Wethersfield *and* Ruislip were a failure, but *either* Wethersfield *or* Ruislip might well have been a success.

It may be true that "the arrest and trial of the Six showed up still further how marginal the influence of anarchist thinking was on the majority of supporters," but surely not in the ways suggested. It is difficult to believe that any genuine supporters of the Committee would really have turned Pat Pottle over to the police "with easy consciences," and it should be remembered that the Committee issued a statement supporting his decision to go on the run; indeed, one of the most significant things about this episode was that so many Committee people did support him. The reason why "the only action advocated to help the Six" was "the rather ridiculous one of supporters lining up outside police stations to confess their shared guilt and ask for retribution" was that the Six didn't want any more help, and preferred the Committee to get on with its job; the Committee naturally didn't want either to flout their wishes, or to jeopardize their slight chance of getting off. The reason why "the only protest" against the imprisonment of the Six was "a rally in Trafalgar Square" was that Pat Arrowsmith's proposal to return to Wethersfield was rejected by overwhelming majorities, first by the Committee (January 28, 1962), and then by its supporters (February 9); this may have been a "failure of nerve," but it may have been a recognition of reality. Anyway, the wish to do more than this was not *anarchist*—there were anarchists on both sides—and the decision to do no more than this didn't prove that the Committee was "a still essentially bourgeois-minded movement" (whatever that means); it was after all prepared to do a lot more than any other organization.

Incidentally, we aren't happy about the attempt to distinguish between Committee demonstrations that were "anarchist" and those that were not. It wasn't more *anarchist* for the Committee to demonstrate at the Holy Loch and Wethersfield rather than in Whitehall or Trafalgar Square—it could even be argued that it was *less* anarchist to do so, since there was the implication that the problem of nuclear war was military rather than political. *Freedom*, after all, didn't prefer one kind of demonstration to another, and would always have preferred an *industrial* campaign to either: "Is it not time that all the goodwill present at those demonstrations be used to persuade our fellow workers to refuse to sell their labor to the merchants of death?" (April 1, 1961).

Finally, Diana Shelley is wrong about the part played by anarchists in the Committee of 100 during the early period. From the beginning, many people in and around the Committee were what Alan Lovell called "emotional anarchists"; but it was significant that when he described this phenomenon it was not in an anarchist paper but in the *New Left Review* (March–April 1961), and that he added that "the formal anarchist movement in this country is totally useless and an absolute disaster for any kind of serious anarchist thinking." Now whether he really meant this or not—he was certainly more charitable when he wrote about the DAC two years earlier in the *Universities and Left Review* (Spring 1959), and when he spoke two months later to the London Anarchists (14 May 1961)—the important thing was that, as one of the most influential members of the Committee of 100 at that time, he was typical of the many Committee people who could be labeled as anarchists but were indifferent or actually hostile to the anarchist movement; some of them objected to being labeled as anarchists at all, and to avoid confusion it might almost be better not to call them anarchists—like the groups which appeared all over the country during 1962 and 1963, they were perhaps "libertarian rather than strictly anarchist."

These emotional anarchists or libertarians were a permanent section of the rank and file of the Committee. They were the successors of—and in some cases the same as—a similar section of the rank and file of the DAC. Thus of the two-thirds of the North Pickenham demonstrators who answered a questionnaire in December 1958, 3 percent supported pacifist parties, 7 percent supported the Communist Party, 23 percent supported the Labour and Cooperative Parties, and as many as 67 percent supported no party (*Peace News*, January 2, 1959). This section was the main source of anarchist influence in the Committee, and in a sense it inoculated the Committee against the influence of the "formal" anarchists, as represented by *Freedom*. When special articles about the Committee appeared in *Peace News*—especially "The Relevance of Resistance" (September 15, 1961) and "The Committee of 100 and a New Political Basis" (September 22)—or in *Solidarity*—especially "From Civil Disobedience to Social Revolution," "Civil Disobedience and the Working Class," and "Civil Disobedience and the State"—they were based on close knowledge of Committee affairs, and were read by a large number of Committee people. By contrast, when special articles about the Committee appeared in *Freedom*—especially the "Inquest on the Sit-Down" series (December 16 and 23, 1961, and January 6, 1962)—they were based only on outside observation of Committee affairs, and were read by only a small number of Committee people. Even when *Anarchy* published special articles about the Committee which were based to a greater extent on inside knowledge of Committee affairs—especially in the issues on "Direct Action" (March 1962) and "Disobedience" (April 1962)—they still appealed mostly to people on the fringes of the Committee; and when they appealed to people closer to the Committee, this was usually because they were also based to a great extent on Committee rather than specifically anarchist ideas.

The trouble was that the editors of *Freedom*—and the leaders of the anarchist movement in general—were not so much aloof from the Committee of 100 as out of touch with it; they were interested all right, but not involved. The result was that many of the Committee people who accepted the anarchist label and even joined the anarchist movement did so in spite of rather than because of the efforts of "formal" anarchists. The important thing about most of the Committee anarchists during the early period was that they didn't really care whether they were anarchists or not. At that time the question either didn't arise or wasn't worth bothering about. In joining the Committee they had at last freed themselves from the various movements of traditional politics, and another movement with a traditional ideology and a traditional organization—even if these were actually similar to their own ideology and organization—meant nothing to them. Their anarchism was a brand new, do-it-yourself, instant anarchism. If they were told that they were closer to Bakunin than to Marx, they would say "So what?"—and they were right. The important question wasn't whether such a statement was true or whether it was relevant; and in the early period of the Committee it was completely irrelevant. That was a time for action, not argument: for movement, not *a* movement: for propaganda by deed, not word.

The Committee anarchists couldn't be distinguished from their comrades by being more "radical." Pat Arrowsmith, who was probably the most radical personality in the Committee, was never an anarchist. The Committee anarchists were like the Committee socialists and the Committee pacifists. In nearly every question of organization or action, there were anarchists on both sides, socialists on both sides, and pacifists on both sides. The Committee of 100 was an ideological no man's land. You were identified not by your uniform but by your behavior, not by what you might say but by what you would do. This was true as long as the Committee held the initiative. When the Committee lost the initiative, during 1962 and 1963, many Committee anarchists joined the anarchist movement; but many did not, because they still didn't really care whether they were anarchists or not. They were still indifferent or actually hostile to the anarchist movement; and some of them still objected to being labeled as anarchists at all.

The emotional anarchists or libertarians are still there. Some are still active in the Committee; some are working for *Peace News* or *Solidarity*, or—since 1963—*Resistance*. Some read *Freedom* and *Anarchy*; some do not. We are typical of the ambivalent relationship between the Committee of 100 and anarchism. One of us went into the Committee from the anarchist movement, and the other moved towards an anarchist position while working in the Committee; one of us accepts the anarchist label, and the other rejects it—though we seldom disagree about action. At the moment, neither of us is happy either with the Committee of 100 or with the anarchist movement. But we are both worried by the suggestion in the last sentence of Diana Shelley's article—that "this may be the time for the *real* anarchist infiltration." On the contrary, anything of the kind would do no good either to the Committee of 100 or to the anarchist movement, or—which is more important—to the cause we are all working for.

Originally published in Anarchy *52 (June 1965).*

7
THE SPIES FOR PEACE AND AFTER

THE SPIES FOR PEACE EPISODE AT EASTER 1963 WAS ONE OF THE MOST successful single actions of the old nuclear disarmament movement. It is described here in some detail partly to preserve the memory of such a dramatic event in the recent history of the British left and partly to consider what lessons may still be drawn from it. First let us summarize the achievement, purpose and significance of the people who called themselves the Spies for Peace.

Their main achievement was to make public the secret plans of the authorities for an emergency regional government of the country in the case of nuclear warfare—or of political breakdown. Until they took a hand, these plans were known only to the relatively few people involved and were deliberately concealed from the wider population in whose name (and at whose expense) they had been made. A combination of the criminal law, embodied in the Official Secrets Acts, and of bureaucratic tradition, supported by the media, meant that not only possibly damaging military information but perfectly innocuous civilian material was surrounded by an elaborate curtain of security, and that the only public references to the system were guarded hints in the press.

Their main purpose was not to render assistance to any enemy country or subversive organization, but to provide this information to the general public and at the same time to reinforce the argument of the nuclear disarmament movement that the official preparations for a future war were directed against rather than towards the welfare of ordinary people.

Their main significance was to show that a small underground group could take effective direct action against the power of the establishment, discover and distribute secret information very widely, avoid detection and punishment, and through such propaganda by both word and deed set an example for subsequent exposure of more such material.

CRISIS IN THE COMMITTEE OF 100

The Spies for Peace had nothing to do with any foreign power or any Marxist party, but were a group of libertarian activists in the Committee of 100.

The old nuclear disarmament movement—like all reformist or revolutionary movements—tended from its beginnings soon after the Second World War to be polarized between moderates, who favored constitutional action through conventional demonstrations and pressure on Parliament, and radicals, who favored direct action through unconventional demonstrations and pressure from the people. The moderates were represented by a series of organizations culminating at the beginning of 1958 in the formation of the Campaign for Nuclear Disarmament, which had broad support but was run by a small group of political activists, mainly associated with the Labour Party and later also with the Communist Party. The radicals were represented by a series of organizations leading at the end of 1957 to the formation of the Direct Action Committee Against Nuclear War, which organized small-scale non-violent demonstrations and won little support for a couple of years, and culminating at the end of 1960 in the formation of the Committee of 100, which organized a series of large-scale non-violent demonstrations and won considerable support for a couple of years. The Committee of 100 was particularly successful in attracting radicals both from the old revolutionary left and from the New Left, which had emerged during the late 1950s, as well as old pacifists and new anti-militarists, and also in combining the long tradition of popular protest and resistance with the fresh techniques of non-violent civil disobedience. By the end of 1962, however, the Committee of 100 was in serious and worsening difficulties. The original Committee was based in London, where it held its meetings and maintained a paid staff in a permanent office. Its success during 1961 led to such increase in support all over the country that at the beginning of 1962 it was replaced by a dozen Regional Committees, which took over the organization of action, very loosely coordinated by a federal National Committee of 100, which took over the existing staff and office and the organization of national meetings in various parts of the country. (The development of a bureaucracy was prevented by the authorities through frequent arrests of leading officials!)

This process of devolution increased local autonomy and activity but weakened the sense of unity and direction of the original Committee. At the same time the imprisonment for twelve or eighteen months of six of its most active leaders in February 1962 (for organizing its most ambitious demonstrations at Wethersfield and several other places on 9 December 1961) weakened the sense of confidence and courage of the whole radical wing of the nuclear disarmament movement. The various Committees were increasingly divided by theoretical arguments about non-violence and direct action and broader political aims and by practical arguments about how to regain the initiative and how to restore the sense of identity.

Meanwhile the moderate wing of the movement, represented by CND, was dominated by the need to remain respectable and acceptable in the face of the temporary success of the Committee of 100, and there was considerable discontent among the rank and file over its activity. Its major new policy statement, *Steps Towards Peace* (which was drafted by the New Left leader Stuart Hall and issued in November 1962), was widely considered to betray the cause of unilateralism, and the plan to hold yet another conventional march from Aldermaston to London at Easter 1963, without any radical demonstrations on the way or a dramatic climax at the end, was similarly considered to ignore the developments of the past two years.

The problems of the Committee of 100 were most acute in London. The London Committee, which was inaugurated on April 1, 1962, was by far the largest single organization in the movement. It was the only one apart from the National Committee itself to maintain paid staff and a permanent office, and it also had a Working Group, which met every week and a local convenor system. But it was the most deeply troubled. After the last demonstration organized by the original Committee of 100—a sit-down in Parliament Square on March 24, 1962—it proved impossible to organize a major demonstration in London, other than emergency actions arising from sudden international events (such as the American and Russian nuclear tests in April and August and the Cuba crisis in October). The London Committee decided at its second meeting, on May 13, to organize a large-scale sit-down in Whitehall for September 9; but as late as September 2 this had to be cancelled because of lack of support (only 4,000 pledges were received, against a target of 7,000) and reorganized as a conventional demonstration two weeks later. All of the most important Committee of 100 demonstrations during this period were organized outside London—by the Scottish Committee (at Holy Loch on June 10), by the Oxford Committee (at Greenham Common on June 23–24), and by the East Anglian Committee (at Honington on October 20)—though most of the participants in the last two came from the London region. The most successful of all took place outside Britain—in the Red Square in Moscow, when members of the Committee of 100 held a public meeting during the World Disarmament Conference on July 13.

The position had been made still more serious by the failure of the Committee of 100 generally to respond adequately to the Cuban missile crisis in October 1962, when neither the non-aligned policy nor the non-violent methods of the Committee made much impact. The famous people who had made up most of the original Committee of 100 dropped out—culminating in the resignation of Bertrand Russell in November 1962, when the London Committee dissociated itself from his biased position during the Cuba crisis. Meeting after meeting failed to decide the crucial issues of "future action" because the membership was so deeply divided over the basic issue of what kind of action was appropriate once "sit-downs" had lost their novelty. The other Regional Committees became increasingly impatient with the state of the London Committee—as a meeting of the National Committee of 100 in London on 18–19 August noted tactfully, "It was generally agreed that the London Committee should be regarded as in a state of transition"—and also with the weakness of the National Committee.

This critical situation in the Committee of 100 was the scene of the development of the Spies for Peace, who emerged from the London Committee during the long, cold winter of 1962–3.

"BEYOND COUNTING ARSES"

At the end of 1962 the London Committee of 100 provisionally planned another large-scale sit-down in Central London for May 12, 1963, but it proved impossible to settle the details and even to confirm the principle of such a demonstration. At the beginning of 1963 this became the symbol of the deepening crisis in the Committee movement. On January 14, a meeting of the London Working Group revealed strong dissatisfaction with the planned demonstration; there was a close vote to cancel it, and a general feeling that there should be a major demonstration before Easter, but no agreement about what to put in its place. On January 21 the London Committee held an emergency meeting to discuss the issue. The circumstances were particularly unfortunate: Helen Allegranza—a popular member of the Committee, the only woman among the six imprisoned leaders, and the new secretary of the National Committee—was found dead that day, and the news of her suicide cast a shadow over the whole meeting; and a power-cut that evening meant that it had to be held in virtual darkness as well as extreme cold.

The 3½-hour meeting was dominated by bitter disagreements, which were not resolved by a series of decisions to go ahead with the May 12 demonstration as an orthodox "public assembly" culminating in a traditional sit-down, and also to hold a march to Parliament on Budget Day, April 3. A small group of members present who were strongly opposed to these decisions felt that it had become essential to make some kind of collective stand, which would bring home to the Committee leaders and officials that the rank and file of the movement was dissatisfied with such an unimaginative approach. They met at a pub immediately after the meeting and then at a Soho restaurant three days later, and began a series of frequent meetings to decide how to take the next appropriate opportunity to explain their dissident position and to influence their colleagues. They were begged by the officials of the National and London Committees and other leading figures not to harm the movement, but they decided that the situation had gone beyond polite disagreement and demanded much more radical dissent.

An appropriate opportunity arose immediately. On February 9–10 there was a national "Way Ahead" conference in London—the first of many—to consider the future of the Committee of 100. It was in effect a general meeting of the radical nuclear disarmament movement, most of those present being deeply unhappy in various ways about the way things were going but equally unable to agree about the way to improve them. As usual, nothing concrete emerged from the weekend's talk; but a paper was presented to the conference by the dissident group which defined once and for all the oppositionist line against the accepted forms of Committee activity—especially against the obsessions with non-violence, openness, symbolic actions, arrests, names, respectability, and so on.

The paper took the form of a duplicated eight-page quarto pamphlet called *Beyond Counting Arses*, written by one member of the group on the basis of its discussions and signed by eight others, dated February 6 and circulated on February 7. It began by describing the confusion in the nuclear disarmament movement in general and in the Committee of 100 in particular, singling out "the lack of common ground among its members and supporters" and its organizational chaos. It pungently expressed total dissatisfaction with the established policy of limping from sit-down to sit-down, relying on "the number of arrested arses" and the length of the press reports to keep the whole process going. It insisted that the most significant demonstrations during the previous year—such as that in Moscow's Red Square in July 1962 and some of those in London during the Cuba crisis in October 1962—had taken place "in spite of rather than through the Committee's normal structure." It dismissed "the perennial back-to-the-womb suggestion for a mass sit-down in Whitehall." It listed the assets of the Committee of 100—its past reputation, its experience of illegal activity, and the commitment of its members—and it called for a deliberate continuation of "radical action" and also a move forward into more consciously subversive activity. The general proposal was that "we must attempt to hinder the warfare state in every possible way."

Three ways of doing this were suggested. The first was a campaign of "Civil Disobedience in Print"—to unmask and publicize the most secret preparations of the Warfare State . . . publish the location of rocket bases and what goes on in the germ warfare centers . . . give details about the secret hide-outs of "civil" defense—and the secretly kept lists of those who will be catered for in the event of nuclear war . . . publish the names of the emergency government "gauleiters" and details of phone-tapping and of the activities of the Special Branch.

The general position laid down was as follows:

> As recent events have shown, the Official Secrets Act does not really function to prevent espionage, but to keep the facts from the people of this country. There can be little information that a foreign power cannot obtain by bribery, blackmail or plain observation. We propose that the Committee should deliberately take the lid off these facts, and let people know what the state does in their name. It is clear that activities of this sort would have to involve certain measures of secrecy, analogous to those practised by VND [the Voice of Nuclear Disarmament, the pirate radio system loosely associated with the Committee of 100].

Various other forms of action were proposed or suggested, and the paper ended with the following conclusion: We do not believe in passive martyrdom. We are not in this movement to opt out of a burden on our consciences but to fight for what we believe in.

THE DISCOVERY OF RSG-6

Beyond Counting Arses had no effect on the conference itself, though it irritated or impressed many of those who read it. In the light of this situation, the group—reinforced by some new members who were interested in putting its proposals into practice—decided that if it couldn't influence the Committee movement by argument it would have to do so by action, either by a small but dramatic demonstration of its own or else by the organization of a mass demonstration which it could prepare and then present to the movement as a fait accompli. In either case, it was felt necessary to bypass the inevitable bottle-neck of prolonged discussion and persistent dissent in the Committee by doing whatever had to be done themselves.

On February 15 the group considered various possible actions— to sabotage the parliamentary debate on the Defense White Paper on March 4–5 or the Budget speech on April 3, whether by interrupting the debate or by disrupting it with the release of some noxious substance from the public gallery (the latter plan was eventually put into effect seven years later, when a CS gas canister was thrown into the chamber in July 1970); to organize a "sleep-out" in the Reading streets or a "sleep-in" at the Reading Town Hall on the first night of the Aldermaston March, in protest against the Council's threat to refuse accommodation to the marchers; or else to organize some kind of diversion of the March at a suitable place along the route.

At this point in the discussion it was remembered that political contacts in Reading had once mentioned someone knowing someone who had worked at a secret bunker near the town. This seemed worth following up, so on February 16 four members of the group drove to Reading. The contacts confirmed that the person in question had been a workman employed on installing equipment in an underground bunker just off the A4, the Reading-London main road—that is, the route of the Aldermaston March on its second day. On the strength of this information they immediately searched the whole area. After many hours of driving over ice-covered roads and tramping over snow-covered fields in the middle of the worst winter for years, at the end of the afternoon they finally found what they assumed must be the place, at the east end of the village of Warren Row, a couple of miles off the main road, eight miles out of Reading. They climbed over the low bank by the locked gate to have a closer look. They took photographs of the general view of the place, the ramp, the air filters, the electric cables, the radio masts, and so on. They were just about to leave when one of them tried the boiler-house door and found that it was unlocked. They went in, looked around, and were about to go out again when they noticed another door, which was also unlocked; it led to a steep staircase which led down into a huge office complex. They rushed down, took a quick look round, grabbed what papers they could find on a desk and a notice-board near the entrance, saw from the visitors' book that the boiler-man was due to call in half an hour, and rushed out again.

On February 17, the London Committee of 100 yet again considered future action, and after another long discussion finally decided to cancel the proposed demonstration on May 12 in favor of supporting a demonstration organized by the East Anglian Committee of 100 at the Marham nuclear base on May 11. But by this time it was too late for the group to be diverted from its own activity, and anyway this decision, though welcome, seemed only to confirm that the London Committee was still unable to do anything on its own account.

THE SPIES FOR PEACE

On February 20, the whole group held a crucial meeting to discuss what had happened and to decide what to do next. They first heard a rough account drafted by one of them of what the papers revealed—that they had discovered a Regional Seat of Government (called RSG-6), only about twenty minutes' walk from the Aldermaston route—and they examined the photographs which had been taken. This seemed to be an opportunity beyond their wildest dreams, but before taking it they had to consider its implications. All the members present said in turn what they should now do. The overwhelming majority agreed that they should independently produce a pamphlet about RSG-6 on the basis of the material discovered in Warren Row, and secretly distribute it to the movement in time for the Aldermaston March seven weeks ahead, in the hope that there would be a major demonstration at the site.

There was some disagreement from a small minority, who argued either that such an action would tend to wreck the Committee of 100 and that the function of the group should continue to be that of an open pressure group within the Committee rather than become a secret cell outside on its own, or else that such an action, however desirable it might seem, would inevitably lead to the arrest and imprisonment of those responsible. After a long discussion, the group decided to go ahead, and the minority left the meeting and took no further part in the group's activities. At the same time the group decided to exclude its more prominent and vulnerable members from direct participation, though they would be kept informed of progress, and also not to include any more members for the time being, except to approach outsiders on a "need-to-know" basis for any necessary help with particular details. The people who remained active members of the group at this stage became the Spies for Peace.

There were eight of them, all in their twenties. They were mostly men with middle-class backgrounds, though two were women (one of whom was pregnant) and two were working class in origin. Several of them were drop outs from the educational system, though two of them had Oxbridge degrees. Between them they had one small car and the use of a delivery van. They had all been active in the Committee of 100 in various ways—some of them as full-time workers or local convenors or members of the Industrial Sub-Committee—and they had all been arrested on demonstrations several times. Most of them had previous experience of left-wing politics covering all kinds of groups—CND or the New Left, student or trade unions, Labour or Communist Party, Trotskyist or anarchist organizations—and between them they had a wide circle of contacts all over the country (their closest connections outside the nuclear disarmament movement being with the new Solidarity group and the old Freedom group). They had got to know each other well during the previous year or two, and now shared both a personal commitment to radical action and also a common acceptance of libertarian socialism (though hardly any of them would have called themselves anarchists).

Having decided to produce a pamphlet, they had to settle several other questions. The next decision they made was that the pamphlet should be produced in conditions of complete security, to minimize the chances of the authorities being able either to interrupt their work before it was complete or of catching them afterwards. They were prepared to take necessary risks, but not to offer themselves up for sacrifice. They took into special account the experience of the publication of an analogous official secret five years earlier.

THE "ISIS" CASE

When the Second World War was followed by the Cold War between Communist Russia and the West, the American and British governments (joined by Canada, Australia and New Zealand) made a secret treaty in 1947 known as the United Kingdom United States of America Security Agreement (UKUSA). This established a joint system of Signals Intelligence (SIGINT), concentrating on the surveillance of Russian military radio traffic from bases in Europe and the Middle East. Many of the radio operators involved were National Servicemen taught Russian or Morse and trained as radio operators, who returned to civilian life—many going on to university—and were a potentially weak link in the security network.

During the 1950s there were several occasions when American and British aircraft and ships made deliberate incursions across the Iron

Curtain in order to provoke radio traffic and provide valuable information. This activity was of course top secret, but it was obviously known to the Russians, and on a few occasions they retaliated by attacking and even destroying American or British aircraft, and the resulting international incidents led to considerable publicity and consequent embarrassment. This episode is described in a book on the subject by "Nigel West" (the Conservative MP, Rupert Allason)—*GCHQ: The Secret Wireless War, 1900–86* (1986)—in a chapter with the appropriate title "Russian Adventures."

The British authorities generally managed to cover up the significance of such incidents, but on one occasion their cover was blown. On February 26, 1958 a special H-Bomb issue of the Oxford student paper *Isis* included a short article called "Frontier Incidents—Exposure," which described the SIGINT system and explained the frontier incidents.

> . . . All along the frontier between east and west, from Iraq to the Baltic, perhaps farther, are monitoring stations, manned largely by National Servicemen trained in Morse or Russian, avidly recording the least squeak from six Russian transmitters—ships, tanks, aeroplanes, troops and control stations. It is believed, perhaps rightly, that this flagrant breach of the Geneva Convention can provide accurate estimates of the size and type of Russian armaments and troops, and the nature of their tactical methods.
>
> In order to get this information the West has been willing to go to extraordinary lengths of deception. British Embassies usually contain monitoring spies. When the Fleet paid a "goodwill" visit to Danzig in 1955 they were on board. And since the Russians do not always provide the required messages they are sometimes provoked. A plane "loses" its way; while behind the frontier tape recorders excitedly read the irritated exchanges of Russian pilots: and when the latter sometimes force the aeroplane to land an international incident is created, and reported in the usual fashion. . . . In a moment of crisis irresponsibility of this kind could well frighten the Russians into war. Certainly if Russian planes were to fly over American bases the American reply would be prompt. But there is no controlling the appetite of the statistical analyzers at Cheltenham. . . .

The point of the article was of course that such incidents were more likely to cause than prevent war, and that such information should be made available to the British people as well as the Russian authorities. The authors were two undergraduates who had worked in SIGINT during their recent National Service in the Navy. The article was not signed, but security at *Isis* was poor, and the British authorities soon took their revenge. In March the office was raided and the editor interrogated, and Paul Thompson and William Miller were charged under the Official Secrets Act. They were tried at the Central Criminal Court in July, and after a deal with the prosecution they pleaded guilty and were sentenced to three months' imprisonment (they went on to distinguished careers in academic history and serious publishing respectively). The offending article was immediately reprinted as a leaflet by the Universities and Left Review Club, the main organization of the New Left in London, so the information was widely distributed, at least on the left; but the fate of the victims was a warning of the possible price to be paid for such activity, and the Spies for Peace were determined not to make the same mistakes. (Nigel West's account of this episode is very inaccurate.)

"DANGER! OFFICIAL SECRET RSG-6"

The group then turned to the problem of whether they needed more material for the pamphlet. After further discussion of the risks to be taken and the advantages to be gained, they agreed that another visit to Warren Row was indeed necessary to obtain more information and to make the pamphlet more detailed and convincing. After leaving the material already collected with a sympathetic anarchist who worked in a Communist bookshop in London, they made careful preparations for a second visit to Warren Row on February 23 (a day when there were meetings of both the National Committee and the London Committee in London).

Four members of the group drove to Reading again, checked that the site was clear—noting with interest that there were workmen there during the day, even though it was a Saturday—and then spent the evening in a pub and watched the satirical late-night television program *That Was The Week That Was* before returning to search the bunker at leisure. They arrived after midnight, picked the lock of the boiler-house door (which was shut this time) and spent several hours inside the installation. They found to their astonishment that the RSG was fully operational—the electricity and water were on, there were notices on the boards, signs in the corridors, maps on the walls, directories in the telephone exchange, desks and cabinets in the offices, and papers in the drawers. It was clear that nothing had been touched since it was last used during the NATO exercise Fallex 62 five months before—except that for some reason all the ashtrays had been locked up in an office.

First they explored the whole place, and then they specialized in various activities—one transcribed documents, one traced maps, one took photographs, and one ransacked every room. They took the greatest care to leave no trace of their visit. They wore gloves the whole time; they broke no locks, picking those they had to open; they took away only those papers which had duplicates, and copied those which hadn't; they photographed the signs and maps, and copied the plan of the bunker from a wall-chart. When they had finished, they put everything back in its place and left with a suitcase full of papers and a camera full of pictures. This technique was clearly successful, for when the pamphlet appeared both the authorities and the media assumed that an insider must have made some kind of deliberate leak rather than that some outsiders had simply broken into a sensitive and insecure installation and found all the necessary material right there in situ.

The material taken from Warren Row was looked after by the same bookshop assistant for a few days, just in case anyone had noticed anything. The group met again on February 25 and discussed the new material they had now obtained. Its significance lay not only in that it included far more information about the RSG system—including the locations of all the other RSGs and the identities of the staff of RSG-6 (and also of RSG-4 in Cambridge)—but that in addition it included detailed information about the disastrous results of two recent Civil Defense exercises—Parapluie in Spring 1962 and Fallex 62 in September—The latter had already been the subject of dramatic disclosures in October 1962 by the West German news magazine *Der Spiegel,* which had immediately been prosecuted by the authorities. The group decided that the pamphlet should contain as much information as possible about both aspects of their discoveries, and they immediately set to work to produce it.

They met regularly every Monday evening—that is, at the same time as the Working Group of the London Committee of 100, on the assumption that any likely surveillance would be diverted elsewhere—with more frequent contacts between various individual members in between. Six members lived within walking distance of each other in Hampstead, and the meetings took place in one or other of their three flats. A constant rule was that every single action involved in the operation must have a complete cover story which sounded convincing and could be checked. Another was that the absolute minimum of material was to be kept in writing or said on the telephone. Everything was decided at the meetings, and nothing was recorded. The procedure was completely informal, with no set structure. Decisions were taken by consent rather than vote. (As is so often the case, those who did the most talking tended to do the least work.)

The first task was to write the text of the pamphlet. One member of the group prepared a rough draft based on the material from Warren Row, filled out by research in a reference library, completing it on March 15; a second member then expanded this into a longer draft, adding the postscript, by March 18; a third member then polished this into a final draft, adding the foreword, by March 23. During the same period three other members drew out maps and developed the photographs. The text and form of the pamphlet were discussed and agreed by the whole group on March 25. All the material taken or copied from Warren Row was then burnt, apart from the photographs.

The pamphlet was planned as follows. The group took the dramatic title "Spies for Peace," partly as a serious shorthand summary of their position, and partly as a frivolous joke at the expense of the Communist front organizations which used such titles. The pamphlet was to be typed and duplicated (those were the days before personal computers and cheap photocopying), since this could be done with the least trouble and the least risk. It was to be foolscap size, to minimize the number of stencils and the quantity of paper needed. It would have twelve pages, including four electro-stencils for illustrations. The only photograph used would be that of the outside of the RSG, so that there would be no indication that anyone had been inside it. There would be 4,000 copies, the maximum number stencils would run to. The pamphlet was given the inelegant but striking title *Danger! Official Secret RSG-6* as a way of catching people's attention in the flood of papers and pamphlets always produced at Easter. The front page consisted of the title with the picture of RSG-6 (photographed in the snow). The text began with a short introduction, then described the RSG system, giving the locations (and telephone numbers) of all the known RSGs, described both the outside and inside of RSG-6, adding a list of its main personnel and a plan of its layout, described the two exercises, adding that the RSGs hadn't been activated during the Cuba crisis in October 1962 (with the comment that "in the face of a real emergency, fuck all was done"), and ended with a conclusion, adding on the back page a map of the area with the suggestion of a demonstration there during the Aldermaston March.

The group calculated that the whole operation would cost about £100—about £1,000 today—which they knew they couldn't afford but thought they could probably raise. They decided to go ahead and see about recovering some of their costs from people who could afford it when they had something definite to show them. They bought a cheap old Underwood typewriter, and one member cut the nine text stencils; the electro-stencils were made by taking the photograph and the maps into a commercial firm in the normal way. By the time all this was ready, they realized that they had only enough time and would probably have only enough money for 3,000 copies after all. They then bought ink, staples, envelopes, wrappers and labels in the normal way. They obtained the paper through a sympathetic anarchist who worked in a pacifist bookshop in London and was able to supply the necessary three dozen reams of duplicating paper without awkward questions being asked. All this material was handled only with gloves at every stage; the coldness of the weather fortunately made this particular precaution seem nothing unusual.

Right up to the last moment they expected the pamphlet to be ignored by the mass media, so it was important to distribute it as widely and effectively as possible. Also every single copy—including their own—had to be sent out by post so that there would be no trace of their origin. About 2,000 copies were to be sent to people likely to be on the Aldermaston March and likely to know what to do—the members of the group themselves, other members of the Committee of 100 (bundles going to secretaries of Regional Committees and convenors of local Working Groups), people known to be sympathetic with the Committee of 100 in CND, Youth CND, the Young Socialists, and the New Left. Copies were also to go to all left-wing papers and magazines. This would at least ensure good publicity in the nuclear disarmament movement.

The other 1,000 copies were to go to people who might give it another kind of publicity, whatever happened on the March—national newspapers and magazines, Government ministers and Opposition leaders, right-wing Conservative and left-wing Labour MPs, civil servants, and a long list of "progressive" celebrities in this country and abroad taken from *Who's Who*. Copies were also sent to key people in the area of southern England covered by RSG-6—local papers, local councilors, local government officials, constituency Labour Party and trade-union branch secretaries, army officers, religious ministers, university dons, and, of course, the people listed on the staff of the RSG itself. One copy was sent to the British Museum, but it never appeared in the catalogue. Later a senior member of the Reading Room staff attempted to obtain a copy, but the person he approached refused to supply one if its availability was going to be restricted; no agreement was reached, so no copy was produced.

By the weekend before Easter, April 6–7, everything was just ready. Some members of the group then showed typescripts of the final draft of the pamphlet to people they knew personally who had previously given money to the Committee of 100 and were likely to be sympathetic but not inquisitive. One former "name" in the Committee gave £50, two others gave £10; one relatively rich surviving member of the Committee gave £25. This was just enough. The typescripts were then burnt. Incidentally, Bertrand Russell did not give any money, though he intended to do so and even believed that he had done so. In the relevant passage of *The Autobiography of Bertrand Russell,* he described the work of the Spies for Peace and added: "They had no funds, and appealed to me. I gave them £50 with my blessing" [volume 3, 125].

An approach was indeed made to contacts on Russell's staff, but the answer was that while Russell approved of the project he couldn't contribute to it financially—though the contacts themselves made a small contribution. Only later was it discovered that Russell had actually authorized a payment of £50, which had been prevented by Ralph Schoenman, the most powerful member of the staff.

The final production of the pamphlet was completed during the week before Easter. The sheets were run off on the *Solidarity* duplicator in the premises of the Independent Labour Party in King's Cross Road, a building used by several left-wing organizations known to the group who wouldn't ask any questions. The work took from Sunday to Tuesday, the members taking turns as they could. At the same time the hundreds of labels were typed on the same typewriter. The sheets were assembled and wrapped and labeled in one of their flats from Tuesday evening to Wednesday afternoon, the members again taking turn as they could, some working right through the night and the next day. The stamps were bought in several Hampstead post offices, and again handled only with gloves. On the Wednesday afternoon they began posting the pamphlet at various places all over London, first the bundles being taken from post office to post office in the delivery van and then the envelopes being taken from postbox to postbox in the car.

Before all the thousands of packets could even be sorted, let alone delivered, the incriminating material was being destroyed. Everything that could be burnt was burnt. Of the things that couldn't, the typewriter was thrown into a river outside London, and—as a last touch of political malice—the cardboard boxes were left in dustbins outside the old *Daily Worker* office down the road in Farringdon Road. The photographs were posted anonymously to Bertrand Russell to provide him with any direct evidence he might need if he were approached by the press—as indeed he was; it was later discovered that when the police hunt began they were buried in his garden at Plas Penrhyn in North Wales, where they may be to this day. At the same time details of the staff in RSG-4 were sent to contacts in Cambridge, in the confidence that they would be either destroyed or published in a similar way. The final task was to clear out the flats of the members of the group thoroughly to make sure that there was no physical evidence linking them with the operation in any way.

By the Thursday morning, April 11, when the pamphlet began to arrive all over the country in the post (which was more reliable in those days), there was nothing to show who was responsible. Everything had been disposed of except the pamphlets themselves, the pamphlets had all been got rid of, and they had no fingerprints, no traceable typeface or postmark, and only their contents to help the police with their inquiries. A secret had escaped, and so—they hoped—had the Spies for Peace.

EASTER 1963

There was a couple of days' grace before any public comment on the pamphlet. It arrived after Thursday's newspapers had been published, there were no newspapers on Good Friday, and the radio and television news programs took some time to catch up with it. On Thursday, the day before the Aldermaston March began, there was much discussion of the mysterious document among members of the nuclear disarmament movement—and no doubt among news editors and Government officials as well. When the March began at Aldermaston, on Friday morning, many of the marchers had already received copies, and further copies were quickly distributed among them and also to reporters. Soon the police began to seize it and question people about it, but of course no one knew who was responsible. Some people had already begun to produce reprints and summaries on Thursday, more did so on Friday, and many more during the rest of the weekend, which increased both the circulation of the pamphlet and the difficulties of the police.

The details of the RSG system had been covered in a D-Notice (an official censorship instruction to the media) only two months earlier, and the authorities answered press inquiries by attempting to suppress the story, but in vain. The news of the pamphlet was broken to the general public on Saturday morning, when it was the main item in almost all national newspapers and radio news programs, and it dominated all comment on the Aldermaston March for the rest of the weekend.

On Saturday the March was due to pass along the A4 main road a couple of miles away from Warren Row. On Friday night several marchers explored the area, produced leaflets calling for a demonstration there, and distributed them among the marchers in Reading overnight and along the March during the next morning. On Saturday this demonstration took place, exactly as had been hoped. Several hundred marchers—led by "anarchists, left-wing socialists, and members of the Committee of 100" (as reported by *Freedom*)—turned off the main road during the lunch break at Knowl Hill, despite the noisy attempts of CND marshals—led by the general secretary, Peggy Duff—to discourage them from leaving the March, made their way to Warren Row and over the fences and banks around the site, and surrounded the entrance to RSG-6 for several hours, chanting slogans and singing songs (the latter were later collected in *The RSG Song Book*). This, too, was widely reported, though the media made an elaborate business of not saying exactly where the demonstration had occurred.

The pamphlet dominated the rest of the March and helped to inspire the more radical marchers, coordinated by a March Must Decide Committee, in a series of diversionary activities, culminating on Easter Monday in a huge final demonstration in the West End of London—again led by anarchists, left-wing socialists, and members of the Committee of 100—which brought the weekend to a fitting climax.

REACTIONS AND COMMENTS

The reaction of the radical wing of the nuclear disarmament movement, and indeed of the rank and file of the left in general, was quite as favorable as had been expected. Bertrand Russell issued a statement about the Aldermaston March on 16 April including strong praise: "In particular, the authors of the pamphlet published by the Spies for Peace have performed a public service." The Committee of 100 generally took the same line, with some qualifications about the danger of being diverted from its main activity, and its members and supporters around the country took the lead in all the following activities.

The reaction of CND was much more mixed, as had also been expected. The senior leaders—especially the chairman, L. John Collins, and Peggy Duff—were at first furious at what they saw as sabotage of the March, and only later grudgingly gave their approval. Peggy Duff said in her memoirs—*Left, Left, Left* (1971)—that "the worst year we ever had on the march was 1963" (her account of the episode is very inaccurate). Canon Collins treated the episode differently in his memoirs—*Faith under Fire* (1966)—by ignoring it completely. The younger leaders felt differently. The editor of the CND paper, *Sanity* (David Boulton of *Tribune,* later a prominent figure in Granada Television), naturally wished to publicize the pamphlet. In the special issue prepared on Friday and printed on Saturday for publication on Easter Sunday, the back page had an anonymous article called "The Secret Society of War" discussing the subject in general terms, accompanied by an illustration with a caption identifying it as "The cover picture of the secrets pamphlet, described as 'the entrance to RSG-6, seen from the road that runs through Warren Row.'" This alarmed the CND officials so much that they insisted on first blacking out or cutting out the caption and then tearing out the whole page from all copies distributed. The article was reprinted without the illustration in the May issue, identified as being by Stuart Hall, and accompanied by a front-page article by David Boulton himself, giving some of the detailed information in the pamphlet; and a new illustration showed a marcher's banner with the location of RSG-6 written on it. As for the rank and file of CND, local groups played an active part in distributing reprints and summaries of the pamphlet.

The reaction of the rest of the left was similarly various. The hard Marxists said as little and as late as possible in the *Daily Worker* (Communist Party) and the *Socialist Standard* (Socialist Party of Great Britain). But the annual conference of the Independent Labour Party at the Easter weekend praised the Spies for Peace, as did the ILP *Socialist Leader*. So did the Trotskyist *Newsletter*. The anarchist paper *Freedom* was favorable, as was the syndicalist *Direct Action*. The pacifist paper *Peace News* was strongly favorable, publishing a front-page article called "The Spies were Right" with a detailed account of the pamphlet and a back-page cartoon by Donald Rooum identifying the location of RSG-6 (19 April). The ILP youth paper *New Generation* later also gave a detailed account of the pamphlet (June).

The right-wing press was as hostile as was expected. The so-called left-wing national newspapers, the *Daily Mirror* and *Daily Herald,* were just as hostile, publishing furious condemnations respectively by Cassandra (April 16) and James Cameron (April 17)—the latter groaning, "God save us from our friends." *Tribune* and the *New Statesman,* and most left-wing Labour figures, were very ambivalent. The Labour Party leaders were either silent or hostile. The Conservative Home Secretary, Henry Brooke, had described the Spies for Peace as "traitors"; the shadow Foreign Secretary, Patrick Gordon Walker, followed by saying that "they are spies and must be treated as such." The right-wing journalist Chapman Pincher said in the *Daily Express* (15 April) that they should be treated "with the same rigour as spies for war"—that is, capital punishment! But when Parliament reassembled after the Easter recess on April 23, the Prime Minister, Harold Macmillan, told the

House of Commons that the whole affair had been greatly exaggerated, and the excitement began to subside.

HOW AND WHO?

The lasting effect of the episode remained to be seen, but the immediate effect was a wave of speculation about the source of the information in the pamphlet and the identity of those responsible for it. A deliberately misleading reference in the pamphlet to "at least *one* occupant of at least *one* RSG" was taken as seriously as had been hoped. The general assumption was that the information must have been leaked by an insider rather than discovered by outsiders, and many people involved in the RSG system were subjected to unpleasant interrogation. The undramatic truth doesn't seem to have been guessed by anyone at the time.

As for the identity of the Spies for Peace themselves, they took care to remain as undetected after their operation as before it. The group automatically disbanded when their work was done, and some took a much needed and well earned holiday. Most of them went on the Aldermaston March, but they had nothing to do with the production and distribution of the many reprints and summaries of the pamphlet during the Easter weekend, or with the organization of the demonstrations at RSG-6 and the various other RSGs around the country. Four of them took part in the demonstration at Warren Row on April 13, and enjoyed the knowledge that their plan had worked perfectly. Four of them also took part in the demonstrations in London, which marked the end of the March on April 15 and were partly inspired by their example, and some of them were arrested. But it was clear that virtually no one, whether in the movement or the media or the police, was sure exactly who they were.

Nevertheless it was fairly easy to guess who they might be. Of course a few of their close colleagues knew some of their identities, and some of their many other associates had ideas which were sometimes correct—though often incorrect. As for the authorities, their views will perhaps be better known when the official records are released under the thirty-year rule in 1994—though not necessarily even then. At first, however, they clearly had no realistic ideas at all, and then they made much the same sort of guesses as anyone else. Police activity began at once, with threats and seizures and arrests and minor charges on the March, a break-in at the Committee of 100 office in London on April 13, and interviews with possible suspects from April 15. On April 17 members of the Special Branch raided a score of people in the

London area, including the signatories of *Beyond Counting Arses*—or, rather, those they could trace—as well as some other people suspected of being involved. Nothing significant was found, and no charges were ever made. Several of the actual Spies for Peace were never raided, and indeed seem never to have been suspected; whereas many of those suspected and raided had nothing to do with the operation at all. The problem of the authorities was that, while it proved fairly easy to establish the identities of some of the people responsible for the many reprints, it proved completely impossible to track down those responsible for the original pamphlet, and after a few weeks the official hunt died down.

Public speculation about the Spies for Peace was generally very badly informed. The defense correspondent of *The Times,* Alun Gwynne Jones (later Lord Chalfont), quoted the opinion of "security officials" that they were "supporters, probably communist, of nuclear disarmament" (April 13); the *Daily Express,* quoting the same sources, mentioned "Communist agents" (April 15); and the *Daily Telegraph* referred to "Communist subversion" (April 17); *Tribune* suggested an "agent-provocateur" (April 19); Clare Hollingworth, the defense correspondent of the *Guardian,* went so far as to suggest "enemy agents" (May 13). The main single suspect at the time was Peter Cadogan, secretary of the East Anglian Committee of 100 and convenor of the March Must Decide Committee (later prominent in the humanist movement); in fact he was completely innocent, and he played a valuable part in drawing off press attention for a few days. Subsidiary suspects were Philip Seed, a Committee of 100 activist who was also completely innocent, and George Clark, a prominent activist in both CND and the Committee of 100, who had led a Campaign Caravan around the country during 1962 and claimed previous knowledge of the RSG system, but who wasn't even on speaking terms with the Spies for Peace. The general public were completely bemused, going by a National Opinion Polls survey of Londoners published later in April 1963—asked who they thought was to blame, 50 percent said they didn't know, 1 percent said the Committee of 100, 3 percent the Civil Defense organization, 4 percent the Communists, 5 percent CND, and 37 percent the Government!

Speculation continued afterwards. *Peace News* drew attention to *Beyond Counting Arses* on April 26. The *Sunday Telegraph,* which had good contacts with the security authorities and a good knowledge of the far left, suggested on April 21 that "it would not be surprising if investigation does not bring to light a shrewd political mind directing this brilliant subversive operation," and followed on May 19 with heavy hints about a "master mind behind the Spies for Peace," a "Jekyll and

Hyde character" who was thought to be "a brilliant man who may be doing an important job," and so on; it was easy to see what was behind this nonsense, but nothing came of it. The Conservative Party *Campaign Guide* for the 1964 General Election implicated the ILP; it was actually involved only to the extent that it supported the Spies for Peace and that some of its members in London and Leeds produced reprints of the pamphlet. Herb Greer's unsympathetic early history of the movement—*Mud Pie* (1964)—carelessly asserted that the Spies for Peace were "made up largely of Anarchists loosely attached to the Committee of 100." Christopher Driver's sympathetic early history of the movement—*The Disarmers* (1964)—cautiously suggested that they "might be found among the readers of the Trotskyist [sic] magazine *Solidarity*." Richard Taylor's and Colin Pritchard's sympathetic later history—*The Protest Makers* (1980)—described them as a "group of libertarian socialists and Anarchists," adding a note that "it is clear that the group around the journal *Solidarity* was closely involved." Paul Mercer's unsympathetic later history—*"Peace" of the Dead* (1986)—alleged that "it did not take Special Branch long to identify those responsible" and that "it was an open secret within the Committee of 100" that some members of the Syndicalist Workers' Federation were involved; the authorities were actually never able to establish who was responsible, and the two named people were involved only in producing reprints and had nothing to do with the original group (indeed the named source of this story wouldn't have been trusted by anyone).

The fact is that the identity of only one member of the group has ever been publicly admitted, though a great many outsiders have claimed membership at various times. At the beginning of 1965 there was much interest in the press and amusement in the movement about a man called Trevor Jones ("Jonah"), who alleged that he was one of the Spies for Peace and had caused much disruption of official activity, but he was generally dismissed as a nuisance or a provocateur. And a much later example of confusion may be found in Alan Ryan's book *Bertrand Russell: A Political Life* (1988), which includes references to "the activities of 'Spies for Peace' (who discovered where the government's wartime communications centers were located and published the information in defiance of the Official Secrets Act)," which isn't quite right, and to "the government's efficient use of the Official Secrets Act to send the most determined Spies for Peace to jail for eighteen months," which is quite wrong. The essential point to emphasize is that, by taking simple precautions, the Spies for Peace made sure that there was no material evidence against anyone, so that no one was arrested, let alone imprisoned.

EFFECTS AND RESULTS

The original pamphlet, which appeared just before Easter 1963, was followed by a literally incalculable number of reprints and summaries produced by various groups and individuals over the Easter weekend and then during the next few weeks. There were certainly at least a hundred separate versions, most duplicated but a few surreptitiously printed. It was estimated that about 10,000 pamphlets and about 30,000 leaflets summarizing the pamphlet had been distributed by the end of the March, on Easter Monday, and Vanessa Redgrave's speech at the closing rally in Hyde Park that afternoon repeated its main contents.

The largest known edition was a printed version, which was produced in London on April 22 in a run of 18,000 copies. (This was one of several that expurgated the remarks about the Cuba crisis to say that "damn all" or "nothing at all" was done.) One summary was distributed at the annual conference of the National Union of Students at Keele University during the weekend after Easter by Martin Loney, then a student leader (and later general secretary of the National Council for Civil Liberties and then an academic sociologist). A particularly interesting version appeared in the French left-wing paper *France Observateur* on April 18. The story filled the front and back pages, with the comment: "Treason ceased to be treason when it became a public service. The boldness of the Spies for Peace has promoted the peace march from the level of British folklore into an event of international significance"; and the two middle pages were filled with facsimiles of the pamphlet. (The issue was banned in Britain.) Copies of the pamphlet soon travelled further afield, and by June versions were being produced as far apart as Australia, New Zealand and the United States. Also in June the London Committee of 100 began producing a series of duplicated editions which it sold at one shilling, and various other versions continued to appear for the rest of the year.

In exactly the same way, the demonstration at RSG-6 on April 13 was followed by demonstrations organized by local nuclear disarmament groups at almost every other known RSG in the country on almost every weekend during the next couple of months. As had been hoped, the Committee of 100 and indeed the radical wing of the movement in general took on a new lease of life. All these events were reported in the press much more widely than had ever been hoped. No doubt this was partly because of their intrinsic interest; but it was much more because the press during that period bore a bitter grudge against the Government—following the imprisonment in February of two reporters for refusing to disclose (nonexistent) sources of information for (imaginary) stories about the Vassall spy case to an official tribunal, and the denial in March by the Minister of War, John Profumo, of rumors about his relationship with Christine Keeler which everyone in Fleet Street knew to be true (the resulting sex-and-politics scandal revolving around Stephen Ward dominated the political scene for the rest of the summer). All the capitalist newspapers wanted the Spies for Peace to be caught and punished; but meanwhile they were delighted to be able to embarrass the Government from a new angle.

Despite specific police threats, detailed accounts of the pamphlets and the demonstrations appeared in some papers of the libertarian left. What was more surprising and significant was that, despite official and unofficial pressure and all the political implications, the *Daily Telegraph* finally broke ranks in the Establishment—by printing on April 19 what was alleged to be the transcript of a program broadcast by Radio Prague the previous day, including substantial quotations from the Spies for Peace pamphlet. On the same day *Private Eye* published a full-page parody of the pamphlet—with the title "Top Secret: Do Not Read This Page" and spoof details of "Holes in the Ground" (HIGs)—and on the next day the pamphlet was shown and discussed on the television program *That Was the Week That Was*. And the case was used as the theme of an episode in the Granada Television serial *The Odd Man* (Edward Boyd's "The Betrayal of Ambrose Leech"), broadcast on Independent Television on May 17. The Spies for Peace had entered the folklore of political culture—and not only in Britain. The pamphlets and demonstrations were praised by the Situationist movement on the Continent as an exemplary instance of the destruction of spectacle and creation of situations, made the subject of an art exhibition called "The Destruction of the RSG-6" held in Odense, Denmark, during June and July 1963, and held up as a model for further revolutionary action—which they were.

DEVELOPMENTS

But the important thing was how the situation would develop in practice. Soon the ripples began to spread as the lessons sank in. The information about RSG-4, which had been sent to contacts in Cambridge, was published in a similar though much shorter pamphlet on April 25. On May 2, a typed leaflet appeared stating that the communications system connecting the RSGs and the central Government was located in underground bunkers near Chancery Lane underground station in London, with surface entrances in Furnival Street and High Holborn.

At the same time secret telephone numbers and addresses were being passed round by word of mouth, and for several weeks members of the nuclear disarmament movement used them to harass and, if possible, to disrupt the communications system.

One unfortunate episode occurred after the demonstration at RSG-12 in Dover Castle on May 5. Local activists broke into the site and discovered further secret papers about the RSG system. However, lacking confidence in their own ability to make use of the material and knowledge of who else might be able to do so, they handed the papers over to the secretary of the National Committee of 100 and the editor of *Peace News*—both of whom had expressed support for the Spies for Peace at Easter. But these two leading figures in the anti-war movement not only destroyed the material, but even rebuked those responsible for this skilful and entirely successful action, so a valuable opportunity was wasted.

The Spies for Peace episode and work continued to be the subject of both private and public discussion during summer 1963. In June the text of *Beyond Counting Arses* was reprinted by *Solidarity* to provide documentation for this discussion. Also in June, a pamphlet with the acronymic title *Resistance Shall Grow* was published by a coalition of groups in the libertarian left—the ILP, the London Federation of Anarchists, Solidarity, the Syndicalist Workers' Federation, and a section of the London Committee of 100—and was also included in *Anarchy* 29 as "The Spies for Peace Story." Subtitled "The Story of the Spies for Peace and Why They Are Important for Your Future," this compilation of anonymous articles described the events of Easter 1963 and the various repercussions, with particular attention to the reactions of the authorities, the media and the orthodox left, and with the hopeful conclusion that the episode might be "the basis of a genuinely revolutionary mass movement."

In September Nicolas Walter's *The RSGs, 1919–1963* was published as a Solidarity pamphlet to fill in the historical background of the emergency regional government system since the First World War (though he didn't go back as far as its slightly earlier origins during the First World War). One interesting point to emerge was that the revived RSG system had not only been fairly widely known for some time but had actually been discussed openly in the press on several occasions and described in some detail in the *Daily Mail* in February 1961; indeed Bertrand Russell himself had drawn attention to its significance (in a speech to the Midlands Conference for Peace in Birmingham on March 11, 1961, reprinted as the pamphlet *Win We Must*). By this time, the authorities, having failed to lay their hands on the Spies for Peace, drew a practical lesson from them instead, and also in September an official report on Civil Defense gave detailed information about the RSG system to the general public for the first time. Already the structure had been modified to provide for the likely dismemberment of the regions by nuclear attack and the establishment instead of Sub-Regional controls (as reported by *Sanity* in August), and soon the Civil Defense structure was completely dismantled, though a skeleton system survived. In a way, then, the Spies for Peace succeeded completely.

REVIVAL AND FAILURE

But the Spies for Peace had aimed at something much more than merely discrediting or even destroying the Civil Defense system, and by the autumn of 1963 they resumed their work. The group had kept constantly in touch, and had also remained active in other ways. Members were among the representatives of the nuclear disarmament movement who confronted Bernard Levin with the pamphlet on *That Was the Week That Was* on April 20, and among the hecklers at the public meeting organized by the London Region of CND on April 28 when leaders of the nuclear disarmament movement offered their belated approval to the Spies for Peace (and made an idiotic appeal to give themselves up!) Several members took part in the Committee of 100 demonstrations during the summer at Marham (in May) and Porton (in June), during Greek Week (in July) and the subsequent Committee convoy to Greece, as well as in the Cuban Embassy demonstration (in July) and the Notting Hill anti-eviction struggle (in August). But, when the London Committee once more relapsed into the same paralysis as had afflicted it before Easter, the group was re-formed at the end of August.

At this point two members dropped out of any further activity, and two new members were brought in to replace them. At various times during the following period other people took part in specific activities on a temporary basis, and there was a growing network of contacts in several parts of the country, but the hard core remained almost unchanged.

The aim of the Spies for Peace remained the same; but now their task was more difficult. It would not be sufficient to repeat their work; it was necessary to move forward and do better than before. They had discovered and exposed the emergency regional government system; now they set out to discover and expose the emergency central government system behind it. They had acquired the essential trust in each other and the basic expertise and experience for this kind of activity; but they were determined not to take any unnecessary risks, which limited their freedom of action. So once more they withdrew from other activities and resumed work.

The first area to be explored was the deep shelters in London which had been constructed during the Second World War. Papers found in Warren Row had shown that the RSG system had not been activated during the Cuba crisis in October 1962, a few weeks after the Fallex 62 exercise, which proved the uselessness of the whole system. The group decided to see what been done with the deep shelters, and they picked on the one near Belsize Park underground station as being the easiest to break into without risk of detection. The shelter was raided on September 28, 1963, and they discovered that it not only had been unused during the Cuba crisis but was unusable at any time, since its fittings were all either dismantled or derelict. But nothing much could be made of that on its own.

The next area to be explored was the enormous military complex near Corsham, just east of Bath on the main London-Bristol road and railway. Contacts at the CND annual conference in October reported local suspicions that this was the site of the emergency central seat of government, and this coincided with hints in the press that in a war the Government would go underground "somewhere in the West." The group decided to see what could be discovered. A preliminary visit was made in November, and two thorough searches were made during December. The whole area was combed, and several installations were broken into; but the group found it impossible to get far enough into the complex to confirm their strong suspicions about it without taking excessive risks, and the operation was temporarily suspended.

Instead the group turned to the London communications system near Chancery Lane underground station. Attempts were made to break into various places during January 1964, but again they found it impossible to penetrate the system without more drastic measures. At several meetings the group discussed—both alone and with sympathetic contacts—the possibility of cracking the system in other ways, whether by planning a public demonstration to draw attention to it and trying to get in during a diversion, or else by mounting a more determined assault altogether. But in the end it was decided to proceed no further because the operation seemed unlikely to succeed without taking unnecessary risks or using undesirable methods.

Another visit was made to the West Country in February, this time in the area of the Mendips, where other contacts had suggested the central seat of government might be located. A long search ended with the discovery of a mysterious site at Temple Cloud, but when this was raided it turned out to be only a Home Office Supply and Transport Store. A great deal of equipment was found in it, but no important papers. Yet another visit was made to the West Country in May, but again nothing was discovered.

By this time attention had been turned elsewhere, as a result of independent work by another group active in East London. In March 1964 the Ilford Civil Defense headquarters was broken into, and some of the papers found there were passed on to the Spies for Peace. References were found to a site near Kelvedon Hatch in Essex which sounded interesting. The site was located after a short search, and was broken into on March 29, Easter Sunday, at the time of the Easter March. Kelvedon Hatch turned out to be an intriguing place, since it combined a Sub-Regional headquarters in the RSG system with a Group headquarters in the Royal Observer Corps system. A great deal of material was removed from the huge bunkers at Kelvedon Hatch, and much of it was found to be interesting; but most of it related to the ROC structure and its exercises, which were hardly worth the trouble of exposing.

One particularly significant item of information that did emerge was that the London Region, whose RSG was strangely missing from the material found in Warren Row, had apparently been eliminated from the system altogether, and divided up between the Eastern, Southern and South-Eastern regions, so that London was to be ruled by Regional Commissioners in Cambridge, Warren Row and Dover; the various sectors of the capital were to be administered from several Sub-Regional headquarters, of which Kelvedon Hatch was the one for East London north of the Thames. The implication was that in the event of nuclear war, London would be virtually abandoned to its fate—but this was no news for anyone who had read the original Spies for Peace pamphlet, and again it was not worth the trouble of exposing on its own.

Further developments in East London put an end to work in that area. In May the Wanstead Civil Defense headquarters was broken into. In August three people were arrested and charged with the Ilford and Wanstead break-ins. There was some dramatic publicity for a time, with heavy hints about the identity of the Spies for Peace, but in the event the magistrates' court proceedings were confined to events in East London and the wider implications were obscured. The defendants were given large fines, which were soon raised by sympathizers.

Another area again was Wales, where contacts pointed out suspicious sites in various parts of the country. Visits were made several times during the spring and summer of 1964, large areas were explored, and some sites were examined; but no hard information was ever obtained.

On 16 and 17 October 1964, during the weekend after general election that brought the Labour Party back to power after thirteen years, two final visits were made to the Corsham complex, and the most determined efforts so far were made to break into appropriate sites. But yet again the task proved impossible, and the operation had to be terminated once and for all. This marked the end of the activity of the Spies for Peace as a group.

SCOTS AGAINST WAR

During all this time a parallel but completely independent response to the situation in the Committee of 100 had taken place in Scotland. Some Glasgow activists who had attended the "Way Ahead" conference in February 1963 were impressed by the arguments of *Beyond Counting Arses*, and developed their ideas in a similar way.

The first public indication of this phenomenon was the appearance at the Holy Loch demonstration on 25 May 1963 of a duplicated leaflet called *How to Disrupt, Obstruct and Subvert the Warfare State*, and signed "Scots against War." This was followed by an irregular series of publications over the next couple of years, aimed at stimulating radical activity in the Scottish nuclear disarmament movement.

This activity was not confined to argument, and sabotage became frequent and widespread from 1963 to 1966. Several fires were started at the Holy Loch and Faslane bases, and many Civil Defense and Army offices all over the country were broken into and wrecked. Occasionally some individuals were arrested, but the authorities generally preferred to keep things quiet. Few charges were brought, and only fines were ever imposed. The Scots against War group was never broken, but in the end it faded away.

In June 1966 the Scottish Solidarity group published as its first pamphlet *A Way Ahead*, which was a collection of articles by and about the Scots against War and the sabotage issue printed in both Scotland and London, with editorial comments. The subtitle was "For a New Peace Movement," but the pamphlet actually marked the end of the old one. Nevertheless, the career of the Scots against War, inspired by the same ideas as the Spies for Peace (and frequently in informal contact with them), may be seen as one of the most successful practical assaults on the military system mounted by the whole nuclear disarmament movement.

LAST THINGS

The individual Spies for Peace remained active after the end of their work as a group. During 1964 they had already joined the picnic at Warren Row on August 16. Following the successful pirate radio broadcasts during the general election of October 1964 in South London, they joined a new group of Radio Pirates which set out to combine old methods of gathering information with new methods of distributing it. But they left the group before its first (and last) broadcasts at Easter 1965. The theme of the messages was to be the secret Civil Defense plans for London, and some of the material accumulated by the Spies for Peace was used in preparing the texts. But the treatment was sensationalized and the organizational and technical defects of the group were such that it soon collapsed. Despite this failure to revive the work of the Voice of Nuclear Disarmament, the Spies for Peace joined the demonstration at the end of the 1965 Easter March called for by the broadcasts (whose texts were distributed in pamphlet form). This was at the Rotundas in Monck Street, Westminster, which were suspected of being the site of the London RSG (if any) or even of the emergency seat of government—and where there had also been a demonstration at the end of the Easter March in 1964.

After this the individual members of the group were involved in several appropriate activities. Some helped to produce the fake American dollars bearing slogans against the Vietnam War during 1966 and 1967. Several took part in the Brighton Church demonstration in October 1966. Contacts were involved in the springing of George Blake from Wormwood Scrubs in October 1966. Several took part in the Greek Embassy demonstration in April 1967. Some joined the Committee of 100 demonstrations at the Corsham complex during 1967. And several were involved in the housing struggles that became the squatters' movement in 1969.

At one stage tenuous connections were made with a new tendency on the libertarian left. One of the contacts of the Spies for Peace, who had been prominent in the Radio Pirates, was involved in an attempt to fire a harmless rocket at the Greek Embassy in 1967; the attempt was a fiasco, but also a portent of things to come. And after the first shooting at the American Embassy in August 1967, the police raids of Committee of 100 militants involved a few members of the Spies for Peace. None of the group was in fact involved in the later developments culminating in 1970–71 in the Angry Brigade, but these connections were not entirely coincidental.

In 1968, some of the Spies for Peace joined the Aldermaston March on the Easter Saturday to take part in a YCND demonstration at Warren Row. This commemorated their success five years earlier; but it also marked their failure to achieve any further success, and indeed the failure of the first nuclear disarmament movement as a whole—for that was the last of the first series of Aldermaston Marches, and 1968 also saw the disbandment of the Committee of 100 and its replacement as the vanguard of the radical left by the new student movement and the campaign against the Vietnam War. Some of the Spies for Peace continued political activity for many years, and a few were involved in the revived nuclear disarmament movement of the 1980s, but by that time they had long ceased to have any corporate existence.

EPILOGUE

One of the main successes of the Spies for Peace was the complete absorption into the public consciousness of the information they revealed. This was shown in 1965 when Peter Watkins made *The War Game*, a television film about the effects of a nuclear war that turned out to be so convincing that the authorities put pressure on the BBC not to broadcast it. Its picture of the political system which would be operated during a nuclear war took for granted the RSG system described by the Spies for Peace, although this had actually been radically altered by then. (It was shown in cinemas at the time and then to peace groups all over the country for twenty years, until it was at last broadcast in July 1985.)

Another success was the general assumption that further information of the same kind should be distributed as widely as possible, and quite soon this began to happen quite openly. Peter Laurie wrote a long article on the emergency government system in the *Sunday Times Magazine* (December 10, 1967), and then expanded it into a frequently revised book, *Beneath the City Streets* (1970, 1972, 1979, 1983). Further information appeared in Tony Bunyan's book, *The Political Police in Britain* (1976, 1977), and also in several pamphlets—such as *London: The Other Underground* (1974) by "Anarchists Anonymous," *Region 1* (1978) by Martin Spence, and *Review of Security and the State* (1979) by "State Research."

During the following decade the field was taken over by Duncan Campbell. He first became well known as one of the three defendants in the ABC trial of 1977–8 (which concerned the SIGINT system), who were found guilty of breaches of the Official Secrets Act but were neither fined nor imprisoned. He then turned to the emergency government system. Articles in *Time Out* (March 21–27 1980) and the *New Statesman* (October 2, 1981) were followed by a 500-page book, *War Plan UK* (1982, 1983). This is a very detailed study of "The Truth about Civil Defense in Britain" from the beginnings of the system during the First World War up to its reorganization during the 1970s and the exercises testing it during the early 1980s. Campbell was able not only to work (almost) completely in the open, but also to use the work of a great many other people (including some of the Spies for Peace). He later produced another book, *The Unsinkable Aircraft Carrier* (1984, 1986), a similarly detailed account of "American Military Power in Britain." His work may be said to have completed that begun by the Spies for Peace after a quarter of a century, so that the British people now have all the necessary information about their fate at the hands of the state in a military—or civil—emergency.

Originally published in Raven *5 (June 1988) [revision and expansion of "The Spies for Peace Story,"* Inside Story *8 and 9 (March–April and May–June 1973].*

THE
RSGs
1919 - 1963

by

NICOLAS
WALTER

6D

SOLIDARITY PAMPHLET No 15

8

THE REGIONAL SEATS OF GOVERNMENT, 1919-1963

THE TWO IMPORTANT THINGS ABOUT THE SPIES FOR PEACE PAMPHLET were its contents and its impact. Its impact was well described in the "Spies for Peace Story" (first printed in the pamphlet *Resistance Shall Grow*, and reprinted in *Anarchy* 29), but its contents have received less attention. The two important things in the contents of the Spies for Peace pamphlet were the regional government system and the 1962 military exercises. Exercises Parapluie and Fallex are still shrouded by official secrecy, despite the revelations in *Der Spiegel* and in the Spies for Peace pamphlet itself, but the RSGs are easier to investigate, and the object of this pamphlet is to describe their background as fully as possible.

The information here is not an Official Secret, though most of it was once, but it is little known because it is hard to extract from the various books and papers where it is to be found (for the most useful books, see Appendix 3).

The text of the Spies for Peace pamphlet begins by saying that "the Government has secretly established a network of Regional Seats of Government covering the whole country." This is rather misleading. It would have been more accurate to say that the Government has secretly *re*-established this network. There is nothing new about the regional government system. As Mr. Macmillan and several other people have pointed out, it was used during the last war. It is in fact forty-four years old. But before tracing its history, we must examine its principles.

THE EMERGENCY COMMISSIONER

The regional government system depends on the figure of the Emergency Commissioner—a special official in charge of a special area containing several counties. Most government departments and other public authorities have a system of local administration using about a dozen regions (and there have been proposals that the whole local government system should be changed so that all the counties and boroughs should be swallowed up in regions of this kind). The regional government system described by the Spies for Peace happens to use the thirteen regions of the Civil Defense Department of the Home Office—ten in England, and one each in Scotland, Wales and Northern Ireland.

The Emergency Commissioner is a unique figure in modern English politics. Local government is this country is normally carried out by two kinds of official—officials directly responsible to a local council, and local officials of a central government department responsible to a minister who is responsible to Parliament. The Emergency Commissioner is neither kind. He is the direct representative of the Crown (i.e. the Cabinet) in his area; he is responsible to no elected assembly, and in extremity he is really responsible to no one at all.

This isn't a new idea—in fact it's a very old one. There are several existing local officials who once had the vice-regal authority that now belongs to the Emergency Commissioner. The ceremonial High Sheriff used to be the Sheriff (= "shire-reeve" or royal "servant in a shire") who had civil supremacy in each county from the tenth to the thirteenth century. The ceremonial Lord Lieutenant used to be the Lieutenant (or royal "deputy") who had military supremacy in each county from the sixteenth to the nineteenth century. Each of these officials was the direct representative of the Crown in his county; each of them was responsible to no elected assembly, and in extremity each of them was really responsible to no one at all.

But at the time each of these two officials was part of the normal machinery of government in the county, and the county was (as it still is) the normal unit of local government. The Emergency Commissioner, on the contrary, is the arbitrary ruler of an arbitrary area. The closest analogy is not with the Sheriff or the Lieutenant but with the sort of local official set up by dictators such as Cromwell, Napoleon and Hitler. In 1655, for example, Oliver Cromwell divided England and Wales into eleven regions, each under a military governor with the rank of Major-General; Scotland and Ireland already had a military governor each, so even the number of regions was the same as now! For three years, despite widespread disapproval, each Major-General was the direct representative of the Lord Protector in his region; each was responsible to no elected assembly, and in extremity he was really responsible to no one at all. In the same way, Napoleon Bonaparte divided France into about eighty *Départements*, each under a *Préfet*, and Adolf Hitler divided Germany into about forty *Gaue*, each under a *Gauleiter*. Each of these officials was the direct representative of the First Consul or the Führer in his *Département* or *Gau*; each of them was responsible to no elected assembly, and in extremity each was really responsible to no one at all. And the Major-General, the *Prefet* and the *Gauleiter*, like the Emergency Commissioner, were all arbitrary rulers of arbitrary areas (though the *Prefet* and his *Département* happened to survive).

The Emergency Commissioner in this country has had two fields of action—a national war, and the class war. This double function of the regional government system is shown quite clearly by its history. The present system derives from the system developed during the thirties as part of the Government's plans for dealing with air raids or invasion from abroad; but that system derived from the system developed during the twenties a part of the government's plans for dealing with strikes or revolution at home. To trace this double development, we must go back to the beginning of the system, in 1919.

THE BEGINNING OF THE SYSTEM

World War I was followed by a period of acute internal crisis, with political and economic chaos, growing unemployment, rising prices, and many bitter strikes. Lloyd George's coalition government did its best to smash the strikers, and one of its measures was the establishment of an emergency supply and transport scheme which had been envisaged during the War by the Inspector-General of Transportation, Sir Eric Geddes (later the First Lord of the Admiralty who promised to squeeze Germany until the pips squeaked, and later still the wielder of the "Geddes Axe" against public expenditure). This measure marked the first appearance of the Emergency Commissioner, and is the model of the regional government system we have today.

At the beginning of 1919 the government began to prepare for a major strike. A secret circular was sent to military commanders throughout the country warning them that troops might be needed to break strikes. An Order was issued under the wartime Defense of the Realm Acts to give the Food Controller wide emergency powers. Finally, the country was divided into sixteen "Districts," each under a junior government minister with local emergency powers who was to have the title of "District Commissioner" (the District Commissioner is of course the chief local official in every British colony!).

In January 1919 the Clyde workers tried to begin a general strike, but they were defeated by soldiers and the police. In same month the miners nearly went on strike, but they were bought off by the Royal Commission headed by John Sankey (later Lord Sankey)—whose report in favor of nationalization was later ignored by the Government. In August the police themselves went on strike, but the strikers were sacked. Then in September the railwaymen went on strike against the wage cuts proposed by the new Minister of Transport, none other than Sir Eric Geddes.

When the rail strike began on September 26, the Geddes supply and transport scheme came into operation. The Food Controller, George Roberts, declared a state of emergency and began requisitioning road vehicles. The supply and transport scheme was supervised by an Emergency Committee headed by Roberts and the Parliamentary Secretary for Food, Charles McCurdy, and it was run by civil servants mostly in the Ministry of Food. Local control of the scheme was in the hands of the District Commissioners. At the same time the Government called out troops and raised volunteer "Citizen Guards." But the strike ended on October 6th, and the scheme lapsed.

There was more trouble in 1920. During the summer the Labour Party and the Trades Union Congress set up a "Council of Action" to organize strikes against British intervention in the Russian Civil War, and the TUC also decided to set up a "General Council" to organize joint action by its member unions. The real trouble came in the autumn. On October 16 the miners went on strike for wage rises, and for the first time since the war the "Triple Alliance" of mining, railway and transport unions (which had been formed in 1914) tried to bring the railwaymen and transport workers out in sympathy. Geddes, still Minister of Transport, tried to revive the supply and transport scheme, and the Overseas Trade Secretary, Francis Kellaway, was appointed Chief District Commissioner while the Government rushed the Emergency Powers Bill through Parliament. But the threatened rail strike was called off, and on October 28 the miners went back to work with temporary wage rises.

The government was actually in a stronger position. On one hand the Triple Alliance had failed to carry out its threat, and on the other land the wartime Defense of the Realm Acts had been replaced by the peacetime Emergency Powers Act of 1920. This law—which is still in force—gives the government authority to proclaim a "State of Emergency" if "any action has been taken or is immediately threatened by any person or body of persons of such a nature and on so extensive a scale as to be calculated . . . to deprive the community or any substantial part of the community of the essentials of life." Such a "Proclamation of Emergency" gives the Government authority to issue regulations and appoint officials "for the preservation of the peace . . . and for any other purposes essential to the public safety and the life of the community" (except that the government may not ban strikes or pickets, or introduce military or industrial conscription).

Armed with this new law, the government rejected Geddes's suggestion to make the supply and transport scheme permanent, but it might just as well have accepted it, for there was yet more trouble in 1921. The miners' wage rises were due to run out in March, and both sides prepared for another strike. The new Financial Secretary to the Admiralty, Leopold Amery, took the scheme over from Kellaway, and on March 31 the government proclaimed a State of Emergency. The miners went on strike on April 1, and the Triple Alliance again tried to bring the railwaymen and transport workers out in sympathy. The supply and transport scheme was supervised by another Emergency Committee headed by Geddes himself and was run by Christopher Roundell of the Ministry of Health (which was responsible for local government from 1919 to 1950—the Ministry of Food had been absorbed into the Board of Trade the previous year). Local control of the scheme was again in the hands of the District Commissioners, Amery being Chief District Commissioner. At the same time the government called out troops again and raised a volunteer "Defense Force." But on April 15—"Black Friday"—the Triple Alliance backed down and the threatened general strike was called off, though the miners struggled on until June.

After this both the Triple Alliance and the supply and transport scheme ran down, the former forever and the latter for a short time. On May 23, 1922 Circular 312 of the Ministry of Health told the local authorities that they would be responsible for maintaining supplies and transport in any future emergency. But three civil servants in the Ministry of Health still kept a skeleton scheme in existence, just in case it might be needed again. It soon was.

THE GENERAL STRIKE

In 1922 Lloyd George's coalition government was replaced by Bonar Law's undiluted Tory government, and in 1923 Bonar Law was replaced by Baldwin. Baldwin immediately decided to revive the supply and transport scheme, and gave the job to his new Chancellor of the Duchy of Lancaster, John Davidson (later Lord Davidson). Davidson set up an inter-departmental committee headed by the Permanent Under-Secretary at the Home Office, Sir John Anderson (later Lord Waverley), to make the necessary arrangements. Anderson reported progress to the Cabinet in July 1923. The scheme was much the same as before, but there were to be eleven "Divisions" instead of sixteen Districts, each under a "Civil Commissioner" instead of a District Commissioner—though the Scottish Division was still to be divided into five Districts, each under a District Commissioner (presumably Scotland still counted as a colony, even though Anderson was a Scot!). The whole scheme was to be rather less of a mere supply and transport system, and rather more of a regional government system.

In 1924, Ramsay MacDonald's first Labour Government held power for a few months. The newly revived regional system, far from being destroyed by the party which led the labor movement, was preserved and even used by the party which was so anxious to prove itself "fit to govern." The job went to Davidson's successor as Chancellor of the Duchy of Lancaster, Josiah Wedgwood (later Lord Wedgwood), who remarked afterwards that "the Trades Union leaders disliked a job which might mean getting across with the Trades Unions." It might indeed, since MacDonald's industrial record was as bad as that of all his predecessors.

In January 1924, when the Labour government took power, there was already an ASLEF rail strike, and the government considered using the Emergency Powers Act against it. In February there was a dock strike, and the government prepared to use the Emergency Powers Act against it. In March there was a London tram strike and the threat of an underground strike in sympathy, and this time the government did use the Emergency Powers Act. A State of Emergency was proclaimed on March 31 and. Wedgwood was appointed Chief Civil Commissioner, but the strike was already over. The TUC General Council was said to have threatened a general strike if emergency regulations were used against strikers; but the unions soon had a much tougher opponent.

When Baldwin regained power at the end of 1924, he gave the job of looking after the regional system to his new Home Secretary, Sir William Joynson-Hicks (known as "Jix," later Lord Brentford). Jix reported progress to the Cabinet in November 1924, but the system seems to have lapsed for a time. In the summer of 1925 the miners prepared to go on strike once more against wage cuts, and in the absence of the Triple Alliance the TUC General Council prepared to impose a national coal embargo and also to consider a general strike. But on July 31—"Red Friday"—it was the owners who backed down, when the government promised a nine-month coal subsidy to finance wages and another Royal Commission headed this time by Sir Herbert Samuel (later Lord Samuel).

The reason for this surrender was, as several ministers admitted, that the government simply wasn't ready. But it was determined to be ready next time. The more belligerent ministers, such as Churchill, wanted Geddes to come back and revive the regional system openly. But Baldwin preferred to work secretly; and while the unofficial "Organization for the Maintenance of Supplies" made a great noise, the official Emergency Committee met quietly under Anderson (who was of course directly responsible to Jix). The Emergency Committee quickly produced the "Civil Emergency Organization," which was basically the old supply and transport scheme brought up to date on the lines of the revised version of 1923, with eleven Divisions under Civil Commissioners and Scotland under five District Commissioners.

On November 20, 1925 Circular 636 of the Ministry of Health told the local authorities about the new regional system. This circular stated that the Commissioners were to be "empowered if necessary to give decisions on behalf of the Government," and it named the Division headquarters as Newcastle, Leeds, Nottingham, Cambridge, London, Reading, Bristol, Cardiff, Birmingham and Liverpool, and the Scottish District headquarters as Edinburgh, Dundee, Aberdeen, Inverness and Glasgow. The Commissioners and their staffs were appointed before the end of the year, and they were instructed to go to their posts and take up their duties when they received telegrams containing the single word "Action."

One interesting change was that the system was not in fact kept entirely secret. Jix was one of the more belligerent ministers, and when he was asked about local authorities recruiting staff for the Civil Emergency Organization, he said in Parliament on November 17: "For several years there has been in existence under successive governments an organization for maintaining essential services during a national emergency." Then he added: "When I came into office I found that this organization had always been treated by previous governments, including the last one, as secret . . . I decided that it was only right that as soon as possible that information should be given." But he never gave any more away— the government let very little information out, and the unions never realized quite what they were up against.

The expected crisis came in the spring of 1926, when the miners rejected the Samuel Report (in March) and the coal subsidy ran out (in April). The result was the General Strike of May 1926. On April 30, the Government proclaimed a State of Emergency and issued Emergency Regulations, and Circular 699 of the Ministry of Health told local authorities that the Civil Emergency Organization was about to come into operation and also gave the names of the Commissioners. The Chief Civil Commissioner was the Postmaster-General, Sir William Mitchell-Thomson (later Lord Selsdon), and the other Civil Commissioners were mostly junior government ministers with military experience (for their names, see Appendix 1). The "Action" telegrams went out on the night of May 2, and the Civil Emergency Organization and the Organization for the Maintenance of Supplies both went into operation the next day.

The General Strike began in confusion on May 4 and ended in confusion between May 12 and 14, though the miners struggled on until November. During their ten days of office, the Commissioners ruled their Divisions and Districts under the control of the central government, while Jix raised thousands of special constables. He also appointed a Special Civil Commissioner for the London Docks—Lt Col John Moore-Brabazon (later Lord Brabazon of Tara). But the unions didn't want to take the strike seriously, so the government didn't need to take it seriously either. The strikers didn't put the Strike Committees and the pickets to a real test, so the authorities didn't put the Commissioners and the troops to a real test either. Supplies never quite failed and transport never quite broke down, so the Organization for the Maintenance was never fully stretched and the Civil Emergency Organization was never forced to give decisions on behalf of the government. On the whole the strike organizers shrank from becoming revolutionary leaders, so on the whole the strike breakers were saved from becoming counter-revolutionary dictators—as they could have done at any time.

The general strike had been tried, and it had failed; it was never tried again. The regional government system had also been tried, and it had worked. It had been prepared for seven years and tested for two weeks. It would certainly be used again if there were another threat to normal government. There wasn't another general strike, but there was soon another kind of threat. The Emergency Commissioner had done his duty in the class war, and he was to do it again in a national war. This is a story which also begins in 1919, so we must go back to the beginning again.

BEFORE THE WAR

The Committee of Imperial Defense—the important Cabinet Committee which had been absorbed into the War Council and then the War Cabinet during World War I—was reconstituted in November 1919. One of its new tasks was to consider plans for dealing with air raids. In the past this country had been protected from foreign attack by the sea, but between 1915 and 1918 German airships and airplanes had made about a hundred air raids on towns in southern and eastern England, especially London. The distant danger of an invasion was now overshadowed by the close danger of an air attack.

When invasion had seemed possible in the autumn of 1914, the Government had appointed an Emergency Committee to consider plans for civil organization in such an event. The chairman of this Committee was Herbert Samuel, the President of the Local Government Board, and the secretary was Maurice Hankey, the Secretary of the Committee of Imperial Defense. The Emergency Committee had looked back to the plans made for dealing with Napoleon's threatened invasion of 1803–05 (just as the Government then had looked back to the plans made for dealing with the Spanish Armada of 1588!), and it decided that these plans still applied—that counties and towns cut off from the central government would be ruled by the Lords Lieutenant and the Mayors and Provosts, invested with special emergency powers. But in 1919 the Committee of Imperial Defense realized that new plans must be made to deal with the new danger. Even so, these plans developed very slowly.

In November 1921, the Committee of Imperial Defense asked military experts about the probable scale and effect of air raids in a future war. After two alarming reports it decided to set up a special "Air Raid Precautions Sub-Committee." This was formed in January 1924 and met secretly under the Permanent Under-Secretary at the Home Office, our old friend Sir John Anderson. It wasn't very active during the twenties. It took note of the Civil Emergency Organization in 1925–26. Because London was so vulnerable to air raids from the Continent, it also took note of the idea of moving the central seat of government away—say to Birmingham or Liverpool—in an emergency; but it decided that the advantages of preserving the continuity of the government machine were outweighed by the disadvantages of damaging the morale of the public.

In April 1929, the ARP Sub-Committee became a full Cabinet Committee and was reconstituted as the "Air Raid Precautions (Organization) Committee," still under Anderson. During the '30s it became more active. In 1933, the year Hitler came to power, the ARP Committee appointed Major-General Harry Pritchard as "Air Raids Commandant" of London, and it suggested that the rest of the country should be divided into regions each under a similar ARP official. In 1934 the Government first disclosed the existence of official Air Raid Precautions to the general public, and in 1935 the ARP Committee was again reconstituted as the "Air Raid Precautions Department" of the Home Office.

Pritchard resigned in 1935, when the ARP Department began using "Air Raid Precautions Inspectors" to maintain liaison with the local authorities. By 1935 there were six of these Inspectors, and the Department planned to station thirteen permanently outside London, each in charge of a region closely similar to the Divisions of the Civil Emergency Organization. In June 1937 a special Sub-Committee of the Committee of Imperial Defense headed by the Permanent Secretary at the Treasury and Head of the Civil Service, Sir Warren Fisher, recommended among other things that the ARP Department's plan for a regional organization should be put into effect because "a regional system of administration will be an essential element in the wartime organization." This recommendation was followed when the Air Raid Precautions Act of 1937 compelled the local authorities to cooperate with the Department. During 1938 regional offices under ARP Inspectors were opened at Newcastle, Leeds, Nottingham, Cambridge, Reading, Bristol, Cardiff, Birmingham, Liverpool, Edinburgh and Glasgow—all of which had been Division or District headquarters during the General Strike twelve years before. London and the Home Counties were administered from the Department's office in Westminster.

When Hitler occupied Austria in May 1938, Sir Warren Fisher and Sir Maurice Hankey (still Secretary of the Committee of Imperial Defense, now also Secretary of the Cabinet and Clerk of the Privy Council, and later Lord Hankey) recommended the immediate establishment of a regional government system with Divisions under "Divisional Commanders." In June a special "Committee for the Coordination and Control of Civil Authorities for Passive Defence Purposes in War" met under Fisher, and this direct successor of the Emergency Committees of the twenties soon produced a direct successor of the Civil Emergency Organization. By August it had worked out the Fisher-Hankey recommendations in detail under the name of "Civil Defence Emergency Scheme Y." The Divisions were to become "Regions" and the Civil Commissioners were to become "Regional Commissioners"; the Scottish Region was to keep its five Districts under District Commissioners. At the same time, a list of local figures who might be suitable candidates as Commissioners was prepared.

During the summer of 1938 the ARP Department worked out warning and blackout systems, chose gasmask and stirrup-pump models, and made secret evacuation plans. But when Hitler threatened to invade the Sudetenland in September, the first thought of the authorities was the maintenance of order and the continuity of government. Before the gasmasks and stirrup-pumps were distributed, trenches and first-aid posts prepared, or a Householder's Handbook at last issued to the general public, Scheme Y was secretly and clumsily put into operation. On September 26, the rapidly appointed Commissioners and their staffs went to their posts.

The Commissioners were mostly High Sheriffs or Lords Lieutenant, chairmen of or clerks to local councils, businessmen or magistrates, headed by—guess who!—Sir John Anderson (back from governing Bengal and now a Tory MP). But they never had to take up their duties, because Chamberlain flew to Munich on September 28 and handed the Sudetenland over to Hitler without breaking the rules the next day. When he flew back to London on September 30 bearing peace with dishonor, the Commissioners left their posts.

In those four days it had become clear that Scheme Y was satisfactory, largely because of its secrecy. The regional government system for a national war had reached the stage that the regional government system for the class war had reached back in 1925 after Red Friday. Once again Anderson took charge. He became what Chamberlain called the "Minister of Civilian Defence"—that is, he was to become Minister of Home Security when war began, and in the meantime he became Lord Privy Seal, taking over the ARP Department and using the Lord Privy Seal's small department as a sort of civil general staff. The government decided to disclose the evacuation plans at once and the regional government plans when they were complete. Scheme Y was knocked into shape by Sir Thomas Gardiner, the Director-General of the Post Office, who was to become the Permanent Secretary of Home Security when war began. The Regional Commissioners were to become national rather than local figures, and they were to be appointed before rather than after a war crisis broke.

On February 2, 1939, Circular 20 of the ARP Department told the local authorities about the regional government system, and on February 7, Chamberlain answered questions about it in Parliament. On March 1, Anderson answered more questions and insisted: "There is nothing sinister behind these plans. They are founded on nothing but plain common sense." Much of the press and the public remained unconvinced; there was nasty talk about Major-Generals and *Prefets* and even Gauleiters; some people asked why Parliament had never been consulted and whether it ever would be. They needn't have bothered.

A fortnight after Hitler occupied the rest of Czechoslovakia in March 1939, the government appointed the first Commissioners and Deputy Commissioners (on April 1 of all dates!). The Deputy Commissioners were mostly local figures—many of whom had been Commissioners during the Munich crisis—and the new Commissioners were mostly politicians, civil servants, businessmen and retired military commanders (for their names, see Appendix 2). When Anderson announced the appointments to Parliament on April 16, it was clear that no one had been consulted and that—as he admitted a few days later—"no attention was paid to the elective principle." At the same time he announced the headquarters and boundaries of the Regions and Scottish Districts. These were the same as in Scheme Y and almost the same as in the Civil Emergency Organization; but Manchester replaced Liverpool as the headquarters of the North-Western Region, and the most vulnerable Region was divided into two—a Greater London region, and a South-Eastern Region with headquarters at Tunbridge Wells. On April 20, Anderson announced the salaries of the Commissioners (up to £2,500) and the Deputy Commissioners (up to £1,000). The ARP Inspectors became "Regional Officers" with special responsibility for ARP in the Regions.

During the summer of 1939 events moved quickly towards war. Military conscription was reintroduced on April 26, and during the next three months the regional government system was tested by secret military exercises (similar to Exercises Parapluie and Fallex of 1962). In July, the Civil Defence Act of 1939 became law. On August 23, the Nazi-Soviet Pact was signed. On August 24, the Emergency Powers (Defence) Bill was rushed through Parliament and Defence Regulations were issued. On August 25, the Regional Commissioners and their staffs went to their posts. On September 1, Hitler invaded Poland, and on the same day the Regional Commissioners Bill among others was rushed through Parliament.

The Regional Commissioners Act of 1939, which wasn't repealed until 1950, didn't establish or even confirm the regional government system, as some people have claimed. The central government had (as it still has) quite enough authority to do this by the normal use of the royal prerogative, and the Regional Commissioners had been legally appointed by Royal Warrant several days before the new law was passed. This law simply gave formal parliamentary sanction for the payment of salaries and expenses to the Commissioners and Deputy Commissioners out of public funds, and removed the usual disqualification from any of them who happened to be members of either house of Parliament.

On September 2, the rest of the Commissioners and Deputy Commissioners were appointed and went to their posts. On September 3, Britain declared war on Germany, and the Emergency Commissioner took up his duties for more than five years.

DURING THE WAR

The Regional Commissioner had a double function during the last war. His ultimate emergency function was to act as the governor of his Region responsible to no one, if he were cut off from the central government by air raids or invasion. But his immediate interim function was to act as the coordinator of civil defense in his Region responsible to the Minister of Home Security—Anderson until October 1940, then Herbert Morrison (later Lord Morrison of Lambeth). In theory, these two functions were separate, but in practice they overlapped and made his position rather ambiguous.

His immediate function was "diplomatic rather than executive," as the North-Eastern Regional Commissioner put it, and involved "a maximum of contact and a minimum of interference," as Anderson put it. But no one could forget that the man who ran civil defense as the regional subordinate of the central government would run everything as the regional dictator if communications ever broke down, and that the regional civil defense headquarters, which had been moved from the regional office to an underground "War Room" at the beginning of the war, would then become a "Regional Seat of Government." This naturally gave the Regional Commissioner great moral authority whatever his legal authority might be—and his legal authority was in fact considerable even before he might have to take over his Region, for it was backed by several Defence Regulations made under the Emergency Powers (Defence) Acts of 1939 and 1940 and by other Orders made under the Civil Defence Act of 1939 and the National Service Act of 1941.

But communications never did break down and, as Terence O'Brien, the official historian of civil defense, put it in 1955: "No Commissioner ever exercised his full powers." This is really the most important thing about the Emergency Commissioner in World War II. The Regional Commissioners never went beyond their immediate function, so their story is rather dull.

The Regional Commissioners' relations with the local authorities in their Regions varied. During the summer of 1939 large Regional and District Councils were set up to maintain liaison, but during the summer of 1940 these proved to be too clumsy, and even smaller Emergency and Defense Committees with the same purpose were rather unwieldy. The military authorities had a simple solution to this problem. In May 1940, the Chiefs of Staff recommended that the Regional Commissioners should take over the civil defense system and run it on military lines without any reference to local authorities. The Government didn't go that far, but it increased the Commissioners' authority by Defence Regulations 16A and 29A of May 31. In June, the Chiefs of Staff again recommended that the Commissioners should have far more authority, and the Government again increased their authority by further Orders. But in general the Commissioners tried to work by persuasion rather than compulsion.

The Regional Commissioners' work during the war fell into three phases—cooperation with the preparations for the expected German invasion of Britain in the summer of 1940, coordination of civil defense during the "Big Blitz" of 1940–41 and the "Little Blitz" of 1944, and cooperation with the preparations for the Allied invasion of France in the summer of 1944. Their function during invasion or counter-invasion preparations was simply to act as the civil arm of the military authorities. Their function during the blitz was to direct the intelligence services during the raids and the rescue and reconstruction services afterwards. Special measures were taken in special circumstances. When Plymouth suffered very heavy raids in April 1941, the Deputy Regional Commissioner set up a temporary headquarters at Tavistock to direct the restoration of normal life. Only one regional War Room was hit—at Bristol in December 1940—and even then the Commissioner didn't have to abandon his post. By and large, the regional organization of civil defense worked well, though a few details were altered from time to time. A Special Commissioner was sent to the Southern Region in April 1941 to deal with the "trekking" (nightly emigration) from Southampton during heavy raids, and a second Regional Commissioner was sent to the Welsh Region in January 1940; and London Region had a Senior Regional Commissioner and two Special Commissioners as well as two normal Regional Commissioners. The problem of London Region leads to the problem of the central seat of government.

During the '30s, several committees reconsidered the idea of moving it out of London, and in 1937 one of them worked out the "Rae Scheme." This had two objects—to strengthen existing accommodation in central London, and to prepare new accommodation outside central London (both in the suburbs and in the provinces). By September 1939, the Office of Works had achieved both these objects, and had also made a plan for the evacuation from London of 60,000 government officials. This was in two parts—a preliminary "Yellow Move" which would evacuate 44,000 subordinate officials to 300 places outside London, and a final "Black Move" which would evacuate 16,000 senior officials and government ministers to a single place outside London.

The Yellow Move was brought into operation as soon as the war began, and it went on for several months; but the Black Move was delayed until London should be seriously threatened. Before this happened, the fall in public morale and administrative efficiency which followed the move of the French government from Paris to Tours and then to Bordeaux in the summer of 1940 persuaded the British authorities to delay the Black Move until the last possible moment—though the Yellow Move aroused occasional suspicions that the government had already left London. In the meantime, a "Black Area" was prepared in the West Midlands and the top brass used the shelters in London— such as the War Rooms under government offices, the "Annexe" by the Admiralty, the "Rotundas" in Monck Street, and so on (including the War Cabinet's "Paddock" near Hampstead, possibly on Primrose Hill).

An interesting sideline is the story of the deep shelters in London. The Government resisted the left-wing deep shelter campaign as long as it could, but the Big Blitz forced a change in policy. In October 1940 the Government decided to build ten deep shelters in London, and early in 1941 the London Passenger Transport Board began work on shelters underneath ten underground stations in three areas—the northern part of the Northern Line (Belsize Park, Camden Town, Goodge Street), the southern part of the Northern Line (Oval, Stockwell, Clapham North, Clapham Common, Clapham South), and the central part of the Central Line (Chancery Lane, St. Paul's). Work was later abandoned at the Oval and St Paul's, but the other eight shelters were completed during 1942. By this time the Big Blitz was over, and none of these deep shelters was ever used by the general public. The Government held them in reserve for a time, and later used them as shelters for civil servants and even as military headquarters.

When the Big Blitz was over the Regional Commissioners' function virtually lapsed, but because of the general law of bureaucratic inertia they did just as much work as before and even employed more staff. The South-Western Regional Commissioner complained that there was too much paper, and on June 11, 1941 Kenneth Lindsay complained in Parliament: "The Regional Commissioner has become a no man's land, and his functions are becoming completely vague. Let us do away with him if he is not necessary."

Herbert Morrison met such criticism with the unanswerable argument that "the Regional Commissioner is a typically British institution," and added that one Regional Commissioner thought the beauty of his office was that "you can jolly well do as you like!" On the next day Thomas Johnston, the Scottish Secretary (formerly the

Scottish Regional Commissioner) claimed: "Here is something that has been superimposed upon the country, which works, and which—and this is the great thing—works by agreement." Anyway, the Regional Commissioners stayed in office.

By the end of 1944, even the authorities agreed that the Regional Commissioners' function had lapsed and they began to resign at the beginning of 1945. Their legal powers were revoked on May 2, and by the end of June they had all gone. The wartime civil defense organization was officially ended by the Civil Defence (Suspension of Powers) Act of 1945. But in August 1945, Hiroshima and Nagasaki were destroyed by atomic bombs. World War II was over, but the Cold War was beginning, and the regional system soon had to be revived.

THE PRESENT SYSTEM

With the end of World War II and the beginning of the Cold War, we begin to approach the territory of official secrecy. As the RSGs pass from history into politics it becomes more and more difficult to find out the facts.

The Emergency Commissioner's two fields of action have continued to exist during the last eighteen years, but normal government has been less threatened by the class war and more threatened by a national war. Attlee's Labour government took the traditional Labourist attitude to strikes—it tried to break them. It had the Emergency Powers Act of 1920, and it also kept many Defense Regulations and other wartime Orders in force for several years after the end of the war—by the Supplies and Services (Transitional Powers) Act of 1945, the Emergency Laws (Transitional Provisions) Act of 1946, the Supplies and Services (Extended Purposes) Act of 1947, and the Emergency Laws (Miscellaneous Provisions) Act of 1948. Order 1305, a wartime measure, prohibiting strikes and lock-outs, was used by the Labour government several times to prosecute employees who went on strike, but not employers who imposed lock-outs.

The Labour government actually used the Emergency Powers Act twice, proclaiming a State of Emergency against a dock strike on June 29, 1948 and against another dock strike on July 11, 1949. In 1948 the government called out troops, and the strike ended before any Emergency Regulations were issued. In 1949 the government again called out troops, but the strike went for a fortnight, so the Government also issued Emergency Regulations and set up an Emergency Committee headed by a former Permanent Under-Secretary at the Home Office,

Sir Arthur Maxwell, to run the docks until the strike ended. There may have been a regional supply and transport system as well, but if so it was kept secret.

Eden's Tory Government used the Emergency Powers Act once, proclaiming a State of Emergency against an ASLEF rail strike on May 31, 1955. There was almost no rail traffic until the strike ended a fortnight later, and road transport was under the control of the eleven existing Regional Transport Commissioners on the staff of the Ministry of Transport. If the strike had spread or continued, there would no doubt have been full Regional Commissioners as well, but if there was ever any plan of this kind it too was kept secret.

There has been no threat of a really serious strike—let alone a general strike—since 1955, and there is no evidence that the Emergency Commissioner has been used against any strike since 1926. But since 1945 the threat of atomic or nuclear war has increased until it now overshadows every other threat to normal government and normal life in general. Soon after the end of World War II the authorities began to prepare for World War III, and the regional government system was revived as part of the official civil defense policy.

The Civil Defence Act of 1948 revived the wartime civil defense organization, but it was some years before the regional government system reappeared. In 1954, Sir Frank Newsam, the official historian of the Home Office, said of the wartime system that "the success of the organization was so complete that its recreation in war is now taken for granted." The Labour Party had already come to this conclusion. On August 1, 1951 Lord Alexander of Hillsborough said in Parliament that the Labour government was considering the "development of the network of control and communications at regional and lower levels." And on 29 March 1955 the Labour Party Civil Defence Committee recommended that the Regional Commissioners "should be appointed now." In fact, the regional government system was recreated during the middle fifties by James Howard, an Assistant Secretary in the Civil Defense Department of the Home Office.

But the system had to be modified. The regional "War Rooms" would become Regional Seats of Government a few moments after war began, and the organization at regional level had to take account of this. Moreover, the Region itself might be broken up so an organization below regional level had to be created as well. In October 1956—just after Suez—Civil Defence Operational Memorandum 1 (CDP 16/12/4) told local authorities about a new "system of operational control within Sub-Regions"—the "Sub-Regions" being industrial areas outside London in which emergency power would be in the hands of "Sub-Regional Controllers" who would be responsible to the Regional Commissioners (and whose headquarters would for obvious reasons be "sited on the outskirts of the Sub-Region"). In July 1957—just after the first British H-Bomb test—Civil Defence Operational Memorandum 2 (CDP 16/31/2) told local authorities about a similar new "system of operational control within Groups"—the "Groups" being rural areas in which emergency power would be in the hands of "Group Controllers" who would also be responsible to the Regional Commissioners (and whose headquarters would present rather less of a problem). These two Operational Memoranda were "concerned with the operation of saving life"—they were "not concerned with the question of reconstruction after a nuclear attack," for this remained in the hands of the Regional Commissioners. They were replaced by a new plan in July 1963; but a lot had happened in between.

The first official hint that the regional government system had been revived appeared in the Defence White Paper of 1961, which was published on February 15. It mentioned "preparations for a scheme of emergency control," and added that "cooperation in exercises and planning between the services and civil authorities at all levels will be further developed." And on March 9, the Home Under-Secretary, David Renton, said in Parliament that "a new system of operational control has been introduced which provides for the establishment of chains of command from regional headquarters down to wardens' posts," and dropped a vague remark about "the provision of premises and communications for the operational chain of command."

In marked contrast to this official vagueness, the *Daily Mail* had already published what it called 'the staggering story of Britain's plans for survival under nuclear attack' in three articles by its Defence Correspondent, Stevenson Pugh. In his first article on February 28, Pugh described the "twelve little governments which . . . have already been set up and staffed to ensure the survival of twelve states of Britain after an H-Bomb war," and he added that such a war "has been rehearsed in exercises many times." He had himself recently visited the central headquarters of the system "not 500 yards from Big Ben" (presumably in the Rotundas in Monck Street) and also one of the regional headquarters "Somewhere in Mercia" (presumably RSG-9 near Kidderminster) during such an exercise. He called the Regional Commissioners the "Big Leaders," said they were "national politicians who, given sufficient warning of the threat of war, would disperse from London to their redoubts," and added that "if, as could happen, they were cut off from each other or from the central government in its own redoubt, each is empowered to act alone." Here, more than two years before the Spies for Peace pamphlet, was the essential truth about the regional government system—though there are thirteen "little governments," not twelve—but no one seems to have taken it in.

Anyway, the radical wing of the unilateralist movement soon found its own way to the truth. When the Committee of 100 organized six demonstrations on December 9, 1961 one of them was at a mysterious structure in York, which happened to be RSG-2. At about the same time, members of the Committee of 100 in Cambridge found another mysterious structure in Brooklands Avenue, which happened to be RSG-4. The Committee people in both York and Cambridge had a pretty good idea of the sort of thing they were on to, and the authorities seem to have had some bad moments. Reports of the York demonstration were officially discouraged, and in February 1962 the Services Press and Broadcasting Committee issued a "D-Notice" covering the regional government system. In the same month, the Defence White Paper of 1962 said that "the scheme of emergency control will be further developed," and added that "there have been a number of joint civil/military exercises in order to test plans for military aid to the civil power, and joint planning for this purpose is continuing."

During the summer of 1962 the Campaign Caravan picked up several unofficial hints about the system as it traveled up and down the country. And then the Spies for Peace sometime, somehow learnt the truth about the RSGs in general and about RSG-6 in particular. On April 11, 1963 the pamphlet *Danger! Official Secret: RSG-6* published what they knew about the regional government system and the military exercises, which had tested it during 1962. There is no need to repeat here the information contained in the Spies for Peace pamphlet, but there is room for a few comments. To begin with, the Spies for Peace were wrong to state that "RSG-5 and RSG-11 are still being built." RSG-11 is the Scottish RSG, which has certainly been built; and RSG-5 is the London RSG, which has presumably been built, but has possibly been used as the central headquarters of the system during the exercises. There are in fact thirteen RSGs, not fourteen as the Spies for Peace implied. The organization of the regional government system seems to be much the same as during World War II, but the new locations of many of the RSGs are interesting. In general, as we might expect, RSGs in highly populated places have moved away from their previous sites to less vulnerable ones. Thus RSG-1 has moved forty miles from Newcastle to Catterick; RSG-2 has moved twenty miles from Leeds to York; RSG-3 has stayed in Nottingham; RSG-4 has stayed in Cambridge; RSG-5 has presumably had to stay in London, though it has probably moved from the Geological Museum in Exhibition Road; RSG-6 has moved eight miles from Reading Gaol to Warren Row; RSG-7 has moved a hundred miles from Bristol to near Kingsbridge; RSG-8 has moved 35 miles from Cardiff to near Brecon; RSG-9 has moved fifteen miles from Birmingham to near Kidderminster; RSG-10 has moved thirty miles from Manchester to near Preston; RSG-11 has stayed in Edinburgh; RSG-12 has moved 45 miles from Tunbridge Wells to Dover Castle; and a new RSG has been built at Armagh. The drastic move of RSG-7 is particularly interesting, for it seems to bear on the old problem of the central seat of government. All the Spies for Peace said about the central headquarters of the regional government system was that its telephone is on the ABBey exchange in Westminster. A site in Westminster was also clearly implied by Stevenson Pugh. The authorities certainly have a great many suitable sites in central London—not only the shelters under government buildings or the special shelters elsewhere, but also the huge shelter system built in the early fifties under a two-mile-long area stretching from Holborn to Victoria. This postwar system was mentioned in *Peace News* on July 12, 1963 and part of it was described in the leaflet about the Furnival Street communications centre in May 1963. But more detailed accounts have appeared in newspapers as different as the *Daily Worker* and the *Daily Express*.

An article in the former by Frank Gullett and another in the latter by Chapman Pincher give a clear picture of the system. Gullett said on September 8, 1951 that "some 2,000 building workers are engaged in burrowing an extensive network of atom-bomb proof tunnels under London," added that "stretching from Holborn to Westminster a mile away, these secret tunnels are designed not for London's population but for Cabinet ministers, top civil servants, and defense chiefs," and described the various entrances to the system. Pincher said on January 21, 1960 that "many hundreds of civil servants are working in deep underground tunnels built below London as atom-bomb shelters but now largely abandoned for this purpose as not being H-Bomb proof," and added that "the tunnels, below Whitehall, Holborn, Victoria and Leicester Square, have been secretly converted into offices to house special security staff and overflow from service ministries, the Works Ministry, Post Office, and other staffs."

Gullett was writing before the system had begun, Pincher after it had been overtaken by events. The "Whitehall Moles" Pincher described were no longer the key staff, and at the end of his article he said that "in the event of emergency the key Moles would be evacuated to a much deeper underground government headquarters being hollowed out far away from London." In fact, as we would expect, a new Black Move has been planned to take place when or if possible before a nuclear war begins, and a new Black Area is being prepared. This too has been described in the press—once more in the *Daily Express*.

In an earlier article on December 28, 1959 Pincher said:

> A chain of underground fortresses from which the government could control Britain and mount a counter-offensive in the event of an H-Bomb attack is being built far outside London. It replaces ten miles of reinforced tunnels built under London after the last war at enormous cost. These tunnels, which run below Whitehall, Leicester Square, Holborn and Victoria, are not deep enough to withstand a near miss with an H-Bomb. The new forts, which have already cost more than £10,000,000, are excavated so deep in rock that they could withstand anything but a direct hit.

He added that "they would enable many hundreds of key people to live for weeks below ground in the event of intense radioactive fall-out," and ended with the comforting news that "the forts are being equipped to house the nation's art treasures in the event of emergency, but they will not be available as shelters for the public!"

In an article on the Spies for Peace pamphlet on April 15, 1963 Pincher said that "there is a bomb-proof underground citadel for the central government," and added this time that it is "somewhere in the West." The new Black Area is clearly not the same as the old one in the West Midlands (which may have been connected with the present RSG near Kidderminster), and the RSG-7 move reinforces the rumors that would place the new one in North Somerset. It wouldn't be surprising if the Spies for Peace have turned their suspicious eyes to the Mendip Hills. The omission of any information about the central seat of government from their pamphlet was disappointing. Another disappointing omission from the Spies for Peace pamphlet was the names of the Regional Commissioners. This suggests that they haven't actually been appointed yet, or else that they haven't been taking part in the exercises. Perhaps the Principal Officers have been standing in for them. Anyway, the regional government system is still far from complete. The Home Secretary, Henry Brooke, has stated that less than a quarter of the estimated cost of £1,600,000 has yet been spent. And the system is still being modified in the light of the 1962 exercises (and possibly in the light of the Spies for Peace pamphlet as well).

In July 1963, Civil Defence Circular 17/63 told local authorities about a new system of operational control below regional level to replace the system described in the two Operational Memoranda of 1956–57. The Sub-Regions and Groups have been replaced by new Sub-Regions, and the Sub-Regional and Group Controllers have been replaced by more powerful "Sub-Regional Commissioners" whose "responsibilities will not be limited to the control of life-saving operations but will extend to the coordination and control (subject to the Regional Commissioner) of all the services necessary to survival." So now even the Regions are too big, and—like the country of which they are divisions—they must be broken up into sub-divisions small enough to be run by a single headquarters after a nuclear attack. But are even these areas small enough? Are there enough emergency dictators to go round? What will their next crazy plans be? Whatever it is, we may be told more of the truth than before. On September 17,1963 an official Report on the State of Civil Defence Today gave as the first of "ten vital points in the civil defence plans for Britain" the fact that "wartime regional headquarters have been provided and equipped in England and Wales, and similar centers in Scotland" (for the five Zones which have replaced the Districts). And the Report specifically mentioned "headquarters from which Regional Commissioners would operate in a war emergency." The regional government system for World War III has now reached the stage that the regional government system for World War II reached back in 1938, after Munich, and the authorities are trying to restore public confidence by pretending to disclose new information. But "none of the information has been deliberately declassified," as the *Sunday Times* said on September 22: "Most of it has been available piecemeal through Parliamentary answers, Home Office booklets, or by courtesy of Spies for Peace!" We shall never be told the whole truth. The Report still tried to hide the real purpose of the regional government system. It repeated the old story that "the emergency chain of control . . . is an essentially civilian organization," but it failed to explain why there are so many servicemen in the RSGs; and it invented a new story that "Parliament has made provision over the years for these preparations," but it failed to explain why there were so few MPs who knew about them.

The conclusion is simple. For forty-four years, our rulers have been making plans to stay as our rulers even if we can't stay to be ruled. These plans have always been secret. The officials in charge of them have often kept them from most of the government as well as from Parliament, the press, and the rest of the population. They have never been discussed in public or even disclosed to the public until they have been completed, if then. The Spies for Peace changed all this. They released a secret and our rulers never caught it. Now our rulers can't be sure it won't happen again. They can't trust one another any more, let alone the rest of us. They can't fool all of the people all of the time. One day, perhaps, they won't fool any of the people any of the time. We must make sure it does happen again, and soon. "There may be more revelations to come," concluded the *Sunday Times*. There may indeed. Our best chance against our known and unknown rulers alike is that there are plenty more "spies" for peace. After all, there are plenty more secrets to release. It is time that we destroyed not just the regional government system, but the whole emergency organization which helps to make nuclear war more bearable, and so more probable. "Catch-22 says they have a right to do anything we can't stop them from doing," wrote Joseph Heller. Who says we can't stop them? We know that during the last year resistance has grown. Let us make sure that *resistance shall grow*.

APPENDICES

1. The Civil Commissioners in the General Strike

1   Northern Sir Kingsley Wood, Parliamentary Secretary to the Ministry of Health
2   North-Eastern Captain Douglas Hacking, Home Under-Secretary
3   North Midland Captain Douglas King, Financial Secretary to the War Office
4   Eastern Major Sir Philip Sassoon, Air Under-Secretary
5   London Major William Cope, Lord Commissioner of the Treasury
6   South Midland Major Lord Winterton, India Under-Secretary
7   South-Western Lord Stanhope, Civil Lord of the Admiralty
8   South Wales Lord Clarendon, Dominion Under-Secretary
9   Midland Lt. Col George Stanley, Parliamentary Secretary to the Ministry of Pensions
10   North-Western Major George Hennessy, Vice-Chamberlain (later Lord Windlesham)
11   Scotland William Watson, Lord Advocate (later Lord Thankerton)

2. The Regional Commissioners in World War II

1   1939–45 Sir Arthur Lambert, former Lord Mayor of Newcastle
2   1939–41 Lord Harlech, former Tory Colonial Secretary
     1941–45 General Sir William Bartholomew, former GOC Northern
     Command
3   1939–45 Lord Trent, boss of Boots
4   1939–45 Sir Will Spens, former Secretary of the Foreign Trade
     Department of the Foreign Office, Master of Clare College and
     Vice-Chancellor of Cambridge University
5   Senior 1940–41 Captain Euan Wallace, MP, former Tory Civil
     Lord of the Admiralty and Home Under-Secretary
     1941–45 Sir Ernest Gowers (see below)
5   Junior A 1939–41 Sir Ernest Gowers, former Permanent Under-
     Secretary for Mines, Chairman of the Board of Inland Revenue,
     and Chairman of the Coal Commission
     1941–45 Charles Key, MP, later Minister of Works in the Labour
     Government
B   1939–45 Admiral Sir Edward Evans, former naval hero "Evans of
     the Broke"—and C-in-C the Nore (later Lord Mountevans)
6   1939–42 Harold Butler, former Tory Minister of Labour and
     Director of the ILO 1942–45 Sir Harry Haig (see below)
7   1939–40 General Sir Hugh Elles, former Director of and Military
     Training and Master General of Ordnance at the War Office
     1940 Sir Geoffrey Peto, former Tory PPS to the Board of Trade and
     Chairman of the Food Council
8   1939–40 Lord Portal, former Director of Organization at the Air
     Ministry, later AOC-in-C and Chief of Air Staff
     Joint 1940–44 A Colonel Sir Gerald Bruce, boss of the Wales
     and Monmouth Industries Association and Lord Lieutenant of
     Glamorgan
B   Robert Richards, MP, former India Under-Secretary in a Labour
     Government
9   1939–45 Lord Dudley, former Tory MP and Chairman of the
     British Iron and Steel Corporation
10   1939–40 Sir Warren Fisher, former Permanent Secretary of the
     Treasury and Head of the Civil Service
     1940–42 Sir Harry Haig, formerly of the Indian Civil Service
     1942 Lord Geddes (see below)
     1942–45 Hartley Shawcross, KC, later Attorney General in the
     Labour Government (and still later Lord Shawcross)

11 1939–41 Thomas Johnston, MP, former Scottish Under-Secretary, later Scottish Secretary

1941–45 Lord Rosebery, former Liberal MP, Lord Lieutenant of Midlothian, later Tory Scottish Secretary

12 1939–41 Sir Auckland Geddes (brother of Sir Eric), former Tory Minister of National Service, Minister of Reconstruction, and President of the Board of Trade (later Lord Geddes)

1941–45 Lord Monsell, former Tory Civil Lord and First Lord of the Admiralty

3. Books containing useful information

George Glasgow, *General Strikes and Road Transport* (1926) [the source for the General Strike Commissioners]

W. H. Crook, *The General Strike* (1931)

Allen Hutt, *The Post-War History of the British Working Class* (1937)

G. M. Young, *Stanley Baldwin* (1952)

Leopold Amery, *My Political Life*, vol. 2 (1953)

Frank Newsam, *The Home Office* (1954)

Terence O'Brien, *Civil Defense* (1955) [the source for the World War II Commissioners and for the map]

Charles Loch Mowat, *Britain Between the Wars* (1955)

Richard W. Lyman, *The First Labour Government, 1924* (1957)

Julian Symons, *The General Strike* (1957)

V. L. Allen, *Trade Unions and Government* (1960)

Originally published in Solidarity *15 (1963).*

9

FIFTY YEARS OF THE PEACE PLEDGE UNION AND *PEACE NEWS*

THE MAIN PACIFIST ORGANIZATION (THE PEACE PLEDGE UNION) AND the main pacifist paper (*Peace News*) in Britain both began in 1936, and their joint fiftieth anniversary gives a good opportunity to consider their history from the anarchist point of view. There have been pacifist organizations in this country since the emergence of the Society of Friends (Quakers) during the English Revolution of the mid-17th century, and there have been moderate peace organizations since the formation of the Peace Society during the Napoleonic Wars in the early 19th century. But the modern movement began with the establishment of the National Peace Council in 1904 and the development of a more militant pacifist movement in the opposition to the First World War in 1914 and especially in the resistance to conscription in 1916. After the end of the war in 1918, the particular campaign against conscription (led by the No Conscription Fellowship, but also joined by the specifically anarchist Anti-Conscription League) was transformed into a general campaign against another war (led from 1921 by the No More War Movement and also by the War Resisters' International, which was based in Britain from 1923), and the traditional peace movement (led by the League of Nations Union) was overtaken by increasingly militant pacifism.

The pace was quickened during the early 1930s by the growing warmongering activities of the new dictatorships—Fascist Italy, Nazi Germany, Imperial Japan—and several new initiatives were tried. A Peace Army to intervene in international disputes was proposed in 1932 by Maude Royden and again in 1935 by Joyce Pollard; the organization which became the Progressive League was founded in 1932 by C. E. M. Joad; new Christian pacifist organizations were founded during 1933 and 1934 by several denominations. Then in October 1934 Dick Sheppard, a charismatic Anglican priest, launched a new movement based on a simple pledge: "I renounce war and never again, directly or indirectly, will I support or sanction another." This grew dramatically during 1935, and what was first known as the Sheppard Peace Movement was formally established as the Peace Pledge Union on May 22, 1936. This quickly gathered a remarkable group of prominent sponsors (including Bertrand Russell and Aldous Huxley, Laurence Housman and Rose Macaulay) and gained remarkable support. In 1937 Max Plowman became general secretary, the PPU absorbed the No More War Movement and became the British section of the War Resisters' International, and it became the main pacifist organization in the country.

All the peace organizations had their own papers, and although the PPU began without one it soon acquired one. The Wood Green Peace Study Group, a non-denominational religious organization in North London, found difficulty in selling existing pacifist publications, and in 1935 its members decided to produce their own popular weekly newspaper. It became the Peace News Group, and after several months of discussion and preparation they produced a specimen issue of *Peace News* on June 6, 1936—a fortnight after the formation of the PPU. This was described as "The Only Weekly Paper Serving All Who Are Working for Peace," and it was edited by Humphrey Moore, a Quaker journalist. The first issue won wide approval, and weekly publication began on June 27. Almost at once the new paper was approached by the PPU, and from July 25 it was adopted as the paper of the organization, although it retained editorial independence, and it became the main pacifist paper in the country. The new organization and paper represented a genuine mass movement on a scale never known by pacifists before or since. The main inspiration was religious, although the movement was kept nondenominational, but there was a strong socialist influence. The PPU had a membership of well over 100,000—at first only men, as those potentially subject to military conscription (an ironical reversal of later sexual separatism in the peace movement), and later about one-third women. *Peace News* had a circulation of well over 20,000, rising to 40,000 at times of crisis (such as the Munich conference in autumn 1938 or the beginning of world war in autumn 1939). The PPU developed a system of more than a thousand local groups, and *Peace News* developed a system of more than a thousand local street-sellers. Both operated as semi-commercial enterprises, employing (badly) paid staff and occupying permanent premises. The PPU acquired its own property in Bloomsbury in 1939, and has stayed there ever since. *Peace News* was at first produced from Moore's home in Southgate; for a time it was published from the PPU office and then from a small office in Holborn, but in 1938 it moved to Finsbury Park, where it stayed for more than twenty years. The PPU and *Peace News* flourished partly because they appealed to many groups and individuals with very different ideas about war and peace and because, although differences of belief and behavior were not suppressed, they were not pressed to the point of division. Both Stuart Morris, who ran the PPU for most of the time from 1939 to 1964, and the various editors of *Peace News* during the same period tried to act as peacemakers within the movement as well as beyond it, and sectarianism was kept to a minimum. From the beginning there were definite libertarian tendencies in the movement. Most pacifists were relatively conventional in their politics, but some were concerned not just with traditional opposition to war but also with the examination of the political and social structures involved in war and with the exploration of ways violence could be replaced and non-violence could be extended between and within countries. In particular there was much interest in non-violent resistance (as practiced by Gandhi in India and preached by Richard Gregg in the United States) and in non-violent revolution (as advocated by anarchists in the international peace movement, especially Bart de Ligt in the Netherlands). But the main unifying factor in the increasing crisis of the late 1930s—the Japanese attack on China, the Italian attack on Abyssinia and the Spanish Civil War (which brought total war back to Europe in July 1936)—was the campaign to prevent world war. In this both the PPU and *Peace News* were tempted by the policy of appeasement, which infected pacifists as well as orthodox political parties, but the temptation was resisted and finally removed by the coming of the war in September 1939.

The beginning of the Second World War was a terrible blow to the whole peace movement, but support for pacifism actually increased for several months. To people like George Orwell pacifism might seem "objectively pro-Fascist," but pacifists themselves were mainly concerned to prevent Britain following Europe into Fascism as part of the war effort. An initial "Stop the War" campaign was very popular, and in early 1940 the membership of the PPU reached a peak of more than 130,000 and the circulation of *Peace News* reached a peak of more than 40,000. But neither the organization nor the paper was prepared to use this strength to move from negative opposition to positive resistance to the war, and a reaction began with the end of the Phoney War in spring 1940. When the fall of France was followed by the Battle of Britain and the Blitz and the threat of invasion became a serious matter, pacifism lost its appeal and the pacifist movement suffered serious setbacks. Neither the PPU nor *Peace News* was ever banned (unlike some Communist and Fascist organizations and publications), but both came under severe pressure and began to decline.

In May 1940, several PPU officers were prosecuted for displaying a poster saying: Wars will cease when men refuse to fight. What are YOU going to do about it?

In June, the PPU officially withdrew the poster and the officers agreed to be bound over. The intention was to save the PPU from suppression, but the effect was to suspend serious opposition to the war. At the same time *Peace News* was suddenly boycotted both by its printers and by its wholesalers. The issues of May 17 and 24, 1940 were hand-printed by Eric Gill's press in High Wycombe, and from May 31 it was printed by Ashley and Hugh Brock in West London. The loss of the trade distribution halved the circulation, and the reliance on subscriptions and street-selling reduced the paper's influence.

Meanwhile the more radical tendency in the movement was expressed by the Forward Movement, appearing within the PPU during the first months of the war, calling for more positive opposition to the war and at the Annual General Meeting in April 1940 for "a revolutionary movement on a non-violent basis." This failed to convert the organization or the paper, but its members pursued a courageous campaign of open-air speaking which brought repeated prosecution, conviction and imprisonment. Some of the members turned to the anarchist movement and took an important part in the work of the Freedom Press (Fred Lohr, John Hewetson, Tony Gibson). The PPU went so far at the Annual General Meeting in April 1945 as to pass a resolution supporting the imprisoned editors of *War Commentary*, but the pacifist movement remained committed to non-violence rather than revolution.

In July 1940 the editorship of *Peace News* was taken over by John Middleton Murry, the well-known writer and editor, and he maintained a high level of journalism for the rest of the war. But the paper and the movement were restricted by caution to campaigning on secondary issues—the status and treatment of conscientious objectors (there were 60,000 during the war, the proportion of conscripts falling from 2 to 0.2 percent), the policy of unconditional surrender, the use of terror bombing, refugee assistance, famine relief, and so on. By the end of the war in 1945 *Peace News* had almost restored its circulation to 20,000, but the PPU never regained anything like its old membership.

After the war both the PPU and *Peace News* faced the new situation of the Cold War and the nuclear bomb, the struggle against colonialism abroad and racialism at home. In 1946 Frank Lea succeeded Middleton Murry (none too soon, since the latter's doubts about pacifism had become an embarrassment), and in 1949 Bernard Boothroyd became editor. In 1951 he was succeeded by J. Allen Skinner, and then in 1955 Hugh Brock, who had provided printing in 1940 and had been assistant editor since 1946, became the most important editor for a decade. Meanwhile Harry Mister, who had been a member of the original Peace News Group and had joined the staff in 1940, became the general manager in 1948, and during the 1950s the paper and its publications and the associated enterprise of Endsleigh Cards and Housmans Bookshop were developed into an efficient business. The peace movement was pushed in two directions by the development of nuclear weapons and by the use of non-violent resistance in India, South Africa, Sicily and the United States. On one hand there was a shift in policy from opposition to war in general to narrower opposition to nuclear weapons, and on the other hand there was a shift in technique from conventional demonstrations to civil disobedience. Pure pacifism continued to decline, the PPU losing members and *Peace News* losing readers for a decade, but during the 1950s these two new influences began to increase and to converge. The testing by Britain of the atom bomb from 1952 and of the hydrogen bomb from 1957 prompted the growth of a movement specifically for nuclear disarmament, and the use of civil disobedience spread in this movement more readily than in the old peace movement. The PPU leadership resisted these tendencies, but *Peace News* supported and indeed helped to stimulate them.

In 1949 the PPU formed a Non-Violence Commission to study the subject, but in 1951 some of its members started "Operation Gandhi" to initiate a program of non-violent direct action. During 1952 this organized the first anti-nuclear sit-down in London (at the War Office), the first demonstration at Aldermaston, the first sit-down at an American nuclear base (at Mildenhall), the first demonstration at Porton, and so on. In 1953 'Operation Gandhi' became the Non-Violent Resistance Group and continued to widen its activities. In April 1957 the Emergency Committee for Direct Action against Nuclear War was formed to help Harold Steele enter the British nuclear test area in the Pacific, and in November 1957 this was transformed into the Direct Action Committee against Nuclear War. These initiatives were led by the *Peace News* staff and organized in the *Peace News* office. At the beginning of 1958 the same group began to organize the first Aldermaston March, and the more conventional Campaign for Nuclear Disarmament was formed. The two wings of the nuclear disarmament movement began to win the sort of support known by the peace movement before the war. At the first Aldermaston March in April 1958 it dramatically entered the political stage and also acquired its universal image in Gerald Holtom's semaphore ND Symbol.

After a series of large legal demonstrations organized by CND and small illegal demonstrations organized by DAC, the Committee of 100 was formed in October 1960 to organize large illegal demonstrations, and the radical wing began a major confrontation with the authorities with the support of *Peace News* but the disapproval of the PPU. This theoretical difference led to a practical division in April 1961, *Peace News* becoming a completely independent paper. Meanwhile it had acquired a sympathetic printer at the Goodwin Press in Finsbury Park in 1953 and suitable premises in King's Cross in 1959, and it now became a separate organization in the peace movement. The PPU had published other papers at various times—the *PPU Journal* from 1946 to 1952 and then an internal newsletter until the end of 1960, and also *Non-Violence*, the bulletin of the Non-Violence Commission, from 1956 to the end of 1960. From April 1961 it published the *Pacifist*, which still appears and has maintained the old PPU pacifist line while *Peace News* has followed other paths.

These developments had a considerable effect not only on the left in general but on the anarchist movement in particular. There had always been an overlap between anarchism and pacifism, occupied at various times by people like Ethel Mannin and Reginald Reynolds, Herbert Read and Alex Comfort, and the growth of the nuclear disarmament movement increased this phenomenon. More militants appeared who were strongly anti-militarist without being strictly pacifist and strongly libertarian without being strictly anarchist, and the revival of anarchism attracted many members of the peace movement. *Peace News* itself, which was the main spokesman of the radical peace movement throughout the period of its greatest activity, drifted steadily away from traditional pacifism towards non-violent anarchism. It even supported the Spies for Peace in 1963—more than it knew, since it unwittingly supplied the paper for the pamphlet *Danger! Official Secret! RSG-6*—though it was not yet prepared to reprint the sort of information, which later became the common coin of left-wing journalism. In 1964 J. Allen Skinner was briefly editor again, the American writer Theodore Roszak took over for a year, and then Rod Prince was editor from 1965 to 1967; but in 1967 an editorial collective was formed, and since then *Peace News* has been in effect a libertarian paper with special interests in pacifist, feminist, communitarian, and ecological topics.

In 1974 *Peace News* made two drastic decisions—it changed from weekly to fortnightly publication, and became a magazine rather than a newspaper; and it moved from London to Nottingham, leaving behind Housmans Bookshop and the Goodwin Press. The latter decision followed the decentralist tendency of the time, but its permanent effect was to isolate the paper from current events and national developments. It has continued to have notable successes—the exposure of a strike-breaking army in 1974, the support for the British Withdrawal from Northern Ireland Campaign when it was prosecuted in 1974–5, and the exposure of "Colonel B" during the ABC official secrets trial in 1977—but it has failed to become the general forum of the revived nuclear disarmament movement since 1979, it has fallen into sectarianism in several areas (feminism, religion, animal liberation, peace camps, affinity groups, non-violence), and it sometimes seems to represent an introspective group rather than the expanding movement.

But if *Peace News* can no longer be said to be "serving all who are working for peace," it still provides a better service than any other paper; and if the Peace Pledge Union now seems rather marginal, it still keeps the pacifist faith alive better than any other organization. They both deserve good wishes for their fiftieth anniversaries, and for the next fifty years.

Originally published in Freedom, *June 1986.*

10
BERTRAND RUSSELL AND THE BOMB

BERTRAND RUSSELL IS CERTAINLY A VERY REMARKABLE MAN. HE BECAME a Fellow of Trinity College, Cambridge, when he was twenty-three years old, and in a few weeks he will be ninety. His first book was published in 1896, and since then he has written nearly one a year; most of them are very good, some are brilliant. He is one of the most famous living Englishmen, distinguishing himself in such fields as mathematical logic, epistemology, the history of philosophy and political thought, popular science, education, atheism, politics, and so on. He comes from a leading Whig family, he inherited an earldom, he belongs to the Order of Merit, and he won a Nobel Prize for Literature; he was the President of the Campaign for Nuclear Disarmament and is now the President of the Committee of 100. The glory and gadfly of the state—a curious mixture of Socrates and Voltaire.

His great virtues as a thinker have been extreme candor, clarity and elegance of expression, and a disconcerting and highly effective gift for sarcasm. His vices have been superficiality, unoriginality, and an unfortunate tendency to oversimplification and overstatement. He should be seen, perhaps, as an old-fashioned rationalist radical, a Utilitarian. He might easily have lived a century and a half ago when deceptively dangerous opinions were fashionable among clever rich men. In our more complicated age he sometimes seems quite out of his depth in politics at least. On the one hand he can write an admirable analysis of the practice and theory of Bolshevism forty years ago or of the policy of nuclear deterrence today, and on the other he seems to have no inkling at all of the reasons why Bolsheviks and Cold Warriors behave as they do. In abstract discussion or straight description he is unrivalled—no one can explain Einstein's theory of relativity or Hume's theory of knowledge more clearly—but the more concrete his argument becomes, the less convincing it seems. Despite the profound intellectual sophistication of this great thinker, he seems to suffer from a strange emotional naïveté.

During the last few years his chief political preoccupation has been unilateral nuclear disarmament by the British government as a first step to the prevention of war. (He is, incidentally, one of the Labour peers in the House of Lords, but it is difficult to believe that his work is much appreciated in Frognal Gardens.) Russell's contribution to the unilateralist *movement* has been invaluable for a number of reasons, the most important being that he is a very fine and famous old man with charismatic qualities who is, as Pat Pottle said at the Old Bailey, "an inspiration to us all." But his contribution to unilateralist *thought* has, I think, been far less useful—even harmful. This may seem a rather hard thing to say, and even rather absurd, considering Russell's intellectual stature and reputation, but if anyone doubts it the best thing you can do is to read what he has actually written on the subject. Apart from several articles in all sorts of papers, there is a booklet called *Common Sense and Nuclear Warfare* (1959), another booklet which reiterates the same arguments called *Has Man a Future?* (1961), and the last part of a collection of essays called *Fact and Fiction* (1961).

Now *Common Sense and Nuclear Warfare* is full of interesting and illuminating information about and discussion of the course of the nuclear arms race, the growing probability of disaster if this arms race continues, and the consequent necessity of an end to the arms race and so on. But he begins as follows: "It is surprising and somewhat disappointing that movements aiming at the prevention of nuclear war are regarded throughout the West as left-wing movements." Well, it may be somewhat disappointing, but how on earth can it be surprising to anyone at all? Again: "It is a profound misfortune that the whole question of nuclear warfare has become entangled in the age-old conflicts of power politics." Has become entangled? Surely not—nuclear warfare *derives* from power politics and cannot possibly be disentangled from it, nor should it be. This sort of attitude runs through the whole book. Nuclear war is considered as some extraordinary disease that has attacked human society from outside and can somehow be cured without altering the form of society in more than a few details. This is why Russell can, rightly be called irresponsible—because he proposes certain measures without realizing how utterly revolutionary they are and without apparently being prepared to answer for what would happen if they were put into effect.

It is important to recognize that Russell isn't a pacifist: "I have never been a complete pacifist and have at no time maintained that all who wage war are to be condemned. I have held the view, which I should have thought was that of common sense, that some wars have been justified and others not." Fair enough. Nor is he an anarchist—indeed all his proposals for British unilateral disarmament and subsequent multilateral disarmament depend on the existence of strong national governments to carry them out and finally on the establishment of a world government to ensure that they are carried out properly. Fair enough again. But his rejection of pacifism and anarchism leads him into a highly inconsistent position. I am referring not to the fact that he thought America should threaten Russia with atomic war after the defeat of Nazi Germany in order to enforce international agreement about atomic weapons and now of course thinks nothing of the kind—his explanation that he has changed his opinion because circumstances have changed is perfectly acceptable—but to the fact that he would put the responsibility for *disarmament* in the hands of the very institutions (and people) who already have the responsibility for *armament*.

This seems to me to be a fatal flaw in Russell's unilateralism. Of course if the rulers of the world were governed by common sense, as he certainly is, they would immediately meet and disarm. In the same way, if the rich of the world were governed by common sense, they would immediately distribute their wealth among their poorer neighbors; and if the scientists of the world, and the writers and workers and all the rest, were governed by common sense, they would join and refuse to support any wars. So what? Everyone knows this, and most people also know that the problem is that very few people in fact *are* governed by common sense.

One particularly interesting side of Russell's unilateralism is his view of demonstrations organized by CND and now by the Committee of 100. He sees them as "a form of protest which even the hostile press will notice," and comments that "for a time, Aldermaston Marches served this purpose, but they are easing to be news," so "the time has come when only large-scale civil disobedience, which should be non-violent, can save populations from the universal death which their governments are preparing for them." What I want to know is how such civil disobedience furthers the cause of world government. It is intended to be a publicity gimmick, but apparently it is also a way by which people can resist their belligerent government; then isn't it—or something like it—a far more promising way of preventing war by undermining the power of national states than any complicated program of conferences and compromises leading to the emergence of a supranational state? Has Russell without realizing it lent his name to a movement whose end is not world government but world anarchism? If so, he would certainly appreciate the irony of the situation. Anyway, I find the last three pages of *Fact and Fiction* more convincing than the whole of his two booklets and indeed all of his unilateralist propaganda written before the formation of the Committee of 100, and I have a feeling that he does too.

So I think the proper reaction to Russell (or Tolstoy or Gandhi or anyone that kind) is to pay more attention to his manner of thinking than to the matter of his thought. The actual details of his proposals aren't nearly as important as his dedication to the central issue and his determination to tell the truth. Some people see his work for CND and the Committee of 100 as a symptom of senile decay. Although I disagree with much of what he says, I see this work as the culmination of his long and magnificent career, as his finest hour. I hope I have half his courage and integrity at half his age.

Originally published in Freedom, *April 21, 1962.*

11
THE NEW SQUATTERS

THE LONDON SQUATTERS' CAMPAIGN, NOW SIX MONTHS OLD, IS AN IN-teresting example of an extremist political movement with no official support which therefore depends very much on the attention of the mass media; and it has had plenty. Every stage in its development has been fully reported in the press and on radio and television, and there have been several attempts to fill in the background. The most thorough have been two documentary programs broadcast in the BBC2 *Man Alive* se-ries in March and April.

The present squatters' movement has many affinities with the great movement of 1946, and there are a few direct links; one person who took part in the old movement wrote an account of it for a broadsheet produced by the new one. Obvious parallels are the growing concern about housing, the emergence of the movement under a Labour govern-ment, which has proved unable to deal with the situation, and the in-volvement in it of political activists. But the divergences from 1946 are more significant. For one thing, the housing situation today—however bad it may be—is not as desperate as it was just after the war, so there is not the same kind of spontaneous mass action; no one expects to see 40,000 people squatting this year as there were twenty-three years ago. And instead of Communists taking over a large movement, this time there are various kinds of anarchists, libertarian socialists and radicals starting a small one.

The movement has two natural sections—the homeless people, and the people who are trying to help them. The homeless belong to a rec-ognizable type—what Audrey Harvey called "casualties of the welfare state" in the title of her Fabian tract of 1960. They are working class and under-educated, they have many children, and they cannot rely on help from friends or families in emergency—they are people without shock-absorbers. Often a single misfortune gives the push towards disintegration; a breadwinner falls ill or loses a job, bills become debts and rent runs into arrears, the family is evicted and driven from place to place, it loses its place on the council waiting-list and ends with the father in lodgings and the mother and children in a hostel (and frequently some children in care).

Very few can be properly described in that crushing phrase, "problem families." As Jim Radford put it on *Man Alive,* "There are families with problems, whose basic problem is that they haven't got a home. That's the problem from which most other problems stem, and we want to help them solve it."

After all, when there are fewer homes than families, someone is bound to go without, and, whatever acceptable form of words expresses it, the basic reason for homelessness is lack of homes, which is not the fault of the homeless. It is cruelly ironical that so many of them are unemployed laborers—exactly the people who could solve the problem by building more houses if our society worked efficiently.

Television is an effective medium, but you really have to visit the accommodation provided for homeless people to appreciate the full extent of the humiliation they suffer. Add to this the attitude of those in authority, and no wonder some of them are taking a short way out. Asked if she was frightened of squatting in Ilford, Carol McNally replied: "No, not now. It's gone too far now, I'm fed up with waiting, I'm desperate." And asked about the child they were taking with them, Danny McNally said: "I've got four children in care, they won't get this one." Margaret Beresford put it another way: "We don't mind it being hard, it will be a change from here anyway." And Ben Beresford added: "The years I fought for this country, and to think I come back to this, and have to bring up my children in this state." A single conversation on *Man Alive* conveyed the bitter feeling behind the squatters' movement.

"Excuse me, where have you come from?"

"Nowhere. I don't live nowhere, that's why I'm here."

"And how long have you been homeless?"

"Seven years."

"What made you decide to come and squat here?"

"No one else will help—they're the only people who's tried to help me—no one, they don't want to know."

The political activists, who are mostly working class as well, also belong to a recognizable type. Though they were for some reason described on *Man Alive* as "an odd mixture," they actually belong to what is known as the libertarian left, which has been a normal part of the political scene for several years. Most of the leading figures got to know one another in a similar movement—the Committee of 100—and have been involved in such *groupuscules* as the East London Libertarian Group, Solidarity, Socialist Action, the North Kent Socialist League, the London Anarchists, and so on. The accusation that they are trying to exploit the growing concern about housing is refuted by the fact that they helped to create this concern; the libertarian left has a strong tradition of participation in the homeless struggle. Back in 1963, for example, there was a Solidarity pamphlet on the subject, a Committee of 100 demonstration at the Newington Lodge hostel in Southwark, and a violent struggle over an eviction in Notting Hill. But the crucial experience was the year-long campaign by and for the homeless people in the King Hill hostel at West Malling, which ended in 1966 with complete defeat for the Kent County Council and considerable discredit for the Labour government.

The point was that direct action had been shown to work, and if it worked once it could work again. The King Hill campaign was followed by similar campaigns at the Abridge hostel in Essex in 1966, at the Durham Buildings halfway accommodation in Battersea in 1967, and at the Coventry Cross council estate in Bromley-at-Bow in 1968. The activists in the homeless struggle built up a pretty big fund of experience and good will before the squatters' campaign began. They are also committed enough to be prepared to break whatever laws they consider unjust, and to go to prison rather than back down when there is trouble. They are obviously an essential factor in the movement, but it would be wrong to infer that it has been created by outside agitators. The King Hill campaign began spontaneously among the hostel inmates, and when outsiders joined it a general principle was that decisions should be taken by the homeless people themselves and the activists should confine their part to giving advice, gathering information, getting publicity, and raising support; and this pattern has been repeated in every subsequent campaign. Anyway, as Jim Radford pointed out, for the activists "it's not a question of 'them' and 'us'—it's just us." When the activists decided last autumn that the time had come for a more radical form of direct action, they were already in touch with families in several homeless hostels and slum estates, and there were plenty of people who wanted to move from crowded into empty accommodation, whether they got outside help or not.

One should also look at the situation in a wider perspective. The King Hill campaign was also followed in 1966 by the first showing of *Cathy Come Home* and the establishment of Shelter. Jeremy Sandford, the author of *Cathy,* had been writing about homelessness since 1961, and has been involved in some of the campaigns. In the same way Audrey Harvey, the author of the Penguin Special *Tenants in Danger* as well as the Fabian tract, has been writing about the problem since 1957 and has also been involved in some of the campaigns; before that she took part in the Committee of 100, like so many of the activists. Nor should one forget, for example, Stanley Alderson's bitter Penguin Special on *Housing.* Political extremists are by no means the only people who feel strongly about homelessness and despair of orthodox methods of curing it. The squatters can count on widespread sympathy, if not outright support. A man watching a demonstration in Ilford, who was asked if he sympathized with the squatters, said simply: "My sympathy is with anyone who wants a house." There is a profound feeling that a home is not a commodity to be bought or hired, or a concession to be granted, but a basic social right.

The London Squatters' Campaign was formally established in East London last November. Three stages were planned—first a symbolic demonstration to launch the movement, then some token occupations to prepare the ground, and finally the real takeovers. The organization seemed rather chaotic to anyone who saw any of it, but it worked, and escalation was rapid. The opening demonstration was at a block of luxury flats in Wanstead on December 1 and several occupations followed in both East and West London that month. The first takeover came in Notting Hill in January, and the main takeovers began in Ilford in February. The West London squatters were eventually given tenancy by the Greater London Council. The East London squatters were at first involved in litigation with the Redbridge borough council; it then gave in and even offered to make its empty houses available to other London councils for their homeless; but it later resorted to brutal evictions, in some cases without court orders.

So there have been some setbacks—a few evictions, the usual business of people being arrested or sued on one pretext or another, and the unusual business (shown on a *Twenty-Four Hours* program in February) of empty houses being wrecked by council workmen to make them uninhabitable. But there have also been successes—several families enjoying a home life again, the security of tenure granted in West London, the formation of more squatters' groups in North, South, and South-East London, and outside London in Harlow, Reading, Leeds, Edinburgh and Belfast, and the wide (and almost entirely favorable) publicity in all the media. So far so good, but what is the next step? As Jim Radford said, when Horace Cutler of the GLC promised the McNallys a home:

"We're glad about that, but we're concerned with the millions of families who can't come on television programs, and in many cases are afraid to squat." Nevertheless, the squatters are largely encouraged by their first six months. There are new takeovers in the London area nearly every week, most of them without any publicity, and many of them with little or no help. To quote Jim Radford again, "People are now going ahead and starting to do this in their own localities—that's the whole point of it."

Of course squatting provides only a short-term solution in most cases, simply because the houses taken over are due to be demolished soon. Even so, as Maggie O'Shannon, the pioneer Notting Hill squatter, emphasized, "They're only going to stand for two or three years, but two or three years in the life of a child at five or six years of age means a hell of a bloody lot." In the meantime, far from jumping the housing queue, as they are often accused, the squatters are actually stepping out of it. Ron Bailey pointed out that, if the London councils did decide to put homeless people into their derelict property, they could empty all their hostels. But what about long-term prospects? Jim Radford said rather hopefully: "I hope it's going to end in massive reform. If it doesn't, then it may lead to revolutionary change."

But, whichever way it goes, he insisted: "This works—that's the main thing, squatting works. It worked in 1946, it's working again in 1969."

There is no ambition to build the campaign up into a mass movement under political control. The activists are trying to establish an example to follow rather than a leadership, and they are populist rather than elitist. Their attitude is expressed in Jim Radford's comment on a scene showing a child-care officer threatening to take the Beresfords' seven children into care: "We identify with the families. We don't go in like that patronizing child-care officer, trying to find out how we can make this family fit into our pattern. We go in to see if we can help that family." More precisely, perhaps, to see how they can help the homeless help themselves. Helping themselves to an empty house may restore their self-respect and put them back on their feet. The first thing is to go to the people and show what can be done. Asked if he was an interfering trouble-maker, Ron Bailey replied: "I *am* an interferer, and I *am* going to make trouble. Isn't it about time that some trouble was made?" Similarly Maggie O'Shannon said: "They might call me a troublemaker. OK, if they do, if I'm a troublemaker by fighting for the rights of the people, then by all means I'll be only too glad to be called one."

The squatters have two simple aims—to do what they can in a few places, and to encourage other people to do what they can in other places. The first priority is direct action—to get some homeless people into empty houses by their own efforts; the second priority is propaganda by deed—to spread the idea of squatting by the news of what has been done rather than by talk of what might be done. As Ron Bailey put it, "If it catches on as we hope it will catch on, it will start to rehouse people. People will start taking over houses in their hundreds, thousands and, we hope, tens of thousands. We hope that people from slums and hostels will rise up in one united protest."

What the new squatters are saying is that, if you think something should be done, do it yourself. They are certainly reminding us that something should be done about homelessness in this country. Can we go on accepting a situation in which twice as much is spent on "defense" as on housing, in which millions of people are living in slums (nearly two million in places officially described as unfit for human habitation), and nearly twenty thousand people are in homeless accommodation (over half in London)—when half a million houses are empty—and it is worth keeping property empty to make a bigger profit later? This situation is actually worse now than when *Cathy Come Home* was first shown. Cathy has taken matters into her own hands, and more and more people are deciding that it is not stealing to squat in an empty house, but stealing to *own* an empty house—or even a full one. When property is seen as theft, squatting is seen as the beginning of justice.

Originally published in Anarchy *102 (August 1969) [full version of article previously printed in* Listener, *May 1969]*

12
THE SOLIDARITY GROUP AND ANARCHISM

ONE OF THE MOST NECESSARY BUT MOST UNCOMMON THINGS IN THE present revival of anarchism in this country is the discussion of first principles. The development of consciousness and the discovery of action are common enough, but the definition of theory which should follow tends to get left out. An impressive attempt to fill this gap is made by a leaflet called *The Meaning of Anarchism*, which was produced at York University last autumn and has been reprinted in the current issue of *Insurrection*.

The Meaning of Anarchism is indeed so impressive and yet in some places so peculiar that it raises suspicions about its origins—which is not surprising, since a closer look shows that it is in fact a careful copy of the Solidarity statement *As We See It*, which was produced in London in spring 1967, was printed in *Solidarity*, and has frequently been reprinted as a separate leaflet.

The authors of *The Meaning of Anarchism* have simply used nine of the ten points of *As We See It*, leaving out the one which deals with working-class consciousness, suppressing the references to Solidarity and "workers' power," disguising the quotation from Marx, substituting the words "anarchism" and "anarchist" for "socialism" and "socialist," and making a few other alterations (for the worse) in the original text. The result reads well, even in this mangled form; though it is surprising to be told that "anarchism is not just the common ownership and control of the means of production and distribution" when no one ever suggested it was (change "anarchism" back to "socialism" and the sentence makes sense).

As We See It is a typically excellent statement of libertarian socialism, derived from a syndicalist development of Marxism. There is a wide overlap between this form of socialism and true anarchism, and the

Solidarity line is certainly relevant to anarchism and worth discussing by anarchists—but surely not in this form, wrenched out of its context and dressed up as some kind of anarchism. Are we so really hard up for ideas that we have to take them (without acknowledgment) from Solidarity and then pretend they are ours? If so, no wonder we get jeered at by libertarian socialists who are not anarchists.

Originally published in Freedom, *December 28, 1968.*

13
LISTEN, SOLIDARIST!

TEN YEARS AGO A GROUP CALLED SOCIALISM REAFFIRMED WAS FORMED and began producing a paper called *Agitator*. After a few issues the paper became *Solidarity*, and after a few years the group took the same name. It is one the best of the groups that emerged from the Communists and Trotskyists after 1956. Its main achievement has been the production of more than sixty issues of an excellent paper and also more than thirty excellent pamphlets (by the original group alone—good papers and pamphlets have also been produced offshoots in various parts of London and in Manchester, Glasgow and Aberdeen); and it has just brought out its third and best book, Maurice Brinton's *The Bolsheviks and Workers' Control, 1917 to 1921*, a detailed exposure of the Bolshevik destruction of the workers' control movement in the Russian Revolution.

Solidarity has always been very small and has had little direct impact on events, but it has exerted a considerable influence in the left, especially on the many people who have found themselves in the no man's land between Marxism and anarchism. This has been one of its problems. Moving from Marxism towards anarchism, in many ways it still remains much closer to the former than to the latter. It pursues a tough libertarian line which has meant that several anarchists at various times have found it rewarding to work with the group, but it remains strongly anti-anarchist. Moreover, in order to prove its revolutionary socialist respectability to its competitors—especially to the Trotskyists—it feels obliged to print sneers at anarchism in all relevant (and in many irrelevant) contexts, at the same time as the sneers it prints at the various brands of Marxism it is so inordinately proud of growing out of.

This has been found necessary even in their new book, which relies to a considerable extent on anarchist sources and which triumphantly reaches the same interpretation of events that the anarchists established half a century ago. Readers of *Freedom* may remember a rather undignified dispute I had with the Solidarity group two-and-a-half years ago over their misrepresentation of the anarchist position in the Russian Revolution. There have been plenty of other cases, as anarchist readers of their publications will know. Now there is another interesting example of their apparent inability to discuss anarchism rationally or responsibly, however hard they try.

In the current issue of *Solidarity*, there is a review of the pamphlet *Listen, Marxist!* by Ian Mitchell. We need have no quarrel with most of the article, which is an intelligent criticism of Murray Bookchin's intelligent criticism of Marxism, published in the United States last year. But at the end of the article Mitchell switches to an attack on Bookchin's defense of anarchism which is much less intelligent and which includes several idiocies, of which I shall mention just two.

One of these is the remarkable claim that Kropotkin was "a consistent supporter of French Imperialism," which will be news to most students of Kropotkin's writings and which I challenge Mitchell to substantiate with proper reference to the sources. The other is a revealing passage that runs as follows:

> So great is the attachment of most anarchists to the romance of their past, and to their label of "anarchist" that they will side with anyone who shares the label, even though he shares none of their ideas. Semantics thus becomes a substitute for politics. There is no need to think, only to use the right incantations. The absolute refusal of the anarchists to split their movement means that it remains forever paralyzed by contradictory tendencies and that it will never develop a dynamic of its own.

The unconscious humor of this splendid piece of dialectical splittism is heightened when it is realized that last year the Solidarity group set out to split the International Socialist movement, and only succeeded in splitting itself. Thus splinter groups in South and West London began publishing their own papers, and forced the original group to call itself Solidarity (North London) although it includes people all over the London area and the paper is actually published in Bromley (Kent)! One significant little fact is that, of the five Solidarists who signed the letters against me in *Freedom* during our last controversy, no less than three have left the group—two of them to join International Socialism! As *Solidarity* might put it, is there no lesson to be learn from all this? Isn't one of the virtues of the British anarchist movement possibly to be found in the fact that so long as we can agree on basic principles we see no point in letting disagreement on other points come between us.

To adapt the last paragraph of Bookchin's excellent pamphlet: "Listen, Solidarist: the organization we try to build is the kind of society our revolution will create. Either we will shed the past—in ourselves, as well as in our groups—or there will simply be no future to win."

Originally published in Freedom, *September 12, 1970.*

14
CORNELIUS CASTORIADIS:
AN OBITUARY

CORNELIUS CASTORIADIS, WHO HAS DIED AT THE AGE OF SEVENTY-FIVE, was one of the most impressive and influential intellectuals on the French left, traveling over half a century from Stalinism through Trotskyism and Leninism and finally past Marxism itself, away from prevailing forms of socialism towards a more autonomous and libertarian approach to politics altogether. He was best known to English-speaking anarchists as the ideological inspiration of the Solidarity group during the 1960s and 1970s.

Kornêlios Kastoriadês was born on March 11, 1922 to a francophile Greek family in Istanbul which soon moved to Greece, and he grew up in Athens where he studied law, economics and philosophy. He was drawn to left-wing politics as a boy and joined the Young Communists in 1937 and the Communist Party in 1941, but he soon turned against the party line and joined an extreme Trotskyist fraction in 1942. He was also involved in the resistance movement against the German occupation of Greece. He ran into personal danger from enemies on either side, and in 1945 he made his way to France, where he spent the rest of his life.

By profession he was a statistical economist, and from 1948 he worked as a senior official at what later became the OECD (Organization for Economic Cooperation and Development) in Paris. But by vocation he was a revolutionary propagandist, and during the same period he wrote prolifically for left-wing publications and held regular meetings in Paris. In 1946 he joined the French section of the Trotskyist Fourth International, the Parti Communiste Internationaliste, but he formed a dissident fraction which left it in 1948. He became a founding editor of the paper *Socialisme ou Barbarie*, which from 1949 acted as the focus of one of the most active groupuscules of the New Left, campaigning against all actually existing forms of socialism, whether reformist or revolutionary, and for a new form of socialism which would bring real liberty, equality and fraternity. As "Pierre Chaulieu" or "Paul Cardan" or "Jean-Marc Coudray," he produced a series of essays which appeared as articles and then as pamphlets, were translated into several languages, and reached small but active groups in other countries.

In this country his influence was exerted through the Solidarity group, founded in 1960, which attempted to play a similar part in the British left (and whose main leader coincidentally came from a Greek family and used various pseudonyms). During a period of more than twenty years, conscientious translations of the writings of "Paul Cardan" (often improved versions of the originals) appeared as articles in Solidarity magazine or as Solidarity pamphlets or books, and introduced his ideas to the English-speaking world—and beyond, since they were widely read not only in Britain and America but in many parts of both Western and Eastern Europe. Revolutionary and libertarian socialists of all kinds in all places were impressed by such texts as Socialism Reaffirmed, Socialism or Barbarism, The Meaning of Socialism, The Crisis of Modern Society, Modern Capitalism and Revolution, History and Revolution, Redefining Revolution, History as Creation, and were stimulated to rethink their ideas.

His key doctrines were that class society is divided not according to the ownership or control of property but according to the possession or exertion of power (essentially between order-givers or directors and executants or order-takers), that the various attempts at political and social revolution (especially by Communist Parties) have succeeded only in replacing the old bureaucracies by new ones, that Marxist analysis itself shows that all the varieties of Marxism (including that of Marx himself) cannot succeed, and that other ways must be found for individuals to take power over their own lives, based on the principles of autogestion—self-management—and autonomy.

His influence was most obvious in the "events" of 1968 in France, many of whose leaders—especially Daniel Cohn-Bendit—were impressed by his critical approach to all old politics, though as it happened the Socialisme ou Barbarie paper and group had ceased a couple of years earlier. In particular his concept of autogestion had a wide appeal for the rebels outside the established political parties. Eventually he abandoned not only Marxism but socialism, and by the end of the 1970s he adopted the term "autonomous society" instead. His line clearly converged with that of anarchism, but although he made occasional references to the anarchists, like many former Marxists he had little respect for them, and in return anarchists took little notice of him. This was probably a mistake, since many of his positive as well as negative ideas are highly relevant to the work facing the anarchist movement in the contemporary world. In 1970 he retired from the OECD and became a French citizen. He turned to psychology and became a psychoanalyst in 1974, associated with the "Fourth Group" of dissident Lacanians. He began to achieve recognition as a leading intellectual, was an editor of two leading magazines—Textures (1971–5) and Libre (1976–80)—and in 1980 he became a director of studies at Ecole des Hautes Etudes en Sciences Sociales at the University of Paris. He conducted an ambitious program of work and, at last able to write freely under his own name, he produced a score of books. A series of cheap collections of his early writings appeared from 1973 to 1979, accompanied by *L'Institution imaginaire de la société* in 1975, and followed by a series of collections of later writings order the general title *Carrefours dans la labyrinthe* from 1978 to 1997.

At the same time he became better known in the English-speaking world with the appearance of American translations of some of his writings—*Crossroads in the Labyrinth* (1984), *The Imaginary Institution of Society* (1987), a three-volume collection of *Political and Social Writings* (1988–93), an anthology of *Philosophy, Politics, Autonomy* (1991), *World in Fragments* (1997)—and another anthology, *The Castoriadis Reader* (1997), just before his death. But he was still virtually ignored by the political and intellectual establishments in the English-speaking world.

Towards the end of his life he turned increasingly to linguistics and mathematics, ancient history and pure philosophy. He developed an idiosyncratic humanist position which emphasized the part played by individual imagination and creative culture in human affairs and which included a remarkable "ethic of mortality," arguing that the absence of any kind of divinity above humanity and of any kind of existence after death made it all the more important to accept a tragic sense of both private and public life and to concentrate on the development of autonomous individuals in an autonomous society here and now. He always opposed all kinds of intellectual obscurantism, though he never escaped the obscurity of modern discourse in French, and his style became increasingly esoteric and neologistic. At his worst he might be arrogant and abstract, but at his best he could be inspiring and realistic. He always had a wide circle of friends, to whom he was known as "Corneille" and with whom he enjoyed furious arguments, and he also earned increasing respect from a larger public. He will probably be remembered for his negative work, which helped to destroy some of the most harmful myths of our time, rather than for his positive work, which tried to construct a new world in their place; yet now that the former task is completed, the latter task becomes increasingly urgent. "Whatever happens," he said at the end of his life, "I shall remain first and foremost a revolutionary." Other revolutionaries still have much to learn from him.

Cornelius Castoriadis died in Paris following a heart operation on December 26, 1997, and was the subject of long obituaries in the French press. Obituaries appeared in this country in the *Guardian* and *The Times* (the latter being an abridged and expurgated version of the present article).

Originally published in Freedom, *February 7, 1998.*

15
CORNELIUS CASTORIADIS:
A REVIEW

WHEN CORNELIUS CASTORIADIS DIED, AT THE END OF 1997, HE RECEIVED long and serious obituaries in his adopted France, just as his books had received long and serious reviews there, and he was acknowledged as a major figure of the left-wing intelligentsia. In Britain, it may be assumed, few people had even heard of him; but some attempts were made to introduce him to a wider English-speaking public, if only posthumously, through obituaries in a few papers (*The Times* and *Guardian*) and also reviews in a few others (*Times Literary Supplement, London Review of Books, New Statesman*). An obituary appeared in *Freedom*, and now here is a review.

Castoriadis was a prolific writer for more than half a century, from the time he went to France from Greece in 1945. While he remained stateless he wrote under a series of pseudonyms in periodicals—especially in *Socialisme ou Barbarie* throughout its existence from 1949 to 1965—but after he obtained French citizenship in 1970 he produced a score of important books under his own name, first reprints of those earlier writings, and then collections of later writings. Some of his most important political writings had been published in English versions by the old Solidarity group, and later several of these and later writings were also published in English translations.

From the 1980s there have been American editions, either translations of individual books or new anthologies, and some of these are available in paperback. The most ambitious is the three volume collection of *Political and Social Writings*—Volume 1 (1988), "From the Critique of Bureaucracy to the Positive Content of Socialism," 1946–1955; Volume 2 (1988), "From the Workers' Struggle against Bureaucracy to Revolution in the Age of Modern Capitalism," 1955–1960; Volume 3 (1993), "Recommencing the Revolution: From Socialism to the Autonomous

Society," 1961–1979. These cover much the same ground as the cheap paperback collections published in France during 1973–9, and contain all the important writings—mostly first published in *Socialisme ou Barbarie* and including those published by Solidarity—which trace his passage from Trotskyism through Marxism and socialism towards his eventual libertarian system.

The Imaginary Institution of Society (1987) is a translation of *L'Institution imaginaire de la société* (1975), which contains other writings dating from 1964 to 1975 and traces his passage onwards into psychoanalysis and linguistics. During the last twenty years of his life he produced a series of five books with the general title *Les Carrefours du labyrinthe* (1978–97), which collected his current writings and trace his passage onwards into mathematics, ancient history and pure philosophy. Only parts of these have appeared in English—*Crossroads in the Labyrinth* (1984) is a translation of the first volume; *World in Fragments* (1997) contains translations of items from the other four volumes. Meanwhile *Philosophy, Politics, Autonomy* (1991) contains translations of other writings dating from 1986 to 1991. Finally there is *The Castoriadis Reader* (1997) in the impressive "Blackwell Readers" series, a big British anthology covering the whole range of his work from 1949 to 1996.

This work falls into three stages—or rather, states—as he wrote by turn in the persona of politician, psychologist, or philosopher. For ordinary readers, Castoriadis seemed to emerge from obscurity into clarity and return to obscurity again. The writings of his early period (roughly the 1940s and 1950s) are so dominated by Marxist terminology as to alienate non-Marxists, and those of his late period (roughly the 1980s and 1990s) are so dominated by esoteric terminology as to alienate non-academics, whereas those of his middle period (roughly the 1960s and 1970s) are more likely to appeal to a wider audience. The *Political and Social Writings* provide the most accessible if excessive introduction to the best of him, and *The Castoriadis Reader* provides the most convenient and comprehensive perspective of all his work.

One problem is that most of these books have been presented by David Ames Curtis, an American academic who is a totally dedicated impresario but not an entirely satisfactory editor or translator. (The leading figure in Solidarity, to whom the *Reader* is dedicated by way of his pseudonym "Maurice Brinton," did better with the old versions of "Paul Cardan," which were often improvements on the originals.) Curtis has done an enormous amount of impressive work, supplying useful introductions and bibliographies as well as producing actual translations, but the combination of translatorial jargon and editorial schematism often seems to be in danger of burying the essential Castoriadis.

What is his essence? He reinterpreted Marx to argue that the essential division in modern society is a matter not of property or production but of power, between order-givers and order-takers. He transcended Marx in arguing that this system is maintained by the emergence of ruling bureaucracies and that the solution is not a violent revolution or any kind of dictatorship, or perhaps even socialism at all. He emphasized the importance of individuality and imagination, of creativity and culture. He valued not so much liberty or equality as autonomy (self-direction) and *autogestion* (self-management), private as well as public. And he looked forward to the development of genuinely free individuals in a genuinely free society. At the same time he looked backward to the thoughts and deeds of ancient Greece and inward at the nature of the human individual and outward at the principles of human society—like, as it happens, his near contemporary libertarian Murray Bookchin who, as it happens, is the subject of *The Murray Bookchin Reader* also published in 1997.

When so many people pay superficial tribute to false prophets, how much better it would be to pay serious attention to this true thinker. Above all, perhaps, he recognized that the socialist project takes on a new meaning in a secular age. If nothing is safe or sacred, if there is nothing after death and nothing above humanity, if we are alone in time and space, it is up to us ourselves to make the best of our own lives, alone and together, here and now. He was in a way his own worst enemy; he is never easy and often very difficult, and he was too clever for his own good and for his readers' comfort, but he is always rewarding and sometimes inspiring. Yet what would such a person, so much aware of mortality, have thought of the fact that he is getting such attention only after his death, or, so much attached to the printed and spoken word, have thought that the quickest and simplest access to his work is now through the Internet?

Originally published in Freedom, *August 15, 1998.*

16
RE-READING READ

HERBERT READ (1893–1968) PROVIDES AN INTERESTING EXAMPLE OF the damaging tendency in the anarchist movement, as elsewhere, for excessive attention to be given to sympathetic intellectuals. He was for thirty years the best-known anarchist in Britain—best-known outside the movement, that is, because his direct participation in political activities was small and brief. This position was at best ambiguous, at worst absurd. Read came from the landed gentry and became a prominent member of the intellectual establishment. After serving as an officer in the First World War, he worked for twelve years in the civil service, then spent thirty-five years as a professional academic, editor, publisher, and writer. Apart from producing poetry, fiction, autobiography and criticism, he played an important part throughout his career as a publicist of the modern movement in art and as a popularizer of art in general, for which he was knighted in 1953.

Despite his professional success, Read always held unorthodox political views. Before the First World War he had favored pacifism and Guild Socialism (the middle-class version of syndicalism), and after the Russian Revolution he flirted with Communism. In the 1930s he moved back to the libertarian position where he had begun, and during the Spanish Civil War he became involved in the anarchist movement.

From 1938 onwards Read contributed articles and pamphlets to the anarchist press, and from 1945 to 1949 he was chairman of the Freedom Defense Committee (a libertarian counterpart to the National Council for Civil Liberties, which was then a Communist front). His acceptance of a knighthood ended his formal connection with the movement after fifteen years, but he maintained his anarchist views for another fifteen years; he was even a member of the Committee of 100 during its first few months.

There is no doubt that Read had a significant influence on British anarchism during the mid-twentieth century, but there is room for doubt about the nature of that influence. In general it affected non-anarchists rather than anarchists, drawing outsiders towards libertarian ideas rather than developing libertarian ideas. This is a useful function, and he performed it skillfully for much of his life, rather as Paul Goodman did in the United States; but it is not certain that his performance is worth a revival.

Read provides an interesting example of another damaging tendency in the anarchist movement—the failure of anarchist authors to write books. This may seem a ridiculous statement in face of the fact that he produced something like a book every year for fifty years; but virtually all of them were actually collections reprinting miscellaneous items, some of which appeared in several collections at various times (Kropotkin's record is similar).

Anarchy and Order, which is Read's main anarchist book, is typical of this pattern, being not a single work but a collection of a dozen essays and a hundred shorter pieces. It contains *Poetry and Anarchism*, itself a collection of seven essays dating from the 1930s, first published together by Faber in 1938 and republished by Freedom Press in 1941; *The Philosophy of Anarchism*, a pamphlet published by Freedom Press in 1940; "The Paradox of Anarchism," an article reprinted in the collection called *A Coat of Many Colours* (1945); *Existentialism, Marxism and Anarchism*, a pamphlet published by Freedom Press in 1949, together with a series of sixty passages extracted from previous writings under the general title "Chains of Freedom"; and "Revolution and Reason," first printed as the introduction to the book, to which was also added a series of another forty passages of "Chains of Freedom."

Anarchy and Order was first published by Faber in 1954; an American paperback edition was published by the Beacon Press in 1971 with a new introduction by Howard Zinn; it has now been republished by the Souvenir Press with no new introduction but with the addition of Read's last political essay, "My Anarchism," which has already been reprinted in the posthumous collection called *The Cult of Sincerity* (1968). Apart from this addition, the new edition has been reproduced from the first, with all its mistakes and misprints.

Read says in his preface that "this volume assembles all the various essays that I have written specifically on the subject of Anarchism." In fact several other pieces were not included twenty years ago and have not been added now—such as his speeches on the disaffection case of 1945 (printed as a pamphlet called *Freedom: Is It a Crime?*) or his call for civil disobedience against nuclear weapons in 1961—and the book is rather a collection of those writings on anarchism which he wanted to be remembered by.

If the bibliography of these writings is a complex problem, a more serious problem is their quality. When Read wrote about literature, or art, or education, or himself, he was concerned with particular writers, painters, practices, events; when he wrote about politics he was inclined to be vague and general. Stuart Christie, reviewing the new edition of *Anarchy and Order* in *Time Out*, described its contents as "little master-pieces of the libertarian credo," but when they are examined carefully they seem to say little that has not been said as well by non-anarchist intellectuals like George Orwell or non-intellectual anarchists like Colin Ward, and to say much that is not really worth saying at all. Read's arguments belong to abstract philosophy rather than to practical politics, and his style is a good instance of modern academese, flat and flabby, littered with clichés and quotations.

Anarchists have been reluctant to criticize Read, possibly because criticism of a well-known anarchist may appear to be criticism of anarchism itself (again, Kropotkin's record is similar). Indeed he has been praised by some who seem unlikely to have much in common with him. Thus Christie described the remarkable occasion when Read gave a public lecture on anarchism in Buenos Aires in June 1962. That was a bold gesture for the official guest of a repressive regime; but Christie made it more than a gesture when he called the lecture "a full-blooded exposition of revolutionary anarchism."

In fact it was a bloodless exposition of philosophical anarchism, which went only as far as agreement with Gandhi and approval for non-violent civil disobedience, and it is hard to believe that Read's insistence on pacifism could really have much appeal for an editor of *Black Flag*. Moreover, to turn from theory to practice, a few months before giving the lecture Read had resigned from the Committee of 100, after taking part in two of its sit-downs in London, because he thought that its planned sit-downs at nuclear bases were un-Gandhian and non-non-violent!

Christie suggested that Read played a contradictory role in society, as an academic Dr. Jekyll and an anarchistic Mr. Hyde; but this phenomenon seems contradictory only in a narrow British context. In the Latin countries of Southern Europe and South America, for example, it has been normal enough for even established intellectuals to have libertarian beliefs and to take some part in anarchist activity. But Read did little more than flirt with political unorthodoxy, taking a brave line but never following it through to its more uncomfortable conclusions.

It is hard to take seriously a radical who rebukes the working class for seeking material comfort but enjoys it himself, a socialist whose disillusionment with the Russian Revolution begins with the persecution of intellectuals, a pacifist who fights in one world war and supports another, a libertarian who calls for the victorious nations to dismember Germany by force, an anarchist who attacks the state but accepts honors from it. It is hard, in fact, to avoid the conclusion that Read's anarchism was something of a pose—taking an attitude rather than making a commitment, joining the political avant-garde rather as he had joined the artistic avant-garde.

Here, perhaps, is the clue. For Read, anarchism was part of art, his position derived from aesthetics rather than politics. (In this, as in much else, he followed the romantic tradition—compare Shelley, Ruskin, Wilde, Morris.) He was concerned with culture rather than society. From beginning to end, he was an intellectual addressing intellectuals. At the time his work had some value, through its influence rather than any intrinsic merits; but few readers will get much out of *Anarchy and Order* any more. Read may have been worth reading, but he is not worth re-reading.

Originally published in Wildcat 5 *(January–February 1975).*

17

REMEMBERING HERBERT READ

THE ONLY CONTACT I EVER HAD WITH HERBERT READ WAS THREE YEARS ago, when I sent him a copy of the questionnaire which my wife and I were distributing to all the people we could trace who had belonged to the Committee of 100. He was one of the original members, and one of the famous people (the "names") who gave the Committee its great initial appeal. It may be significant that, of all the "names" we contacted, he was the only one who bothered to complete the questionnaire. He returned it in January 1966 with a friendly letter (beginning "I have submitted to your inquisition . . ."), and I don't think he would have minded my quoting from it after his death.

The main conclusion that emerges from his replies is that he was very much unlike most Committee people, and I suspect that in this he was like most of the other "names." For one thing, he was older (born in 1893), and for another, he had done military service (in the First World War, when he was decorated, which he didn't mention). But more important, he wasn't involved in the active political life, which was typical of most Committee people. The only political paper he read, apart from *Freedom* and *Anarchy*, was the *New Statesman*. He had not belonged to any political group or taken part in any political activity before joining the Committee (he didn't mention his former relations with the anarchist movement), and this extended to his support for nuclear disarmament; thus he went on no Aldermaston Marches, and took no part in CND or Committee work.

His year-long membership of the Committee of 100 was therefore a break in the pattern of his political life. He said simply that he joined it because "the Committee got in touch with me" and because "I sympathized with its aims." He went on two sit-downs—the first one, at the Ministry of Defense on February 18, and the biggest one, in

Trafalgar Square on September 17, 1962—but was not arrested. He said he had left the Committee, but gave no reason (it was in fact because he opposed the Wethersfield demonstration on December 9, 1961). He described himself as an anarchist, a libertarian, and a pacifist, but acknowledged no influences on his ideas, and offered no proposals for future action.

His attitudes to the Committee of 100 are predictable enough. He thought that the best thing it had done was "non-violent mass demonstrations," and that the worst thing was "aggressive trespass of airfields, etc." He thought that it declined because of "lack of direction and discipline," and the main lesson of its history was the "need for training in the strategy of non-violence," and that its main effect was that it "alienated many people of good will." His attitude to non-violence was one of "complete belief in its efficacy if properly used" and he thought that we could get rid of weapons of mass destruction only through some form of revolution.

Only the first and last of these attitudes hint at the Herbert Read who was an anarchist for fifty years. The rest express the Herbert Read who seemed so far away from most anarchists—an intellectual who took a brave line all his life but never followed it through to its more uncomfortable conclusions.

Originally published in Anarchy *91 (September 1968).*

18
GEORGE ORWELL AND ANARCHISM

1.

ERIC BLAIR, WHO IS MUCH BETTER KNOWN AS "GEORGE ORWELL," WAS born nearly a century ago and died nearly half a century ago. He would probably be generally forgotten by now except that his political satires, *Animal Farm* and *Nineteen Eighty-Four,* have been kept alive as set books for several generations of schoolchildren, that some quotations from them have stayed alive as universal political aphorisms, and also that a dwindling group of aging admirers have contrived to keep his work in print and his reputation alive. In fact, although most of what he wrote is dated beyond recall, much of it is still interesting and important, and he is well worth studying on his own account.

He was born at Motihari in Bengal on June 25, 1903. He belonged to what he called "the lower-upper-middle class," the shabby genteel "poor whites" of the English social system, and his early life was almost a parody of what his background demanded. He was a child of the Raj (the British imperial regime in India), like Thackeray, Kipling and Saki, and for a time he returned to it. His father was an obscure member of a once prosperous English (and partly Scottish) professional family, who spent his working life as an official in the Opium Department in India, and he himself served as a policeman in Burma for five years. His mother was a half-French member of a commercial family in India. She returned to England with her three children in 1904, and her husband retired to England in 1911, though he served in the army during the First World War.

Eric Blair was educated at St. Cyprian's, an unpleasant but successful preparatory school in Eastbourne, from 1911 to 1916; then, being clever enough to win scholarships, he went to Eton College, the leading "public" school, from 1917 to 1921. In later life he said that he wasted his time there and that it had no influence on him, but he might have been a very different person if he had gone to a more conventional school (such as Wellington College, where he won another scholarship).

By the time he went to Burma in 1922, he had assembled a fine collection of chips on his shoulder. He had been sent away from home for most of his childhood, like so many children of so-called civilized middle-class parents; he had been taken by his prep school at a reduced fee in the hope that he would win credit for the school with a good scholarship (which he did); he was sickly, and thought he was also ugly and unpopular (which he wasn't); then he didn't do very well at Eton and didn't go to Oxford or Cambridge, where he might have done very well, but went out to the East instead; and, of course, he was that unhappy animal, a bourgeois intellectual doing uncongenial work.

In 1927, when he was twenty-four, he resigned his post in Burma, after acquiring on the one hand the material for a novel and some of his finest essays, and on the other "an immense weight of guilt that I had got to expiate." It would be fair to say that he spent the second half of his life trying to do just that. He worked hard to become a writer, first living rough in Britain and France, then working in London as a private schoolteacher in 1932–3 and as a bookshop assistant in 1934–6. He began publishing articles in 1928 and then books, adopting the pseudonym "'George Orwell'" for the first one, the semi-autobiographical *Down and Out in Paris and London* (1933).

He was for a time a fairly successful journalist, producing efficient reviews and impressive essays, and a fairly unsuccessful novelist, producing *Burmese Days* (1934), *A Clergyman's Daughter* (1935), *Keep the Aspidistra Flying* (1936), and *Coming Up For Air* (1939). He became a well-known left-wing writer when he toured the industrial North of England in January–March 1936 and wrote about it in *The Road to Wigan Pier* (1937). He married Eileen O'Shaughnessy in June 1936, and they took a village shop in Wallington until 1940. He went to Spain to see and join in the Civil War from December 1936 to July 1937, and wrote about it in *Homage to Catalonia* (1938). He had always suffered from lung trouble, and tuberculosis was first diagnosed just before the Second World War. He was out of action during 1938–9, first in a sanatorium and then in French Morocco. During the war he lived in London. Although he was unfit for military service, he served in the Home Guard from 1940 to 1943. He worked as a radio Talks Assistant and Talks Producer in the Indian Section of the Eastern Service of the BBC from 1941 to 1943, and then as Literary Editor of the socialist weekly *Tribune* from 1943 to 1944. He and Eileen adopted a son in 1944, but she died during an operation in 1945.

He achieved real fame with the publication of *Animal Farm* (1945) and added to it with *Nineteen Eighty-Four* (1949), which was completed with great difficulty because of his worsening illness, but he didn't live to enjoy it. He spent much time on the Scottish island of Jura from 1946 to 1948, but he was increasingly ill from 1944 and in and out of sanatoriums from 1947. He went into hospital in London in 1949, married Sonia Brownell in October 1949, and died on January 21, 1950 at the age of forty-six.

After his death his fame grew steadily, and after becoming a classic in his own lifetime he became a name known by virtually everyone who reads books and by many who don't. His own radio version of *Animal Farm* was broadcast on the BBC Third Programme in January and February 1947, and in 1955 a cartoon film version was made by Joy Batchelor and John Halas, who had produced an illustrated edition of the book in 1954. Nigel Kneale's BBC television version of *Nineteen Eighty-Four* had an enormous public impact when it was broadcast in December 1954. (It was following this that *Picture Post* published the special feature on George Orwell, including some of the photographs by Vernon Richards and Marie Louise Berneri, on January 8, 1955.) Michael Anderson's and Michael Radford's films of *Nineteen Eighty-Four* in 1955 and 1984 respectively were worthy but weaker successors.

The "Uniform Edition" of his writings began in 1948 and continued until 1965. Almost all his books were continually reprinted, in both cloth and paperback editions, and two of them—*Animal Farm* and to a lesser extent *Nineteen Eighty-Four*—became favorite set-books and are repeatedly named among the key works of the 20th century. A one-volume omnibus edition of all his fiction was published in 1976. Most of his shorter writings were eventually reprinted in convenient editions—first in various separate volumes, then in the inferior and unsatisfactory one-volume omnibus *Collected Essays* (1961), and then in the superior but still not satisfactory four-volume *Collected Essays, Journalism and Letters* (1968).

There have been many studies of his work, but few are more than useful and most are less than useless. Orwell himself asked that no biography should be written, and none appeared for more than twenty years after his death. But again, there have been many studies of his life, the most valuable material being personal reminiscences by some of the people who knew him well, nearly all the rest being valueless or worse. Two useful collections of broadcast reminiscences were published in

1984 as *Remembering Orwell* and *Orwell Remembered*. Apart from sheer ignorance and irrelevance, one major problem was always that Orwell's widow, whom he married just before his death and who controlled both his copyright and his papers, refused to allow either a full account of this work with all the necessary quotations or a full account of his life with all the necessary information, although she founded the Orwell Archive at University College London in 1960. This frustrating situation changed in 1972, when the first installment of a two-volume study of Orwell's early life by Peter Stansky and William Abrahams managed to be at the same time so detailed and so dreadful that she at last authorized a proper biography by Bernard Crick, Professor of Politics at Birkbeck College, London, and a well-known democratic socialist and literary journalist.

The result, which was published as *George Orwell: A Life* (1980)— and republished in a revised American edition in 1981 and a re-revised Penguin edition in 1982—is by far the best single book yet on Orwell's whole career. Crick's most obvious advantage was that he was the first person to have complete freedom of quotation from the whole of Orwell's published and unpublished writings and of access to the whole of the Orwell Archive, so his book was based on a much wider range of material than ever before. A less obvious but just as serious advantage was that he shared many personal and political characteristics of Orwell, and was both genuinely well informed about and generally well-disposed towards his subject. His book didn't entirely supersede the Stansky-Abrahams pair—*The Unknown Orwell* (1972) and *Orwell: The Transformation* (1979)—since their coverage of Orwell's life up to 1938 was twice as full as his and they used a few sources he didn't; but it immediately became and has subsequently remained the standard biography.

There have been a few alterations to the situation and additions to the canon. Sonia Orwell died in 1980, a few weeks after the publication of Crick's biography, and control of Orwell's papers and copyrights passed to literary agents who proved more lenient. J. West produced two volumes—*The War Broadcasts* (1985) and *The War Commentaries* (1985)—containing the texts of many unpublished and indeed unknown broadcasts produced by Orwell during his time at the BBC, which mostly reinforced rather than revised the prevailing view of his work. Michael Shelden produced *Orwell: The Authorized Biography* (1991), described as "authorized" because it was approved by the agent for the Orwell estate, and distinguished for patronizing its predecessors. These books did add a few new facts, and also prompted an interesting and entertaining appendix in another revised edition of Crick's *George Orwell: A Life* (1992), but they didn't alter the now familiar picture.

Meanwhile *The Complete Works of George Orwell*, edited by Peter Davison—who produced the facsimile edition of *Nineteen Eighty-Four* (in 1984)—was inaugurated in 1981. The first part of this project consisted of the establishment of authoritative texts of the nine main books, both to correct editors' and printers' errors and also to restore so far as possible the author's original intentions, derived from letters, typescripts or proofs, before the original publishers' censorship (additionally having the profitable effect of extending the copyright term). After many misadventures, these versions were published in 1986-7, and soon also appeared in new Penguin paperback editions. The second part of this project consisted of the replacement of the four-volume *Collected Essays, Journalism and Letters* with an eleven-volume collection three times as long of essays, articles, reviews, talks, scripts, letters, diaries and notes, containing as nearly as possible a virtually definitive edition of all his shorter writings. After many more misadventures, the final result was published in 1998, making available a more extensive account of George Orwell than of any other twentieth-century British writer, and making possible the most intensive examination of his personal and political career.

2.

Of all modern writers, George Orwell is the easiest to get hold of, and at the same time the easiest to get to grips with. All his writing has a style and structure that are so spare and simple and a personality and purpose which are so peculiar and powerful that introduction and explanation are virtually unnecessary. In a way, then, there is no need to read *about* Orwell at all, only to read Orwell. But there are some puzzles about him, such as the precise nature of his political (and religious) opinions.

One aspect of George Orwell's life and work that is obscure is his relationship with anarchism and anarchists. There are of course several other cases of what could be called anarchist fellow-travelers among British intellectuals (William Godwin, P. B. Shelley, William Morris, Oscar Wilde, Edward Carpenter, Augustus John, E. M. Forster, Herbert Read, and so on), and in such a case it is wrong to go too far in either direction—to say either that the person in question was essentially an anarchist all the time, or that he never really had anything to do with anarchism. It is necessary to work out both just how close he was to and just how far he was from anarchism, and to make a fair judgment of the final relationship. It should always be remembered, anyway, that Orwell was never a conformist adherent of any ideology, rejecting what he described in his essay on Charles Dickens as "all the smelly little orthodoxies which are now contending for our souls" (*Inside the Whale*, 1940).

In Orwell's particular case, the former mistake was made, for example, by Julian Symons, the writer who was associated with anarchists during the Second World War and remained sympathetic to anarchism for the rest of his life, and who was a close friend of Orwell. In an article in the *London Magazine* (September 1963), he drew public attention to Orwell's own association with anarchists at the same time, but he went on to argue that Orwell continued to support libertarian socialism for the rest of his life, and that this ideology "was expressed for him more sympathetically in the personalities of unpractical Anarchists than in the slide-rule Socialists who made up the bulk of the British Parliamentary Labour Party." George Woodcock, the writer who was associated with anarchists during and after the war and who was also a close friend of Orwell, described this view as being "substantially correct" in his book *The Crystal Spirit* (1967), which is one of the few worthwhile studies of Orwell's work. Woodcock continued: "Conservatism and socialism form the two poles of Orwell's political thought. What holds them together is the never wholly abandoned strain of anarchism . . . Anarchism remained a restless presence in his mind right to the end." How far is this really true? Woodcock himself had in his earlier essay on Orwell described him as "an independent socialist with libertarian tendencies" and even as "an old-style Liberal" (*Politics*, December 1946). E. M. Forster saw him as "a true liberal," Fenner Brockway as a libertarian socialist. Crick preferred to see him as a left-wing democratic socialist. Kenneth Allsop took a more unpolitical, almost anti-political, line in his article in *Picture Post* (January 8, 1955). He suggested that Orwell was both a socialist and an individualist. He quoted the famous prophecy from *Nineteen Eighty-Four*, "If you want a picture of the future, imagine a boot stamping on a human face—for ever," and he commented: "What Orwell hated and fought was They, 'the sober citizens in bowler hats who are always anxious to stop you doing anything worth doing.'" *Nineteen Eighty-Four* is not particularly anti-Russian: it is anti-boot state, anti-They; They wherever They exist and under whatever ambiguous political label They masquerade.

With Orwell, it is always important to begin at the beginning, since he himself drew so much of his inspiration and his ideology from his own childhood and youth—or rather, from what he made of his childhood and youth in later life. His writings about early life at home or at school are often contradicted by the memories of his family or friends, but they do have the authority of his own authorship; and even if they don't tell the truth about his beliefs at the time he was writing about, they presumably do tell the truth about his beliefs at the time he was writing. The primary source for his early ideas is the extraordinary essay about his preparatory school, thinly disguised as "Crossgates." "Such, Such Were the Joys" seems to have been written by May 1947, but it wasn't published until after his death, and then only in the United States—first in *Partisan Review* (September–October 1952) and then in collections of essays, *Such, Such Were the Joys* (1953) and *The Orwell Reader* (1956). It contains several revealing passages. He described the conformist atmosphere of the school, and commented: "I was not a rebel, except by force of circumstances. I accepted the codes that I found in being . . . I did not question the prevailing standards, because so far as I could see there were no others.

"I could not invert the existing scale of values," he continued, "but I could . . . make the best of it." And he added, more interestingly: "At the time I could not see beyond the moral dilemma that is presented to the weak in a world governed by the strong: Break the rules or perish. I did not see that in that case the weak have the right to make a different set of rules for themselves."

And he concluded: "But I never did rebel intellectually, only emotionally."

Later, however, it is clear that he became an intellectual as well as an emotional rebel. He was remembered by his contemporaries at Eton as a leading member of an "antinomian" party, rejecting all religious and political orthodoxies, and then by his colleagues in Burma as a discontented member of the British establishment, repelled by social and national prejudices.

Orwell himself, in the equally extraordinary political autobiography which fills the second half of *The Road to Wigan Pier* (1937), mentioned that by the time he left Eton he "was against all authority," and that by the time he left Burma he had "worked out an anarchistic theory that all government is evil, that the punishment always does more harm than the crime, and that people can be trusted to behave decently if only you will let them," immediately and characteristically adding that "this of course was sentimental nonsense." Yet, from a slightly different, increasingly personal, perspective, this was his position when he first set out to be a writer:

> I had reduced everything to the simple theory that the oppressed are always right and the oppressors are always wrong: a mistaken theory,

but the natural result of being one of the oppressors yourself. I felt that I had got to escape not merely from imperialism but from every form of man's dominion over man. I wanted to submerge myself, to get right down among the oppressed, to be one of them and on their side against their tyrants.

False consciousness, perhaps, yet a form of consciousness which is better than unconsciousness and which is capable of development. Hence on a personal level his adventures as a tramp or down-and-out which are so vividly described in some of his earliest and best writings. And hence on a political level his emergence as a leading socialist intellectual.

Orwell's first recorded reference to anarchism came in an early book review, when he recalled witnessing a demonstration for Sacco and Vanzetti in Marseille in 1927 and protesting against English onlookers who assumed that they were guilty and that "you've got to hang these blasted anarchists" (*Adelphi*, May 1932). At that time, when he was beginning to make his way into left-wing journalism in London, he was apparently describing himself as a "Tory anarchist"—according to his friends Rayner Heppenstall, in *Four Absentees* (1960), and Richard Rees, in *George Orwell: Fugitive from the Camp of Victory* (1961)—although when he described his political position in public he always seems to have identified himself with some kind of socialism.

The most significant developments in Orwell's politics came in his mid-thirties. The first event was his journey to the North of England to investigate poverty for his book *The Road to Wigan Pier*, which was republished for the Left Book Club and in which he expressed his unrestrained and unequivocal commitment to socialism. The first part of the book was a semi-documentary account of conditions in the depressed areas, and the second was a semi-autobiographical account of his idiosyncratic view of left-wing politics. He expressed a very particular and peculiar kind of socialism, neither Marxist nor Fabian, neither egalitarian nor bureaucratic. He began with the assumption that the "underlying ideal of Socialism" is "justice and liberty" or "justice and common decency," and that the "mark of a real Socialist" is the wish "to see tyranny overthrown." He repeated that "Socialism means the overthrow of tyranny," and from this he could reasonably argue that "any decent person, however much of a Tory or anarchist by temperament," must "work for the establishment of Socialism." He continued to identify socialism as "common decency" in *Homage to Catalonia* and in writing to Humphry House (letter, April 11, 1940), and as "justice, liberty and common decency" (*Tribune*, June 21, 1940). He later identified it rather with "human brotherhood" (*Time and Tide*, April 6, 1940; *Tribune*, December 24, 1943; *Observer*, May 9, 1948).

This simple and even simplistic view of socialism was Orwell's basic political position for the rest of his life. The problem with it from the point of view of other socialists was that his widely read discussion in *The Road to Wigan Pier* included a vicious attack on the actually existing socialism of the 1930s, including the notorious obsessive sneers at "the middle-class Socialist," "the outer-suburban creeping Jesus," the "youthful snob-Bolshevik," the "prim little man with a white-collar job, usually a secret teetotaller and often with vegetarian leanings," the "cranks" and "mingy little beasts," "all that dreary tribe of high-minded women and sandal-wearers and bearded fruit-juice drinkers who come flocking towards the smell of 'progress' like blue-bottles to a dead cat," with the climactic claim that "the mere words 'Socialism' and 'Communism' draw towards them with magnetic force every fruit-juice drinker, nudist, sandal-wearer, sex-maniac, Quaker, 'Nature Cure' quack, pacifist and feminist in England," and the crushing conclusion:

> We have reached a stage when the very word "Socialism" calls up, on the one hand, a picture of aeroplanes, tractors and huge glittering factories of glass and concrete; on the other, a picture of vegetarians with wilting beards, of Bolshevik commissars (half gangster, half gramophone), of earnest ladies in sandals, shock-headed Marxists chewing polysyllables, escaped Quakers, birth-control fanatics and Labour Party backstairs-crawlers.

This sort of rhetoric, expressing Orwell's alienation from many kinds of socialist, encouraged the alienation of many kinds of socialist from Orwell throughout the rest of his life and long after his death.

The problem with Orwell's basic political position from the point of view of anarchists is that, while such a view is essential to anarchism, anarchism is not essential to such a view. The second significant event, however, was his journey to Spain at the end of 1936 to investigate and indeed to intervene in the Civil War. There he was involved not with half-hearted "anarchistic" theories or so-called "Tory" anarchism, not with the relative poverty of down-and-outs or the Depression, not with middle-class socialists of one kind or another, but with real live anarcho-syndicalists and other socialists fighting to establish a political and social revolution in the middle of a bitter war, between the Nationalists and Fascists in front of them and the Republicans and Communists behind them. His experience in Spain once and for all convinced him on the one hand of the truth of socialism—thus he wrote to Cyril Connolly, "I have seen wonderful things & at last really believe in Socialism, which I never did before" (letter, June 8, 1937)—and on the other hand of the fact that the two equal and opposite enemies of socialism were Fascism and Communism. At the same time, and for the first time, he also considered anarchism as a serious subject, though his view was coloured by the particular nature of Spanish—or rather, Catalan—anarchism.

When Orwell returned to Britain in July 1937, after narrowly escaping death first in the fighting in Barcelona in May 1937 and then from a serious wound at the Aragon front in June 1937, and then narrowly escaping arrest in the purge of the non-Communist left in Barcelona in June 1937, he became one of the very few people in this country who had actually been to Spain and who would publicly defend the Spanish revolutionaries, including the anarchists, a task he pursued with relish. He pointed out that there were three versions of the Spanish situation—"the Communist version, the Anarchist, and the 'Trotskyist'"—and commented that "we have learnt a little of the 'Trotskyist' version and next to nothing of the Anarchist version, while the Communist version is, so to speak the official one" (*New English Weekly*, July 21, 1938); and he had previously said that "the Anarchists and Syndicalists have been persistently misrepresented" (*Time and Tide*, December 11, 1937), and that "it is almost impossible to get anything printed in favour of Anarchism or 'Trotskyism'" (*Time and Tide*, February 5, 1938). He contributed more than anyone else to the effort to change this situation.

Orwell went to Spain (as he had gone to the North of England a few months earlier) under the auspices of the Independent Labour Party, and he therefore fought in a contingent of its Spanish allies, the revolutionary Marxist POUM (Partido Obrero de Unificatión Marxista). But he wrote in his manuscript "Notes on the Spanish Militias" that "had I had a complete understanding of the situation I should probably have joined the CNT militia" (1939?). He wrote privately to his friend Jack Common: "If I had understood the situation a bit better I should probably have joined the Anarchists" (letter, October 1937). And he wrote publicly in his book on Spain: 'As far as my purely personal preferences went I would have liked to join the Anarchists' (*Homage to Catalonia*, 1938); yet at one time he tried to join the International Brigades, although they were controlled by the Communists, because they seemed to be more determined to fight Franco. At the same time he insisted that "most of the active revolutionaries were Anarchists" (*New English Weekly*, July 29, 1937) and that "the Anarchists were the main revolutionary force" (*Time and Tide*, July 31, 1937), "notoriously the best fighters" (*Homage to Catalonia*) and "the real enemy" of the Communists (*Controversy*, August 1937). On the other hand, he had no illusions about the anarchists, frequently commenting on the defects of their beliefs and behavior, and later remarking that Spanish anarchism "shaded off into Utopianism at one end and into sheer banditry at the other" (*Observer*, November 10, 1946). He also acknowledged not only the equal determination of POUM to win the revolution but the equal determination of the Communists to win the war.

Despite his public sympathy, he never showed much knowledge of anarchist history or understanding of anarchist theory. John Sceats, a political colleague, later reported that in 1938 "he had already decided he was not a Marxist, & he was more than interested in the philosophy of anarchism," but there is no direct evidence of this. He often mocked those who thought that anarchism is the same as Communism or that anarchism is the same as anarchy, but he seldom went further. He contributed a puff to Rudolf Rocker's book on *Anarcho-Syndicalism* (1938), which was published by Secker & Warburg at the same time as *Homage to Catalonia*, commenting that it was "of great value" and that "it will do something towards filling a great gap in political consciousness"; but there is no sign that he actually read it.

Nevertheless, his personal commitment to socialism had become almost a personal commitment to anarchism. Indeed Emma Goldman, the main public representative of the Spanish anarcho-syndicalists in Britain, did her best to recruit him to the cause. She persuaded him to become one of the sponsors of the Solidaridad Internacional Antifascista (International Anti-Fascist Solidarity) committee which she organized in 1938 as a front organization, and this brought him for the first time into contact with anarchists in Britain. Among his fellow sponsors were such libertarians as Ethel Mannin, Rebecca West, John Cowper Powys, and also Herbert Read, who had recently adopted anarchism as a result of events in Spain. In this milieu he also met Vernon Richards, who had been producing *Spain and the World* since 1936, and thus came into personal contact with the formal anarchist movement in Britain.

But Orwell was still a pretty obscure writer, and for taking his revolutionary and libertarian line on Spain, and especially for emphasizing the Communist treatment of the rest of the Spanish left, he risked becoming even more obscure. He was boycotted by his publisher, Victor Gollancz, and by one of his editors, Kingsley Martin of the *New Statesman*, both of whom were part of what he rather unfairly described to Rayner Heppenstall as "the Communism-racket" (letter, July 31, 1937). His articles appeared mainly in little magazines, and *Homage to*

Catalonia which was published alongside other non-Communist left-wing books by Secker & Warburg, was one of his most unsuccessful books. The first edition of 1,500 copies still hadn't sold out when he died twelve years later—the remainders were acquired by the Freedom Press—and, despite some controversy at the time, it and other books like it were swamped in the flood of Liberal and Marxist historiography which was checked only several decades later by honest writers such Pierre Broué and Emile Témime, Burnett Bolloten and Noam Chomsky. Yet Orwell had some value for the anarchists themselves. As Emma Goldman wrote to Rudolf Rocker about *Homage to Catalonia,* "For the first time since the struggle began in 1936 someone outside our ranks has come forward to paint the Spanish anarchists as they really are" (letter, May 6, 1938, International Institute of Social History). For this alone, anarchists owe Orwell a great debt of deep gratitude.

Despite his sympathetic attitude, however, it is significant that Orwell didn't join any specifically anarchist organization. When he came back from Spain, he contacted the Peace Pledge Union in December 1937 and joined the Independent Labour Party in June 1938, clearly believing that the most urgent political priorities were peace and social-ism. Indeed for more than a year his position was as much pacifist as socialist, and he contributed to *Peace News* as well as the *Socialist Leader.* This phase coincided with his first serious attack of tuberculosis, which put him out of action for a year. The most remarkable episode came at the beginning of 1939, when he wrote to Herbert Read "about a matter which is much on my mind":

> I believe it is vitally necessary for those of us who intend to oppose the coming war to start organizing for illegal anti-war activities. It is per-fectly obvious that any open and legal agitation will be impossible not only when war has started but when it is imminent, and that if we do not make ready now for the issue of pamphlets etc. we shall be quite unable to do so when the decisive moment comes. At present there is considerable freedom of the press and no restriction on the purchase of printing presses, stocks of paper etc., but I don't believe for an in-stant that this state of affairs is going to continue. If we don't make preparations we may find ourselves silenced and absolutely helpless when either war or the pre-war fascising processes begin . . .
>
> It seems to me that the commonsense thing to do would be to ac-cumulate the things we should need for the production of pamphlets, stickybacks etc., lay them by in some unobtrusive place and not use them until it became necessary. For this we should need organisation and, in particular, money, probably 3 or 4 hundred pounds, but this

should not be impossible with the help of the people one could probably rope in by degrees [letter, January 4, 1939].

Read must have replied discouragingly, for a couple of months later
Orwell wrote on the subject again:

> I quite agree that it's in a way absurd to start preparing for an un-
> derground campaign unless you know who is going to campaign and
> what for, but the point is that if you don't make some preparations
> beforehand you will be helpless when you want to start, as you are sure
> to sooner or later. I cannot believe that the time when one can buy a
> printing press with no questions asked will last forever . . . [letter, 5
> March 1939].

Orwell explained that he expected both the Conservative-dominated
National government and any future Labour government elected in the
near future to prepare for war with Nazi Germany, that there would be
a "fascising process leading to an authoritarian regime" supported by
both right and left, and that the only opposition would come from the
real Fascists and from "dissident lefts like ourselves" who must organize
"some body of people who are both anti-war and anti-fascist":

> Actually there will be such people, probably very great numbers of
> them, but their being able to do anything will depend largely on their
> having some means of expression during the time when discontent is
> growing. I doubt whether there is much hope of saving England from
> fascism of one kind or another, but clearly one must put up a fight,
> and it seems silly to be silenced because one had failed to take a few
> precautions beforehand. If we laid in printing presses etc. in some
> discreet place we could then cautiously go to work to get together a
> distributing agency, and we could then feel "Well, if trouble comes we
> are ready." On the other hand if it doesn't come I should be so pleased
> that I would not grudge a little wasted effort [letter, March 5, 1939].

He suggested approaching independent intellectuals like Bertrand
Russell and Roland Penrose. But Read must have remained discourag-
ing, for nothing came of Orwell's plan.

He supported *Revolt!*, the anarchist paper which followed *Spain
and the World* when the Spanish Civil War ended with Franco's victory
in 1939, and which opposed the coming world war. He also produced
some anti-war material himself in the form of a 5,000-word pamphlet

called *Socialism and War*. This was written in May 1938, and according to Bob Edwards, the commander of the ILP contingent in Spain and later a trade-union leader and Labour MP, writing more than thirty years later, it was offered to but rejected by the ILP for being "too long and absolutist"! Orwell vainly tried for several months to get it accepted by other publishers. At the time of the Munich conference, in September 1938, he signed the ILP manifesto against war, and soon afterwards he wrote to Jack Common: "I wish someone would print my anti-war pamphlet I wrote earlier this year, but of course no one will" (letter, October 12, 1938). And he repeated in his essay "My Country Right or Left" that in his opposition to war he "even made speeches and wrote pamphlet against it" (*Folios of New Writing*, Autumn 1940). *Socialism and War* was never published, and the text seems to have disappeared, but some of it may have bee recycled in his essay "Not Counting Niggers," which argued against supporting the Western democracies in a war against Fascism because imperialism and capitalism weren't worth defending, and advocated "a real mass party whose first pledges are to refuse war and to right imperial injustice" (*Adelphi*, July 1939). This virtually pacifist attitude was strongly expressed at the same time in his last straight novel, *Coming Up for Air* (1939).

But all this was completely superseded by the next significant development in Orwell's politics, which—according to his own account in "My Country Right or Left"—came overnight at the time of the Nazi-Soviet pact in August 1939. He told the story of his dream that war had begun, from which he learnt "first, that I should be simply relieved when the long-dreaded war started, secondly that I was patriotic at heart, would not sabotage or act against my own side, would support the war, would fight in it if possible." As he wrote to Geoffrey Gorer, "It seems to me that now we are in this bloody war we have got to win it & I would like to lend a hand" (letter, January 10, 1940). It was just as well that Read hadn't been persuaded to support Orwell's anti-war campaign! To do him justice, he had already risked his life fighting Fascism in the Spanish Civil War, and he did what he could to fight it in the Second World War. After being rejected by the army for medical reasons, he spent three two years in the Home Guard, characteristically trying to transform it into a "People's Army." His position from now on was what Marxists during the First World War had labeled "Social Patriotism," as opposed to "revolutionary defeatism."

Meanwhile the anarchists and pacifists (and some revolutionary Marxists) conducted the anti-war campaign he had proposed, not just without his help, but indeed against his public opposition. For a time they found his new position hard to understand. Ethel Mannin told him that she was "bitched buggered and bewildered" by his change of front and asked him "for the luv of Mike" to explain himself (letter, October 10, 1939); no reply has survived. Orwell not only abandoned his own pacifism at the beginning of the war, but soon attacked the pacifism of others. During the Phoney War, he included pacifists among those who "are at this moment helping Hitler" (*Time and Tide*, March 30, 1940), and he told Rayner Heppenstall that he wrote a lecture for an Easter conference "attacking pacifism for all I was worth" (letter, April 11, 1940). When the real war began, he repeatedly accused pacifists of being "objectively pro-Nazi" or "pro-Fascist"—a practice which had infuriated him when it was used by Stalinists against anarchists and Trotskyists in Spain—and even alluded to "the overlap between Fascism and pacifism" (*Partisan Review*, March–April 1942) and alleged that "our English pacifists are tending towards active pro-Fascism" (*Partisan Review*, September–October 1942).

To some extent he abandoned socialism, too, at least for a time. He left the Independent Labour Party, and began describing left-wing politics as "almost entirely a form of masturbation" (diary, June 27, 1940) and as "a sort of masturbation fantasy in which the world of facts hardly matters" (*Partisan Review*, Winter 1944–5). Yet in March 1940 he still supported Richard Acland's *Manifesto of the Common Man,* which led to the formation of the socialist Common Wealth party, and he contributed to its paper *CW Review.* In April 1940 he insisted in autobiographical notes for an American reference book that "in sentiment I am definitely 'left,'" though he added that the observation and experience of left-wing politics "have given me a horror of politics."

But things changed again as the war worsened. Writing for Left Book Club members, he looked forward to "the real English socialist movement," which "will be both revolutionary and democratic" (*Left News*, February 1941). His book, *The Lion and the Unicorn* ([February] 1941), which was subtitled "Socialism and the English Genius," looked forward to a democratic form of socialism brought about by a democratic form of revolution—"a specifically *English* Socialist movement" leading to "an English Socialist government"—with a program similar to those of the prewar Independent Labour Party or of the postwar Labour left. (It may be significant that he later included this book among those he didn't want reprinted.) In October 1941 he was even invited by the Hampstead Garden Suburb ward of the Hendon Labour Party to become its prospective parliamentary candidate! And at the end of the war he wrote to the Duchess of Atholl, "I belong to the Left and must work inside it" (letter, November 15, 1945).

Like most socialists, he welcomed the victory of the Labour Party in the general election of 1945; but, like many socialists, he suffered from disillusion with the Labour government, even with Aneurin Bevan, his closest friend among its leaders; and, like many socialists again, he suffered not so much disillusion as despair with the Communist regime in the Soviet Union and its satellites. Following the publication of his great satires of false socialism, *Animal Farm* and *Nineteen Eighty-Four*, it was often said that he had actually ceased to be a socialist; but he repeatedly denied this, and he had several public statements to this effect issued in 1949. He remained a critical supporter of the Labour Party to the end of his life. And his most perfect book, *Animal Farm*, is above all a fable defending the basic principles of simple socialism. At about the same time he established his final view of these principles. At the beginning of 1946 he contributed to the *Manchester Evening News* a series of four articles on "The Intellectual Revolt," based on the premise that "old-style, laissez-faire capitalism is finished" and that "the drift everywhere is towards planned economies and away from an individualistic society in which property rights are absolute and money-making is the chief incentive," but that "simultaneously with this development there has happened an intellectual revolt" in which "a large proportion of the best minds of our time are dismayed by the turn of events and doubtful whether more economic security is a worthwhile objective."

The second article asked, "What is Socialism?" (January 31, 1946), attempting to answer on the basis of recent books on the subject by eight authors, including Arthur Koestler, André Malraux, Ignazio Silone, and Gerrard Winstanley. He began by saying that,

> until the twentieth century, and indeed until the 1930s, all Socialist thought was in some sense Utopian. Socialism had nowhere been tested in the physical world, and in the mind of almost everyone, including its enemies, it was bound up with the idea of liberty and equality.

But, he continued, "after 1930 an ideological split began to appear in the Socialist movement," because of the emergence of a form of actually existing socialism in Communist Russia and also a form of so-called "National Socialism" in Nazi Germany, both involving the worst tyrannies the world had ever known: "Evidently it was time for the word 'Socialism' to be redefined." He then made an attempt to do just this:

> What is Socialism? Can you have Socialism without liberty, without equality, and without internationalism? Are we still aiming at

universal human brotherhood, or must we be satisfied with a new kind of caste society in which we surrender our individual rights in return for economic security? . . .

A Socialist is not obliged to believe that human society can actually be made perfect, but almost any Socialist does believe that it could be a great deal better than it is at present, and that most of the evil that men do results from the warping effect of injustice and inequality. The basis of Socialism is humanism. It can co-exist with religious belief, but not with the belief that man is a limited creature who will always misbehave himself if he gets half a chance . . .

The "earthly paradise" has never been realized, but as an idea it never seems to perish, in spite of the ease with which it can be debunked by practical politicians of all colours.

Underneath it lies the belief that human nature is fairly decent to start with and capable of indefinite development. This belief has been the main driving force of the Socialist movement, including the underground sects which prepared the way for the Russian revolution, and it could be claimed that the Utopians, at present a scattered minority, are the true upholders of the Socialist tradition.

He added further thoughts in the third article, "Pacifism and Progress" (February 14, 1946). He assumed that "Socialists, Communists and Anarchists, all in their different ways, are all aiming at" what he called "the good society," one "in which human beings are equal and in which they cooperate with one another willingly and not because of fear or economic compulsion." He saw pacifist writers as extreme examples of this group, including among them Alex Comfort, Aldous Huxley, and Herbert Read, and he treated them more fairly than he had done during the war.

As for anarchism itself, however, after 1939 Orwell never again defended it and often attacked it. His attacks on pacifism during the war implicitly covered anarchism as well, and the tendency became explicit in the occasional "London Letter" which he contributed to *Partisan Review*, the semi-Trotskyist American magazine. The worst example appeared in an issue published at about the worst time of the war. As well as including both anarchists and pacifists in what he called "left-wing defeatism," he gave an account of the semi-anarchist British magazine *Now* which suggested that it was a pacifist-anarchist front, smeared several contributors for Fascist links or tendencies, and even stated that "Julian Symons writes in a vaguely Fascist strain" (March–April 1942). Vehement replies followed from George Woodcock, editor of *Now* (who mentioned Orwell's previous defense of the Spanish anarchists),

Alex Comfort, and D. S. Savage (September–October 1942). Orwell characteristically became friends with them and also with Symons; but he had another angry encounter with Comfort in *Tribune* (June 4 and 18, 1943), the two exchanging satirical Byronic stanzas, in the course of which Orwell accused Comfort of wanting to "kiss the Nazi's bum" and even attacked at him for using a pseudonym!

He continued to criticize anarchism more generally, too. In a review of a book by Lionel Fielden advocating Indian independence, he included a sneer at what he called "Parlour Anarchism—a plea for the simple life, based on dividends" (*Horizon*, September 1943); half a century later, it would have been based on benefits. He also added a sneer about both anarchism and pacifism that "these creeds have the advantage that they aim at the impossible and therefore demand very little." In his booklet on *The English People* (written in 1944 but not published until 1947), he mentioned that "English people in large numbers will not accept any creed whose dominant notes are hatred and illegality"—among which he included anarchism alongside Communism, Fascism and Catholicism. In a review of Herbert Read's collection of essays, *A Coat of Many Colours*, he argued that Read's version of anarchism "avoids the enormous question: how are freedom and organization to be reconciled," that "Anarchism implies a low standard of living," and that "unless there is some unpredictable change in human nature, liberty and efficiency must pull in opposite directions" (*Poetry Quarterly*, Winter 1945).

After the war he produced two major essays, which included serious criticisms of anarchism. In "Politics versus Literature: An Examination of *Gulliver's Travels*" (*Polemic*, September–October 1946), he said that Jonathan Swift was "a kind of anarchist"—a "Tory anarchist", in fact, as Orwell had once described himself—"despising authority while disbelieving in liberty"; and he added that the fourth part of *Travels into Several Remote Nations of the World*—"A Voyage to the Country of the Houyhnhnms," in which the savage Yahoos (men) are contrasted with the civilized Houyhnhnms (horses)—"is a picture of an anarchist society, not governed by law in the ordinary sense, but by the dictates of 'Reason,' which are voluntarily adopted by everyone." He commented that "this illustrates very well the totalitarian tendency which is explicit in the anarchist or pacifist vision of society" (explicit?—did he mean *implicit?*); and he continued:

> In a society in which there is no law, and in theory no compulsion, the only arbiter of behaviour is public opinion. But public opinion, because of the tremendous urge to conformity in gregarious animals, is

less tolerant than any system of law. When human beings are governed by "Thou shalt not," the individual can practise a certain amount of eccentricity; when they are supposedly governed by "love" or "reason," he is under continuous pressure to make him behave and think in exactly the same way as everyone else.

George Woodcock wrote a strong reply, which was accepted by but not published in *Polemic* and which eventually appeared in *Freedom* (June 28, 1947). He argued that Orwell had only a "superficial acquaintance with anarchist writings," gave "a wholly erroneous view of the anarchist idea of society," wrongly identified anarchism and pacifism, and failed to realize that anarchists opposed the tyranny of society as much as of the state.

Again, in "Lear, Tolstoy and the Fool" (*Polemic*, March 1947), which concerns not so much Tolstoy's view of Shakespeare as Orwell's view of Tolstoy, he took the same line about Tolstoy's religious combination of anarchism and pacifism:

> Tolstoy renounced wealth, fame and privilege; he abjured violence in all its forms and was ready to suffer for doing so; but it is not easy to believe that he abjured the principle of coercion, or at least the desire to coerce others . . . The distinction that really matters is not between violence and non-violence, but between having and not having the appetite for power.

Orwell insisted that "there are people who are convinced of the wickedness both of armies and of police forces, but who are nevertheless much more intolerant and inquisitorial in outlook than the normal person who believes that it is necessary to use violence in certain circumstances"; and he added that "creeds like pacifism and anarchism, which seem on the surface to imply a complete renunciation of power rather encourage this habit of mind."

It is hard to know whether Orwell really believed this sort of thing, which is reminiscent of similar remarks by D. H. Lawrence a generation earlier. He forgot how he himself made a living and almost a profession out of defying public opinion over and over again, from his schooldays until his death, without any fear of persecution in Britain (despite his complaints about censorship by editors and bureaucrats), and he ignored the crucial distinction between holding authoritarian views in theory and having the actual power to put them into practice. After all, the most intolerant and totalitarian ideology or temperament has no effect until someone is able not only to give orders but to get them obeyed, and here even the most objectionable anarchists or pacifists hardly rival the adherents of other ideologies. In his own greatest political books, *Animal Farm* and *Nineteen Eighty-Four,* the worst thing about the tyranny he described is not its moral conformity but its political power, enforced respectively by the ruling pigs or the ruling party, and of course the same was true of Nazi Germany and Communist Russia, and indeed of British India or Republican Spain. It is really very difficult to take Orwell seriously as a critic of anarchism.

Later he refrained from such harsh judgments, but his attitude remained hostile or—even worse—silent. Thus when he reviewed George Woodcock book *The Writer and Politics* he agreed that "anarchism is not the same thing a woolly-minded Utopianism," added polite remarks about some anarchist writers, especially Kropotkin, but concluded dismissively that "anarchism is simply another -ism" (*Observer,* August 22, 1948). Even worse, when describing "Britain's Left-wing Press" for American readers, he completely ignored the anarchist papers (*Progressive,* June 1948).

The curious if characteristic thing about Orwell is that, even when he was attacking anarchism in theory, he was one of the best friends of anarchists in practice. At the very time he was attacking them for following "a line which by implication is by imputation 'revolutionary defeatist'" (*Partisan Review,* March–April 1942), in the very worst days of the Second World War, when it seemed quite possible that Britain would follow most of the rest of Europe and actually be conquered by Fascist invaders, he was going out of his way to help them. While he was working at the BBC, he did is best to encourage a wide variety of opinions, including anarchists as well as pacifists. One amusing example is that he wrote to Reg Reynolds, a socialist pacifist, to confirm a commission for a short talk on Peter Kropotkin, but wrote again a week later to cancel it (letters, November 5 and 12, 1943); he explained, "I have been told that we ought not to give publicity on the air to a notorious anarchist!" Another is that he used to have his hair cut in London by the veteran anarchist Matt Kavanagh. Bernard Crick comments that "he did not accept anarchism in principle, but had, as a socialist who distrusted any kind of state power, a speculative and personal sympathy with anarchists"—like Crick himself, one may add.

Anarchists were even among his closest friends. Throughout the war he kept in touch with Vernon Richards and Marie Louise Berneri, who were leading members of the group producing *War Commentary,* later *Freedom,* the successor of *Spain and the World* and *Revolt!,* and who often reprinted extracts from his writing. And just after the war, when Orwell was looking after his adopted son following the death of his wife, they took the famous series of photographs of him at home. When Marie Louise Berneri unexpectedly died, he contributed to the memorial issue of *Freedom*: "She was always so much alive that it is difficult to believe it can have happened" (May 28, 1949).

Indeed there is even a story that this group, the Freedom Press, could actually have published *Animal Farm* in 1944. Crick repeats the version told by Woodcock, that when the book had been rejected by several straight publishers—including Victor Gollancz, Jonathan Cape, T. S. Eliot (for Faber & Faber)—he offered it through Woodcock to the Freedom Press, but that it was rejected because the group included "many belligerent pacifists." Crick mentioned that Richards "is adamant that it was never submitted," but commented first that "he was in prison at the relevant time and might not have been told" (1980) or later that "the Anarchists were being prosecuted at that time and their affairs were in confusion" (1982). Since this was meant to have happened in July 1944, before the book was accepted by Fredric Warburg (for Secker & Warburg, who had published *Homage to Catalonia*), and since Richards was not arrested and the anarchists were not being prosecuted until December 1944, and the three editors were not imprisoned until April 1945, it seems more likely that Richards is right. Woodcock refers only to the hostile reaction of Marie Louise Berneri, who died in 1949; surviving members of the Freedom Press at that time always agreed that the book was certainly not offered to them and that if it had been it would certainly not have been rejected. There is also a story that the book was nearly published by Paul Potts, the libertarian poet who had a private publishing house, and it does at least seem that Orwell seriously considered having it produced as his own expense; but in the event it was published by Secker & Warburg in 1945, and of course it made him famous.

There is another similar story, which also seems to originate with Woodcock. Crick takes it from what Orwell told Dwight Macdonald, the American radical journalist: "When Queen Elizabeth [wife of King George VI], whose literary adviser was Osbert Sitwell, sent the Royal Messenger to Secker & Warburg for a copy in November, he found them utterly sold out and had to go with horse, carriage, top hat and all, to the anarchist Freedom Bookshop, in Red Lion Square, where George Woodcock gave him a copy" (letter, January 6, 1946). Again, surviving members of the Freedom Press at that time remembered rather that it was a publisher's messenger who came to collect a copy of the book, and Woodcock himself later toned his version down. But it's a good story, even if it's only a story—though the Freedom Bookshop was in Red Lion Street, not Square.

What certainly isn't just a story is Orwell's later support for the anarchists. When the Freedom Press was raided at the end of 1944 and four editors of *War Commentary* were prosecuted at the beginning of 1945 for attempting 'to undermine the affections of members of His Majesty's Forces', he not only protested, but became vice-chairman of the Defense Committee, which was established because the National Council for Civil Liberties was then a Communist front. The committee chairman was Herbert Read and the secretary was George Woodcock. The latter recorded that Orwell, then becoming increasingly ill, contributed time and money as well as his name. Over a period of four years he signed letters, wrote articles and made speeches for it, and also lent it his wife's typewriter. He later became involved in a more ambitious attempt to establish a "League for the Dignity and Rights of Man" with Arthur Koestler and Bertrand Russell, which came to nothing (though some of its ideas were later taken up by the Congress for Cultural Freedom and Amnesty International).

The point of course is that Orwell genuinely believed in the freedom of the press and of speech and assembly not only for people he agreed with but for people he disagreed with. This extended not only to anarchist and pacifists but also to Fascists and Communists. But he never wrote for Fascist or Communist papers, whereas during and after the war he did occasionally write for anarchist papers—an essay on "Looking Back on the Spanish War" in Alex Comfort's magazine *New Road* ([June] 1943), a review of W. McCartney's pamphlet *The French Cooks' Syndicate* in *Freedom* (September 8, 1945), and the essay "How the Poor Die" in George Woodcock's magazine *Now* (November 1946). It is not surprising that when the Freedom Defence Committee was dissolved in 1949, Orwell let the Freedom Press keep the old typewriter (which was sometimes rumored to be the one on which *Freedom* was later typeset!).

One last event linked Orwell and the anarchists. When he was very ill with tuberculosis during 1949, the year between the publication of *Nineteen Eighty-Four* and his death, he had his adopted son brought to stay near his sanatorium in the Cotswolds. Crick records that the boy was kept "in the care of Lilian Wolfe, a 73-year-old veteran of the British anarchist movement who lived at the nearby anarchist and craft colony, Whiteway" (corrected version, 1982). Orwell described it vaguely to Richard Rees as "some sort of Anarchist colony run, or financed, by the old lady whose name I forget who keeps the Freedom Bookshop" (letter, April 17, 1949). How nice to know that at the very end of his life Orwell was helped by a high-minded woman who was not only an anarchist but a pacifist, and also a vegetarian and a teetotaller—a perfect irony to close the case of Orwell and the anarchists!

What really matters, however, is not what Orwell said about this or that kind of anarchism, or did about these or those anarchists, but what he meant when he took as his fundamental political position the form of socialism based on the overthrow of tyranny and the establishment of justice and liberty, the recognition of common decency and the pursuit of human brotherhood, and what he said in his very widely read journalistic and fictional and satirical writings about the implications of such a position. At most, George Orwell may be said to have been an anarchist fellow-traveler; but he was one of the best there ever was.

3.

Far too much has been said by far too many people about George Orwell, and most of what has been said here is quite unnecessary for the appreciation of his work, but it is worth adding a few more words to the record.

His writings seem very straightforward, but he was a very complicated man. It is possible to detect two main driving forces in his career—a sense of compassion and guilt, and a determination to be tested and not to be found wanting. He was always putting himself to the test, forcing himself to endure hardship and discomfort, swallowing disgust and pain, going without proper food during the war and proper medical care after it, wearing down his health and his talent, fighting the evils of the world and the weakness of his body to the day of his death, always striving, striving to tell the truth about what he saw and what he felt.

He had his faults. He often spoke out without verifying his facts and often he was grossly unfair. Hardly any literary or political group escaped his bitter criticism. But he should be seen not just as an angry middle-aged man but as an extreme example of the English middle-class dissenter who, having rebelled against his own group, must always rebel against any group, even a group of conscious rebels. So he was a puritan who despised other puritans, a patriot who despised other patriots, a socialist who despised other socialists, an intellectual who despised other intellectuals, a bohemian who despised other bohemians. He was a man full of logical contradictions and emotional ambivalences, but the point is that this made him better, not worse. He was always able not only to see but to *feel* both sides to every argument, to realize the imperfections of every position, including his own, and his honesty about the difficulties this raised was one of his most valuable characteristics. He was a heretic obliged to betray his own heresy, a protestant protesting against his own faith, a political quaker reduced to trusting only his inner light.

Above all, it is reasonable to conclude that his personal and political qualities were based on an individual form of secular humanism. Vernon Richards said in his obituary that "Orwell was, first and foremost, a humanist" (*Freedom*, February 4, 1950). Evelyn Waugh said in his review of *Critical Essays* that Orwell expressed "the new humanism of the common man" (*Tablet*, April 6, 1946). Orwell himself said that "the basis of Socialism is humanism" (*Manchester Evening News*, January 31, 1946), and frequently emphasized the contrast between the humanist and religious views of the world. He added in his review of George Woodcock's edition of Oscar Wilde's essay *The Soul of Man under Socialism* that "such publications remind the Socialist movement of its original, half-forgotten objective of human brotherhood" (*Observer*, May 9, 1948). And in "Reflections on Gandhi," he referred with approval to "the belief that Man is the measure of all things, and that our job is to make life worth living on this earth, which is the only earth we have" (*Partisan Review*, January 1949).

His most utterly hopeless book, *Nineteen Eighty-Four*, does contain two hopeful passages. First, on the proles: "They were not loyal to a party or a country or an idea, they were loyal to one another . . . The proles had stayed human. They had not become hardened inside."

(This is why "the only hope is the proles.") Then, on Winston Smith's dead mother: "She had possessed a kind of nobility, a kind of purity, simply because the standards that she obeyed were private ones. Her feelings were her own, and could not be altered from outside."

Orwell is describing his ideal type—"the last man in Europe," to use the phrase which was the original title of the book—but he is also describing himself. He may perhaps be seen as the "Man-of-Letters Hero," described by Thomas Carlyle in his book *On Heroes, Hero-Worship and the Heroic in History* (1841):

> This same Man-of-Letters Hero must be regarded as our most important modern person. He, such as he may be, is the soul of all . . . Whence he came, whither he is bound, by what ways he arrived, by what he might be furthered on his course, no one asks. He is an accident in society. He walks like a wild Ishmaelite, in a world of which he is as the spiritual light, either the guidance or the misguidance!

Orwell would have rejected such pretentious stuff with scorn, if only because of the fancy style, but there is something of him in it. We can dig up all the available facts about him and go through all the accessible writings by him, but he remains a mystery, an accident in society; yet he was certainly one of our most important modern persons, one of the few real heroes, true souls, whom our age has seen. Unhappy the country that needs such a person, perhaps, but happy the country that gets it. In one of his last statements, made to his childhood friend Jacintha Buddicom, in the shadow cast by worsening illness and approaching death and in the gloom raised by the Cold War and the publication of *Nineteen Eighty-Four*, he still insisted "Nothing ever dies" (letter, June 8, 1949). Of course, everything does die, but sometimes something lives. Eric Blair's body lies a-mouldering in the grave—in All Saints churchyard at Sutton Courtenay, as it happens—but George Orwell's soul is still marching on.

Originally published in Vernon Richards, ed. George Orwell at Home (and among the Anarchists): Essays and Photographs *(Freedom Press, 1998).*

19
BECAUSE HE IS A MAN:
ALAN SILLITOE

Who are the Rats? Well, they're the people who do nothing about anything, who accept the atom bomb and want the cat back, the civil servants with closed minds and politicians who believe in armaments, all the forms of authority and persuasion which want people to conform into a mass, and all the people who worship the State and submit to over-government. This is nothing to do with politics, because the conformist is found under all banners, under Communism and Capitalism . . . (Alan Sillitoe)

I BEGAN READING ALAN SILLITOE'S NEW NOVEL, *KEY TO THE DOOR,* A FEW hours after hearing he had joined us in the big sit-down, while I was lying on a police-cell floor during the long night of September 17. I can think of no more suitable time and place, for Sillitoe has a voice of pure human dissent, like Sean O'Casey or John Osborne; there are no concessions attached to his total commitment. He offers no comforting message like Forster or Wesker, no prophetic cure like Shaw or Lawrence, no escape into art like Wilde or Behan, no indulgent affection like Orwell or MacInnes. He is just *for* the ordinary people and against their bosses and rulers, without question or quarter.

As everyone knows, Sillitoe made his name with his first novel, *Saturday Night and Sunday Morning* (1958), a debut quite as remarkable as *Lucky Jim* or *Room at the Top*; the original edition has sold over 10,000 copies, the paperback edition has sold nearly a million, and the excellent film must have reached several million more people who had never heard of the book. Who read this book? "Ordinary working-class people," its author replies. It was followed by a collection of short stories, *The Loneliness of the Long-Distance Runner* (1959), some of which—especially the outstanding title story—are even better than the novel. Then came a political fantasy, *The General* (1960), and a book of verse,

The Rats (1960), neither of which I liked very much, despite their admirable sentiments. I remember even having the impertinence to tell the author to go back and write what he knew; this he has now done, and here we have a long novel by present standards, which makes me feel I was right, for it is an important and impressive achievement. Sillitoe has proved that his talent was not just a flash in the pan, like that of so many of the other new writers since the war; his last book stands firmly on the same high level as the first two.

Key to the Door has the function in its author's work that *Of Human Bondage*, *Eyeless in Gaza* and *Dr Zhivago* had in theirs—to make a major statement about the meaning of his life and his ideas in the framework of a large semi-autobiographical novel. Because of Sillitoe's background and his reaction to it, this statement takes the form of a powerful protest against his society—the sort of protest made in *Death of a Hero*, *The Grapes of Wrath* and *From Here to Eternity*. I use these names deliberately; this is a big book. As a much-publicized Book Society choice, it will be enjoyed by many thousands of readers—but I wonder how many of them will understand what it is trying to say. Alan Sillitoe didn't come and sit down in Trafalgar Square for the sake of his health or his reputation, and the reasons he came are clear enough in *Key to the Door*. If the Establishment had any sense it would be worried about this book and its author. If we have any sense we will read the one and listen to the other. Here is the story of the first twenty-one years in the life of Brian Seaton, who was born when Lady Chatterley found her lover, in the same part of England—industrial Nottinghamshire and Derbyshire—and shares with his author the same working-class origins that Oliver Mellors and Paul Morel shared with theirs (indeed, though there is no sign of imitation, the first part of *Key to the Door* reminded me strongly of *Sons and Lovers*). Readers of *Saturday Night and Sunday Morning* will remember its tough hero Arthur Seaton, his brother Fred and sister Margaret, his aunt Ada and cousin Bert; well they are all here, though Brian—the eldest Seaton brother—didn't appear in the earlier book. Arthur's story is set in the '50s, the age of full employment and television; Brian's is set in the '30s and '40s the age of unemployment and war. Here is the background not only of Brian Seaton and his brother, but of Alan Sillitoe and the best of his work, described in satisfying and convincing detail.

As in the earlier book, there is no conventional plot, no real sense of the passage of time, no contrived development or revelation—just a series of vivid episodes piling on top of each other, the last one fitting naturally into its place. The characters don't change much; they grow up, and struggle or give in, and fade away—birth and copulation and death, sometimes with good luck, usually with bad. But in the end Arthur came to some sort of terms with the world he defied; and in the same way Brian, a gentler person, finds the key to his door, though it is cut by everything that has happened to him from the material he was born with. There is no slick dénouement to round off the book; the story is real and its conclusion is real, for there is nothing phony about Sillitoe. There is richness here, more than he has shown before. The child growing up with his brothers and sisters in the shadow of a hot-tempered, foul-mouthed father (very like Walter Morel) and a rather helpless nagging mother (*not* like Gertrude Morel), with interesting aunts and grandparents, all in the deeper shadow of the Depression; his struggle to find knowledge in dictionaries and maps, excitement in *The Count of Monte Cristo* and *Les Misérables,* identity and meaning in the harsh world of the industrial Midlands in the terrible thirties—all this is done with deep feeling and skill.

But *Key to the Door* is no portrait of the artist as an angry young man, or even as a hungry young man. It is far more than autobiographical self-pity. Brian Seaton grows up in a grim age, but he is no more a grim person than his creator. When the hungry years are over he puts them behind him, though—like his creator—he never forgets his early loathing of the people who kept the rotten system going and prolonged the hopeless helpless hunger of his childhood. "I don't know why they have coppers," says young Brian, "they're worse than schoolteachers." "No difference," says his cousin, "it's all part of the gov'ment." Nonsense on the surface, but good sense underneath. Sillitoe does not preach resignation, as Arnold Bennett did, nor does he, godlike, rescue his hero from his predicament, as H. G. Wells did and as John Braine has done.

There is no consolation in religion. "There ain't no bastard God!" his father shouts; and little Brian reflects that "his teacher said that God loved everybody: Italians gassing blackies and mowing 'em down with machine-guns: dole, thunderstorms, school." Nor is there consolation in the nihilism expressed by Arthur Seaton in the earlier book. The only true consolation is in hatred of the top-dogs and solidarity with all other underdogs. When Brian looked at a picture of Shylock in a school edition of Shakespeare, "he knew whose side he was on and who would be on his side if he could suddenly come to life and step out of the printed book"; he admired the caricatured Jew for defying his persecutors.

When Brian buys a copy of *The Count of Monte Cristo,* his father is furious. "Yer've wasted 'alf a crown on a book?" he exclaims—furious not because he is illiterate (although he is) but because he is unemployed and can't afford food, let alone books. But the investment pays off; in his book Brian "heard the patient scraping and scratching of freedom, was shown that even dungeons and giant prisons were unable to keep men in forever." Even bitter poverty is unable to quench his thirst for knowledge and truth. Later he buys *Les Misérables* too, and reads about "the battle between a common man and the police who would not let him be free because he had once stolen a loaf of bread for the children of his starving sister." His own father goes to prison when he steals to feed his family. The problem of literary commitment is no problem for Brian Seaton; Dumas and Hugo are on his side and describe his predicament in imaginative terms—that is enough.

Perhaps it is difficult now to imagine a child who has to say: "My dad's allus on dole . . . Nearly all the kids at school 'ave got dads on dole." But *Love on the Dole* was published in 1933; the last great Hunger March took place just 25 years ago; Wal Hannington's National Unemployed Workers' Movement was pursuing its brilliant campaign well into 1939, when there were still over two million unemployed. We should remember the context of the first part of *Key to the Door*. It would be strange if Brian Seaton (and Alan Sillitoe) were *not* on the far left in politics.

Even after the betrayal of 1931, hatred of top-dogs and solidarity with underdogs meant support of the Labour Party for most people: "Labour was the best thing—and if Brian ever felt distrust for that sympathetic organization it was only because all big names seemed like devil's threats to hold his soul in thrall." How right he was; and in fact he grows up to become a common sort of wartime fellow-traveler who scrawls "LONG LIVE RUSSIA AND STALIN" up by his 137 books and hopes that the 1945 election means the coming of his ideas of socialism—"he knew that all men were brothers and that the wealth of the world should be pooled and divided fairly among those who worked."

Back in the '30s war is welcomed because it means the end of want—what is rationing to starvelings in their hunger or conscription to men without work? But there are no illusions about it. When he asks his grandmother who won the First World War, her answer is simply "Nobody." And when Munich comes, the sadistic schoolmaster reminds the boys that "war is nothing but pain." Nor is there any illusion about Munich. "They'll be no peace in our time," says Brian's mother. "No," agrees his father, "nor in any other bloody time either." Nor later is there any illusion about Churchill—"Owd Fatguts," they call him. He didn't give a bogger about us. It was all his bleeding factory owners he saved . . . It was him and his gang as turned hosepipes on the hunger-marchers before the war.

Cynicism without illusions is necessary for survival. "It's no worse in a war than it is now," Brian is told: "You get boggered from pillar to post and get nowt to eat, just the same." For most people in the world this is the simple truth.

Brian is too young to fight in the war, but he is called up soon after it and volunteers for service overseas, although he has just married the girl he gets into trouble (who is rather like Doreen in *Saturday Night and Sunday Morning*), because he wants to see something of the world before he settles down. The second part of the book alternates between his youth in wartime Nottingham and his experience in Malaya. He discovers the truth of "Orwell's Law" (that the oppressed proletariat of Britain has its own oppressed proletariat in the colored parts of the British Empire—a version of the law that there's always someone worse off than you), he has an affair with a Chinese girl (who is uncomfortably like Suzie Wong), and he meets an example of the familiar species of the anarchic NCO (who reads *The Ragged Trousered Philanthropists* and is very like Jack Malloy in *From Here to Eternity*). Meanwhile we learn about his first jobs at home, and his courtship of Pauline.

Corporal Knotman, the anarchist, is important, since he helps to give shape to Brian's spontaneous political ideas. He is a regular who fought through the war and is almost due for release: "I've learnt to know what freedom means in these last eight years . . . and the bloke who doesn't learn that, sooner or later, isn't fit to be on the face of the earth, because they're the types that end up as the enemies and persecutors of those who know what freedom means." Like all real soldiers he has no hatred for his official enemies: "It's them who shout 'Charge' and 'Up and at 'em lads' who are your biggest enemies." He has evolved his own form of individualism, and he sees a kindred spirit in Brian: "You're not a communist . . . You might be a socialist when you've read more and know a bit about it . . . If you're anything you're a socialist-anarchist." One is reminded of the "anarchist socialism" described in the editorial of the first number of *Freedom*; Brian Seaton, like Alan Sillitoe, is an old-fashioned—a pre-1917—socialist, as interested in liberty and fraternity as in equality.

Knotman adds mysteriously: "History is on our side, so just bide your time: you won't even know when to act; the first thing you'll know you'll be acting—and in the right way." This recalls the end of *The Rats*, and we are led to anticipate a semi-existentialist act of defiance like that in *The Loneliness of the Long-Distance Runner*. But what happens is more than an act of defiance: Brian is more mature than the Borstal boy, and manages to combine defiance of the top-dogs with an expression of solidarity with the underdogs.

The war against the Communist guerrillas begins just before he leaves Malaya, and he is involved in a skirmish with them. Sure enough, he finds himself acting—by deliberately shooting at trees instead of Communists, and even releasing a Communist he has captured by mistake. The only casualty in his unit is a typical middle-class dissenter, who speaks big but shoots straight enough when it comes to the point, and his death might have been Brian's fault. But he knows he was right. He imagines himself telling his father about it. "I caught a Communist and let him go," he says: I let him go because he was a comrade! I didn't kill him because he was a man. This is the key to the book. Brian's moment of decision comes when he is face to face with a fellow-countryman of his mistress, a fellow-opponent of the top-dogs, a fellow human being. His "duty" is to kill him or take him prisoner; but he knows that his real duty is to let him go. Similarly his real duty is to marry Pauline when she becomes pregnant and to go back to her when he gets out of the army, despite his feelings for Mimi, to stay with his own people—his family, his mates, his class—and to be a "socialist-anarchist."

The book closes with Brian on the way home to the England that is struggling out of austerity into affluence, to the busy Nottingham in which the Cherry Orchard (significant name!) where he used to play as a child and where he later used to make love with Pauline, has been built over. He is 21 and he has become a man. "He somehow felt he had the key to the door . . . And with the key to the door all you need to do now," he decides, "was flex your muscles to open it . . . At least my eyes have been opened. All I've got to do now is to see with them, and when one person sees, maybe the next one will as well."

As with Arthur in the earlier book, the time has come to settle down and hand life and liberty on to the next generation: "I'll spend a night or two helping the union, you can bet, because somebody's got to do it, and I feel I'm just the bloke for a thing like that. I'll get to know what's what as well, pull a few more books into the house to see what makes the world tick, maybe read some of those I nicked years ago."

But he hasn't been tamed by any means. It is worth remembering what Sillitoe said about his work on the film of *Saturday Night and Sunday Morning*:

> I didn't want Arthur Sexton . . . getting transmogrified into a young workman who turns out to be an honest-to-goodness British individualist—that is, one who triumphs in the end against and at the expense of a communist agitator or the trade unions. I didn't want him to become a tough stereotype with, after all, a heart of moral gold which has in it a love of the monarchy and all that old-fashioned muck.

In the same way, Alan Sillitoe himself hasn't been tamed. He has refused to be turned aside by the people who would like him to be either responsible or sensational (i.e. conformist or melodramatic). In a way this harms *Key to the Door*. He is so anxious to make himself clear, that he has made his book far too long, and parts of it tend to drag badly without the pressure that drove *Saturday Night and Sunday Morning* along—constructive anarchism is far more difficult to get across than destructive nihilism. Other defects are that Brian is a slightly colorless character and that the sex in his story seems to come to him rather too easily: surely there would have been some obstacles of the kind that Paul Morel encountered fifty years ago? Perhaps a more serious defect is that the symbolism that recurs in the book tends to get lost—the storms, the animals' deaths, the mountain-climb and so on all have important functions in the story, but what these functions are is not always clear.

Nevertheless, the statement made in *Key to the Door* is clear enough, and the book is certainly a vital part of Sillitoe's work. It would be absurd merely to label him as an "anarchist writer" but it would be equally absurd for anarchists to ignore what he has to say—and not only in his novels, stories and poems. Like John Osborne or like Sean O'Casey, he sometimes seems naive and confused, but like them he is in touch with things that matter. Consider his comment on the big sit-down:

> The anti-bomb campaign is, obviously, a political movement. It is also disenfranchised and, as such, is revolutionary, more dangerous than if it had a couple of hundred MPs in Parliament—which would make it useless. The longer it remains unrepresented the more certain will be its complete victory. Everyone who sat down in Trafalgar Square did so for political reasons, and in so doing they threaten (or would do if there were enough of them) the basis on which the present political life of this country stands.

Sillitoe is a revolutionary writer and a writing revolutionary. Brian Seaton is a worthy successor to Frank Owen, and Alan Sillitoe is a worthy successor to Robert Noonan, the unhappy pseudonymous author of *The Ragged Trousered Philanthropists*. Seaton is luckier than Owen, because his comrades have won a better share of life, liberty and the pursuit of happiness; Sillitoe is luckier than Noonan, because of *his* comrades, the people who read his books, and certainly we should be among them, because he too is a comrade, because he is a man.

Originally published in Anarchy *10 (December 1961).*

20

THE SHORT STORIES OF ALAN SILLITOE

ALAN SILLITOE HAS CHANGED LESS THAN ANY OF THE OTHER WRITERS who became well-known during the 1950s. He hasn't sold out or become a snob or retreated into private obsessions or taken refuge in religious or philosophical nonsense. His novels do show an advance from describing young people who aren't intellectuals to describing older people who are intellectuals, but this simply represents the passage of time and the alteration in his circumstances over ten years. Experience and success have scarcely affected him, except perhaps that he is more sure of himself and less concerned about other people's views of his work.

His stories are particularly consistent. First *The Loneliness of the Long-Distance Runner* (1959), then *The Ragman's Daughter* (1963), and now *Guzman, Go Home*—the stories in all three of his collections deal with the same kind of people in the same kind of places in the same kind of way. There is nothing like a Sillitoe story except another Sillitoe story.

This is meant as praise, not blame. After all, Sillitoe is a serious writer, worth reading properly and thinking about carefully, because of his material and his attitude to it, rather than his technique—because of what he has to say rather than his way of saying it. In fact he is at his worst when he relies on technique, when he loses his grip and falls into "fine writing." He is at his best when he writes directly what he knows, and it is good to see him doing just that in six of the stories in *Guzman, Go Home*. Of course this is a technique itself, but the best art is the art that hides art, and in these stories you don't realize how well they are written until you have finished reading them.

There are quarrels between husbands and wives, leading to attempted poisoning (or was it a delusion after all?), to dazed children, to family problems. There is plenty of sex, not in the modern form of arty pornography but as a disturbing and delightful force. *Make love and war* might be Sillitoe's motto. There are beautiful sketches of the kind stories used to be in the days before cleverness became fashionable—a beheaded chicken which runs into the next house, the man who can never forget the girl he picked up when he came out of prison who disappeared when he went to steal some money for her. And there is a fine return to Nottingham and an old girl friend by a man who left them both ten years ago.

These are all vintage Sillitoe with an excellent and unmistakeable flavor. There is also a *tour de force* in the title story, which is largely a monologue by a Nazi who runs a garage in the middle of Spain. It is very good in its way, but this isn't Sillitoe's way, and it is curiously disappointing, while the other stories are curiously satisfying. Writers get it both ways. If they go on writing the same way, they are told that their range is limited and they should develop it; if they write in different ways, they are told that they have no recognizable style and they should establish one. But I think there is no doubt that Sillitoe is best when he is most definitely himself, and that he is read and will be remembered for his most characteristic work. However much he may hate it, he is the man who wrote *Saturday Night and Sunday Morning* and *The Loneliness of the Long-distance Runner*, and it is when he writes in that tradition that he compels our attention.

Originally published in Freedom, *January 11, 1969.*

21
C. W. DANIEL:
THE ODD MAN

C. W. DANIEL IS ONE OF THE FORGOTTEN ODD MEN OUT OF THE 20TH century. He is forgotten because he didn't ever do or say anything particularly dramatic, or follow any powerful person or join any powerful party, or belong to any of the groups of fashionable left-wing biography. He wasn't a member of any socialist or anarchist or pacifist organization; he wasn't female or Jewish or Marxist or working-class; he was a publisher and editor rather than a writer or speaker; he never held any position other than director of his own little company; he never made or lost much money; he didn't write his memoirs.

Nevertheless he deserves to be remembered, for several reasons—as an odd man (which is what he called himself) and as a crank (which he also called himself), who had a great sense of life and fun, but above all as the man who was probably responsible for the publication of more libertarian and other alternative writings in English during the first half of the twentieth century than any other single person. This is an inevitably sketchy and selective attempt to remember him as he deserves, emphasizing his contributions to social and political debate, but neglecting the personal and spiritual sides of his life and work.

Charles William Daniel was born on April 23, 1871 at 35 King's Cross Road in London (near the site of the old Clerkenwell Prison, and also of Arnold Bennett's *Riceyman Steps*). He came from the middle of the middle class. His father's family was of Welsh origin and claimed descent from the Elizabethan poet Samuel Daniel; his mother's family had Dutch connections. He was brought up with nine brothers and sisters in Liverpool Road, Islington. Their father worked for the London publisher, Frederick Warne, but he died of drink in 1883.

Young Daniel left school at once and began to earn his living at the age of fourteen. He worked for a time as an office boy and then as an advertising agent, but eventually he went into publishing, where he stayed for sixty years. He got a job with the London publisher, Walter Scott (no connection with the novelist), now long defunct. The manager of the firm was Fred Henderson, a philosophical anarchist who later ran the well-known "Bomb Shop" in Charing Cross Road and who was at that time a follower of Tolstoy; indeed Walter Scott was the main British publisher of Tolstoy's works. Daniel had through family connections met another Tolstoyan—J. C. Kenworthy, the main British propagandist for Tolstoy's social and political ideas during the 1890s (until he went mad).

The influence of the great Russian writer and thinker nearly a century ago can hardly be overestimated, even though it was exerted quietly on individuals through his writings rather than noisily on the masses through organizations, and Daniel was one of many who fell completely under its spell. He adopted the very unorthodox Christianity, the rejection of both Church and State and of both authority and violence, the abstention from meat and tobacco (though not from alcohol), the prejudice against sex (and against women), and the acceptance of all sorts of unorthodox views about life and health. At the same time he adopted the more specifically economic ideas of Henry George and political ideas of Proudhon. He also accepted the occult, reincarnation, homoeopathy, health food, herbal medicine, organic farming, and many others of the minority ideas which were floating in the air at the end of the last century, some of which are still doing so at the end of this one—all elements of what was later called the alternative or counter-culture. Daniel first entered public life as the main organizer of the London Tolstoyan Society, a short-lived little group of eccentrics who from September 1900 held weekly meetings in the hall of the West London Institute of Music over a shop off the Edgware Road (and who also held open-air meetings in Hyde Park on Sunday afternoons in summer 1901). He soon became one of its main speakers, being listed ten times during the year from December 1900 to November 1901 (mostly on Tolstoy himself, but also on other topics). This tiny organization belonged to the shadowy world between progressive religion and progressive politics, and was close to the then flourishing Ethical Societies.

Daniel's involvement in the London Tolstoyan Society not only began his public life, as I have said, but also changed his private life. He met there Florence E. Worland, a young middle-class New Woman who was leading a bohemian life in a garret in Bloomsbury, and who was first listed as a speaker (on Kropotkin) in September 1901. She impressed Daniel against his will—according to her later account, his comment on her first intervention in the discussion was: "I welcome with joy any sign that the feminine mind is capable of thought" (*Focus*, February 1926)—and they eventually fell in love. The path of love did not run smooth (as is shown by their sometimes painful private letters), but eventually they married—at the Lambeth Register Office on March 23, 1905 (during working hours on a weekday!). More important, in a way, they became close colleagues; for although he was a good manager and organizer, she was a better writer and editor, and she became his professional as well as personal inspiration.

They had only one child, a son born in 1913 who was symbolically called Henry George Daniel; like the children of so many remarkable people, he had a difficult childhood and an unhappy life, and died after a mental breakdown in 1985. It was a rather cruel irony that among his mother's books were such titles as *Of Babies* and *Of Children*. (One of their colleagues later said: "They should never have had real children, they had so many children of the mind.")

In 1902, Daniel began the main thing for which he is sometimes remembered—his own publishing business, the C. W. Daniel Company Ltd, which occupied various premises in the City and Bloomsbury, often with a bookshop as well as an office, for nearly forty years, and which occupied the rest of his life. To begin with, he continued business as an advertising agent, and he also worked closely with other publishers of similar material. He became the London agent for the Free Age Press, which was the main source of English translations of Tolstoy's later works in dozens of editions (under the direction of Tolstoy's leading disciple Vladimir Chertkov); and he co-operated closely with Arthur C. Fifield, then the main British publisher of unorthodox progressive and left-wing material. One of Fifield's projects was several series of pamphlets in tiny sexto-decimo format (roughly A6)—first the "Simple Life" series (from 1903 to 1906), and then the 'Brochure' series (from 1906 to 1907). Many of the titles were taken over by Daniel, who also produced his own "People's Classics" (from 1905 to 1906), which included short works by a score of great writers from the ancient world to the present day. He started several other similar series, and gradually expanded his list of publications as Fifield's contracted, eventually replacing him as the main publisher of unorthodox progressive and left-wing material for several decades. Although it should be remembered that Daniel always produced plenty of ordinary publications, especially if the authors were prepared to pay for them, he was more important as a publisher who generally produced what he approved of—indeed it was said that his imprint was his imprimatur.

At the same time, Daniel and Florence Worland ventured together into the world of periodicals, which occupied him for forty years. They first planned a paper called the *Idealist*, but in November 1902 it appeared as the *Tolstoyan: A Magazine of Practical Idealism* in the same tiny format as the pamphlets. This lasted only until June 1903, partly because—as with the Tolstoyan Society itself—the great man objected to organizations or periodicals named after himself. One of the most useful features of the *Tolstoyan* was their series of articles on Tolstoy's ideas, which were collected as a booklet called *Tolstoy's Teaching: An Epitome, with a Program of Study* by "F.E. & C.W.D." (1912).

In January 1904, the paper was relaunched as the *Crank: An Unconventional Magazine*, and the Daniels were firmly set on the course they followed for the rest of their lives together. The title of the paper was taken from a saying of Henry George—"A crank is a little thing that makes revolutions"—and its intention was to celebrate crankiness as the salvation of the world. The first issue proudly proclaimed: "This little Magazine . . . is published by one Crank, edited by another, and generally conducted, guided, and helped by a committee of Cranks . . ." There was a series of articles on "Historic Cranks," from Socrates to Henry George himself; there was a series of interviews with contemporary "Representative Cranks," most of whom have long been forgotten, but one of whom was Bernard Shaw. Daniel himself wrote most of the editorials, under the heading "Instead of an Editorial," and over the pseudonym "The Odd Man."

In January 1907, the title of the paper was changed to *Ye Crank*, but this turned out to be altogether too cranky, and in July 1907 it became the *Open Road*, taking its place as one of the many little periodicals preaching faith and hope during the period just before the First World War. The title came from one of Walt Whitman's best-known poems— "The Song of the Open Road"—and had already been given to one of the most popular poetry anthologies of the age—E. V. Lucas's *The Open Road* (1899). Soon its many preoccupations grew altogether too many for one periodical, and the health aspect was taken over by a new magazine, *Healthy Life*, which began in August 1911 under the editorship of Daniel's friend Edgar J. Savage (who adopted the more suitable pseudonym of "Saxon"!), and which continued long after Daniel ceased to publish it. The contributors to the Daniels' papers were generally obscure, but they included several writers who later became well known, among them such diverse names as G. K. and Cecil Chesterton, Arthur Ransome and Victor Neuburg, and they are among the few papers of the past which may still be read with pleasure and profit.

The main overt influences on the Daniels remained Tolstoy and Henry George; but a powerful covert influence at least on Florence

Daniel was Mary Everest Boole, who has been almost forgotten (except—following common sexist lines—as a niece of the mountaineer George Everest, the wife of the mathematician George Boole, and the mother of the writer Ethel Voynich). She was a very eccentric thinker, who developed the concept of "mental hygiene," pioneered ideas about the unconscious mind, held an informal London salon for several years, and wrote under several names in the Daniels' papers; four volumes of her *Collected Works* were edited by Eleanor M. Cobham and published by Daniel in 1931. Her writings are an extraordinary combination of good sense and apparent nonsense, and I must confess that I find Boolean psychology almost as incomprehensible as Boolean algebra.

Daniel himself slowly became better known in the wider world. He was one of the founding members of the Cranks' Table, a group of progressive journalists and publishers who met and talked over meals at vegetarian restaurants in central London, and were the subject of amused but admiring comments in more respectable papers. Most of his then well-known associates are now as little known as he is; more interesting now are some of those who were then little known. Let me take one example.

Among the many obscure writers who first appeared in Daniel's columns was Dorothy Richardson, another young middle-class New Woman leading a bohemian life in a garret in Bloomsbury, who later wrote the pioneering feminist "stream-of-consciousness" novel *Pilgrimage*. She contributed to the Daniels' papers from August 1906 to December 1907—just at the time when she was involved in an affair with H. G. Wells (which ended with her pregnancy and abortion during 1907). She kept in touch with the Daniels during her later life; she also described them in *Revolving Lights* (1923), the seventh volume of *Pilgrimage*, which was indeed dedicated "To F.E.W." In one of the long conversations between "Miriam" (Dorothy Richardson herself) and "Hypo Wilson" (H. G. Wells), she praises "George and Dora Taylor" (Charles and Florence Daniel):

> They *are* wonderful. Their atmosphere is the freest I know. . . . You go there, worn out, at the end of the day, and have to walk, after a long tram-ride through the wrong part of London, along raw new roads, dark little houses on either side, solid, without a single break, darkness, a street-lamp, more darkness, another lamp; and something in the air that lets down and down. Partly the thought of these streets increasing, all the time, all over London . . . suddenly you are in their kitchen. White walls and aluminium and a smell of fruit. Do you know the smell of root vegetables cooking slowly in a casserole? . . . You are all

standing about. Happy and undisturbed. None of that feeling of darkness and strangeness and the need for a fresh beginning. Tranquillity
. . . Making every one move like a song. And talk. You are all, at once,
bursting with talk. All over the flat, in and out of the rooms. George
washing up all the time, wandering about with a dish and a cloth, and
Dora probably doing her hair in a dressing-gown, and cooking. It's the
only place where I can talk exhausted and starving. . . . We find ourselves
sitting in the bathroom, engrossed—long speeches—they talk to each
other, like strangers talking intimately on a bus. Then something boils
over and we all drift back to the kitchen. Left to herself, Dora would
go on for ever and sit down to a few walnuts at midnight. . . . But she is
an absolutely perfect cook. An artist. She invents and experiments. But
he has a feminine consciousness, though he's a most manly little man
with a head like Beethoven. So he's practical. Meaning he feels with his
nerves and has a perfect sympathetic imagination. So presently we are
all sitting down to a meal and the evening begins to look short. And
yet endless. With them everything feels endless; the present I mean.
They are so immediately alive. Everything and everybody is abolished
. . . And a new world is there. You feel language changing, every word
moving, changed, into the new world. *But,* when their friends come in
the evening, weird people, real cranks, it disappears . . . But the evening
is wonderful. None of these people mind how far or how late they walk.
And it goes on till the small hours . . .

There is also a vivid account of "Dora" speaking at a meeting of the
London Tolstoyan Society, when "Miriam" says that "I felt I was hearing
the whole truth spoken aloud for the first time," and adds that behind
all the prophets of social and political change: "I see little Taylor, unanswerable, standing for more difficult deep-rooted individual things."*

But the most important person for the Daniels and their papers, of
course, was Tolstoy himself. He was still very much alive, though approaching eighty, holding court among the quarrelling factions of his
relations and disciples at his country estate in central Russia. It is not
surprising that the Daniels sent him their publications; what is surprising is that he responded to them. There are several entries in his diaries referring to them and their papers, and some of their writings were
included in the anthologies he compiled under the general title *The
Reading Circle (Krug Chteniya)*.

Then on January 4, 1907 (December 22, 1906) he wrote a letter
directly "To the Odd Man of the Crank":

---

* The relevant passages from *Revolving Lights* appear in the third volume of the
collected edition of *Pilgrimage* (1967, 1979), 371–4.

Dear Sir,

I thank you very much for the *Crank Magazine*, which I enjoy very much. To-day I have read the last article of Worland: "The Earth for all." It is very good; especially his criticism of Maltus's [*sic*] theory, which, notwithstanding its weakness, has had such a large spreading. I think that true Christianity with its ideal of chastity, is the best remedy for the population. I will take care that it should be translated in russian, if he will allow it. I liked it very much, also your answer to Shaw, as I like all the pages signed by "Odd Man." I would be very glad to know your name and be in direct intercourse with you.

Have you many subscribers to your magazine? I wish the greatest success to your work, so very necessary in our time.

Yours truly,
Leo Tolstoy

P.S. Reading your very good note to the word "anarchism" I remembered on the same matter the saying of Lao-Tze. He says: "When great sages have power over the people, the people do not notice them; if the power is in the hands of sages (not the great ones), the people like them and praise them; if those who govern are less sage—the people are afraid of them; and where those who govern are still less sage—the people despise them."

A corrected version of this letter was published in the *Crank* in February 1907. (It is worth mentioning that Tolstoy himself had thirteen legitimate children, as well as an unknown number of illegitimate ones!)

When proper introductions had been made and true identities established, Tolstoy wrote another encouraging letter on 15 (2) February 1907:

Dear Mrs. Daniel,

I did not answer your letter before, because I was ill, and am not quite well till now. I am glad to hear that you intend to work at your article on land. Though it is very good as it is, it can only gain by it. I appreciate also very much your idea of the connection of the three principles of poverty, continence (as a degree of chastity) and obedience to natural law. And I think and hope that you will express those ideas as strongly as all the articles of Worland, and as simply and shortly as you say you wish to do it.

The sole advise [*sic*] that I should wish to give you is to avoid polemic as much as possible.

I have received also a letter from your husband, I hope he will excuse me if I do not write to him separately and will ask you to be so kind and tell him:

1) That although I like the "Crank" very much, I quite agree with him that it would be very good not only to combine gardening and agricultural work with writing, but to put the foundation of your life in manual work, as I keep publishing work as an accessory. Then he will not be afraid to be too successful.

2) That I hope I will send something for the "Crank" which will be worthy of it.

and 3) That I will be very glad to know his questions and answer them if I feel myself able to do it.
With best wishes for you and your husband.

Your friend,
Leo Tolstoy*

Tolstoy did send a few short items to the *Crank* and the *Open Road* during the next few years. And at the end of 1909 Daniel made the long pilgrimage to Yasnaya Polyana. The *Open Road* reported that "The Odd Man is in Russia, sitting at the feet of Tolstoy" (January 1910). Tolstoy's diaries included several references to his visit, not all of them favorable.

> Had dinner, spoke with difficulty in English. Dan. is a clever, cold person [November 25].
> With Dan. especially hard because of my ignorance or, rather, half-knowledge of the language [November 28].

The master and disciple don't actually seem to have got on very well, and the latter wrote little about the former on his return; but he retained his Tolstoyan convictions, and he also strengthened his friendship with Chertkov, whom he defended when the old man died only a year later (*Open Road*, January 1911).

One of the most interesting features in the *Crank* and the *Open Road* was a series of articles signed F. E. Worland which was collected in a booklet called *Love: Sacred and Profane* (1908), dedicated "To 'My lover, my dear friend,'" and explaining the Tolstoyan doctrine of love and

---

* The relevant passages from the diaries appear in the standard Russian edition of Tolstoy's works (*Polnoye sobraniye sochinenii 56 and 57*, 1937). The relevant letters appear in fairly accurate transcripts of the original English texts in the same edition (ibid., 76 and 77, 1956); the first letter also appears in R. F. Christian's English selection (*Tolstoy's Letters*, volume 2, 1978). The versions here are taken from the originals in the Daniel papers.

marriage for an English audience. It now seems extraordinarily dated in many of its ideas, but it is deeply felt and elegantly written, and it may be taken as expressing the Daniels' feelings for each other.

Daniel's own main preoccupation in the *Crank* and the *Open Road* was the criticism of socialism—not so much the revolutionary movement represented by the Marxists or anarchists as the parliamentary movement represented by the Fabian Society and the new Labour Party, which he saw as just another oligarchy or monopoly long before it got near to achieving political power. His early articles on the subject were often attacked by the young Dorothy Richardson, then influenced by Wells and active in the Fabians (who appear as the "Lycurgans" in *Pilgrimage*). His later articles, which appeared throughout the life of the *Open Road*, from 1908 to 1912, were collected as a booklet called *Instead of Socialism: And Papers on Two Democratic Delusions* (1913).

This was the only book of which Daniel was the author, and it gives a useful summary of his political ideas—or at least of his negative political ideas, for despite the title it offers nothing "instead of socialism," though it does make very cogent criticisms of a centralized collectivist economy. One of the articles was called "Socialism: Its Cause and Cure," echoing Edward Carpenter's famous book *Civilization: Its Cause and Cure*, and this was originally going to be the title of the book; but he discussed the disease rather than the cure. Similarly, he didn't develop his sketchy remarks on anarchism, and they were not included in the book version of the articles. All he definitely advocated was what he called "Thearchy," or the rule of God; but what he meant by "God" was even less clear than what Tolstoy meant, and what he meant by "Thearchy" (which he first discussed in 1907) was even less clear than that. His personal religion was an informal affair, involving no kind of dogmatic belief or external observance; he later preferred to use such formulas as *God = Good* and *Lord = Law*. That "Thearchy" really amounted to was "the rule of universal goodwill"—that we should follow the law in our own hearts, which is to treat others as we wish to be treated ourselves, and to develop a society and an economy in which co-operation and competition are combined on a practical basis. Daniel called himself a "philosophical anarchist"; perhaps he would be better described as a philosophical libertarian, since he rejected some of the basic elements of anarchism. But although he always avoided political activity as such, he maintained some strong negative principles—he would never vote or serve on a jury, for example, and he never supported any violence or war.

Daniel's articles were interrupted by the closure of the *Open Road*, the last issue appearing in January–March 1913. Two other series of articles that were interrupted at the same time for the same reason were also collected in popular books. One was "Where the Road Leads," by Ethel Wedgwood (the first wife of the radical politician Josiah Wedgwood), which appeared as *The Road to Freedom: And What Lies Beyond* (1913). The other was "Liberty Luminants," compiled by Henry Bool and "S. Carlyle" (the former an individualist who had lived in the United States, and the latter a pseudonym of S. Carlyle Potter, a libertarian writer and editor who ended as a London bookseller), which appeared as *For Liberty: An Anthology of Revolt* (1914), and was a rich source for apt quotations (of the kind which used to appear on the masthead of *Freedom*). At the same time, Daniel published British editions of such American libertarian classics as Stephen Pearl Andrews's *The Science of Society* (1913) and Victor Yarros's version of Lysander Spooner's *Free Political Institutions* (1912), and he later published S. Carlyle Potter's digest of Godwin's ideas as a pamphlet called *Reflections on Political Justice.*

Daniel's criticisms of socialism were of course increasingly unfashionable as socialist ideas and organizations gained support. So of course were his criticisms of war, especially when the First World War began. Despite his general avoidance of political activity, he was not only dragged into controversy over the war but twice got into trouble with the authorities through his involvement with anti-war propaganda. He was himself too old to be called up when conscription eventually came in 1916, but he published several pacifist books; including some moving novels about unwilling conscripts (especially by "Herbert Tremaine," the pseudonym of Mrs. Norman Deuchar), and J. Scott Duckers's vivid account of his experiences as one in the hands of the army, *"Handed Over"* (1917).

Eventually trouble came for Daniel himself. At the end of 1916, he was involved in the clandestine production and distribution of an anonymous pacifist pamphlet called *A "Knock-Out" Blow*, a bitter critique of the more aggressive war policy of the new Lloyd George government. Daniel's office was raided by the police, and he and the editor and printer were prosecuted under the Defence of the Realm Act in spring 1917. At the Chief Metropolitan Magistrates' Court in Bow Street on April 28, they were convicted and fined (Daniel's share was £80 and ten guineas' costs). The printer paid up, but the editor (James Evans) and Daniel refused and went to prison instead. Daniel spent two months in Wormwood Scrubs. He later told the story that when he was asked for his religion he gave it as "Christian." "Oh!" he was told, "you can't be that 'ere." "Very well, then," he said, "put me down as No Religion."

Trouble came again a year later. In spring 1918, he published another anti-war novel called *Despised and Rejected*, which contained a new element in his publications. It was generally about a group of people who were involved in the struggle against conscription, but it was especially about two homosexuals in the group—indeed it was one of the very first open fictional accounts of homosexuality in English. The author was given as "A.T. Fitzroy" but was in fact Rose Laure Allatini, the young daughter of an Italian diplomat and an Austrian mother who had already produced several romantic novels under her own name. This particular one had been submitted to Stanley Unwin, who relates in his autobiography, *The Truth About a Publisher* (1960), that he rejected it because he feared it would be prosecuted, and adds that "in view of the subjects dealt with I did not think that any publisher would consider it; the only man who might conceivably do so was C. W. Daniel"—which was indeed the case, with precisely the result Unwin feared.

The initial public reception of the book was mixed; the review in the *Times Literary Supplement* (June 6, 1918) expresses it well enough:

> A well-written novel—evidently the work of a woman—on the subjects of pacifism and of abnormality in the affections. The author's sympathy is plainly with the pacifists; and her plea for more tolerant recognition of the fact that some people are, not of choice but by nature, abnormal in their affections is open and bold enough to rob the book of unpleasant suggestions. As a frank and sympathetic study of certain types of mind and character, it is of interest; but it is not to be recommended for general reading.

The latter feeling spread to official quarters, and Daniel was once more prosecuted under the Defence of the Realm Act. At the City of London Court at Mansion House on October 10, 1918 (only a month before the war ended) he was convicted and fined £420 with £40 costs. The official reason was the pacifist message, but an unofficial one was the even more objectionable homosexual message. Daniel immediately circulated a statement dissociating himself from this aspect of the book, and at the same time his friend Gilbert Sadler, an unorthodox pacifist clergyman, circulated an appeal for help with the fine, which was soon oversubscribed.

Rose Allatini was briefly taken up by the Bloomsbury Group; in 1921 she married the composer Cyril Scott; they were involved in the occultist movement and associated with the libertarian millionaire George Davison, had two children, and separated in 1941; she spent the rest of her life with a woman friend in Rye, and returned to romantic novels, achieving considerable success under the name "Eunice Buckley"; she died only a few years ago. *Despised and Rejected* was reprinted by the Gay Men's Press in 1988 with an informative and entertaining introduction by Jonathan Cutbill.

Daniel's wartime experiences fixed his pacifist convictions more firmly than ever, and afterwards he produced *The Indictment of War* (1919), a big anthology of anti-war extracts from British and American but also many foreign (including German) writers, edited by H. Stanley Redgrove and Jeanne Heloise Rowbottom, which was one of his most impressive publications, and is still a very valuable source of pacifist material.

The major political event after the war was of course the Russian Revolution. At first Daniel took no particular view of it, and in 1920 he published a booklet called *Russia before and after the Revolution* by S. Carlyle Potter defending the Bolsheviks against outside criticism or intervention. (In 1919 he published *Factory Echoes,* the first book by R. M. Fox, later a well-known Communist writer.) But he was soon persuaded by the libertarian critics of the new regime to become one of the main publishers of their writings. In 1925, he was responsible for the first British (and only complete) edition of Emma Goldman's book *My Disillusionment in Russia.* In 1926, he became the British publisher of *Letters from Russian Prisons* (1925), the influential collection of primary documents officially edited in the United States by Roger N. Baldwin, but actually compiled in Europe by Alexander Berkman. Also in 1926 he published a British edition of Berkman's *Prison Memoirs of an Anarchist,* with a new introduction by Edward Carpenter; though he later declined Berkman's *Now and After: The ABC of Communist Anarchism* (1928). Incidentally, the record of these publications didn't prevent Daniel from being invited to Moscow as one of the official British representatives at the national celebration of the centenary of Tolstoy's birth in 1928—just before the cultural life of the Soviet Union fell under the total control of the Stalinist dictatorship.

Daniel continued to publish the same kind of books as before, and he was also the first British publisher of such foreign writers as Søren Kierkegaard, Georg Groddeck and José Ortega y Gasset, but he continued to keep up with unorthodox developments in Britain. When Leslie Paul founded the new left-wing youth movement, the Woodcraft Folk, his first account of the organization was published by Daniel as *The Green Company* (1928). When Nellie Shaw, one of the founders of the libertarian community at Whiteway in 1898, wrote its history, this was published by Daniel as *Whiteway: A Colony on the Cotswolds* (1935); and he himself had several friends there, including Thomas Keell and Lilian Wolfe.

Daniel also ventured into pure literature. He always published novels, plays and poems, though few were successful or memorable. But one project which had some impact was a series of "Plays for a People's Theatre," of which the second was D. H. Lawrence's *Touch and Go* (1920), published at a time when he was an extremely unpopular writer. Later in the 1920s there were serious discussions about forming a publishing company with Lawrence and some of his friends, but they came to nothing—probably fortunately for Daniel, who would have suffered the difficulties involved in any co-operation with Lawrence, and who might have faced a trial of *Lady Chatterley* thirty years early!

It took some time for the Daniels to start a magazine again. But in January 1926 they began *Focus: A Periodical to the Point in Matters of Health, Wealth, and Life*. At the same time he revived the "People's Classics" series (and Dorothy Richardson returned to his columns for a few months). One of the most attractive features of *Focus* was a series of articles called "Meetings and Partings" and signed "FEW," which described the old London Tolstoyan Society (January–May 1926). They incidentally included a nice portrait of Daniel in 1901: ". . . a serious-looking young man of medium height, clean-shaven, with broad shoulders and dark brown hair. He had a fine head, but, in those days, not much sense of humor" [February 1926]. But by then she had fallen ill, and she died of cancer in September 1927. Her friend Eleanor M. Cobham wrote a little pamphlet, *A Tribute to the Memory of Florence Daniel (F. E. Worland)* (1927).

Without her inspiration and cooperation, Daniel himself soon decided to relinquish editing and concentrate on publishing; at the beginning of 1929 *Focus* was replaced by *Purpose: A Quarterly Magazine*. At first it was nominally edited by "John Marlow" (Daniel himself), but he soon handed over to his old friend W. Travers Symons. *Purpose* was a much more conventional and sophisticated magazine than its predecessors, with a more deliberate approach to politics (of the Social Credit variety) and psychology (of the Individual variety), and with a stronger literary side (conducted by Desmond Hawkins). Perhaps most of the political and psychological material has now dated beyond recall, but it is worth recording that in January–March 1940 Herbert Read contributed "A Community of Individuals," a characteristic defense of anarchism, which was reprinted in his book *A Coat of Many Colors* (1945). The literary contributors included such names as W. H. Auden, George Barker, Elizabeth Bowen, Lawrence Durrell, T. S. Eliot, James Hanley, Rayner Heppenstall, Hugh MacDiarmid, Henry Miller, Edwin Muir, John Middleton Murry, Anaïs Nin, Ezra Pound, John Pudney, Kathleen

Raine, Stephen Spender, Julian Symons, Dylan Thomas, and so on. In short, *Purpose* was one of the many serious magazines of the low dishonest decade before the Second World War, which soon brought it to an end with the issue of July–September 1940.

At the same time Daniel had revived his health magazine in June 1934 as *Health and Life*, which was again edited by "Saxon," and which again continued long after he had given up his connections with it. His premises in Great Russell Street in the late 1930s had a well-known shop, to which the Post Office once delivered a letter addressed to "The Bookshop near the British Museum with Health Books in the Window!" That period was probably the peak of his success as a publisher, though he suffered the experience of all small firms, of discovering new writers who moved on to bigger firms when they achieved some fame. He later told a nice story against himself of overhearing one man telling another about "Daniel, the publisher—a nice chap, but a damn fool at business!"

Daniel was as much opposed to the Second as to the First World War, and he experienced a more personal anguish when his son joined the Royal Air Force. He didn't get into any trouble with the authorities this time, but he suffered more directly when his premises were destroyed in the Blitz in 1941. Rather than try to resume activities in wartime London, he moved near several old friends and colleagues in the libertarian colony of The Chase at Ashingdon, a few miles north of Southend. He took a rambling Victorian house which was renamed "Oprodan" (the old telegraphic address for "The Open Road, Daniel"), and stayed there for the rest of his life, along with his few remaining colleagues. He dropped his political and literary publications and concentrated on health books, especially the works of Bircher-Benner, the inventor of muesli, and Edward Bach, the inventor of flower remedies. He read and talked with his friends, worked and sat in his garden, enjoyed the company of his dog and cats, and lived in his memories. He described himself as an anarchist to the end, and always subscribed to anarchist periodicals and purchased anarchist books, though he was virtually unknown to the anarchist movement.

C. W. Daniel died at Ashingdon on January 15, 1955. His death was almost unnoticed in the outside world; though his oldest colleague, Denise Waltham (who had been with him for more than forty years), anonymously wrote and published a little pamphlet *A Tribute to the Memory of Charles William Daniel* (1955). She and a few other colleagues kept the firm going for several years, and in 1971 Daniel's great-nephew Jeremy Goring wrote another little pamphlet, *The Centenary of a "Crank" Publisher: Charles William Daniel (1871–1955)* (1971), and also an article about him in the *Bookseller* (December 18, 1971). This came to the notice of a young London publisher, Ian Miller, who got in touch with the firm and eventually took it over. He continued its work for a time in London, and then in beautiful old premises in Saffron Walden, where it still flourishes as one of the main publishers in the English-speaking world of unorthodox health books and pamphlets. Meanwhile Denise Waltham, now in her nineties, lives at Oprodan with Mary Sweetlove, a niece and former colleague of Daniel, among the many relics of their work together, sharing their memories, keeping up with old and new friends, and looking for a better world of the kind Daniel strove for all his life.*

Jeremy Goring concluded his 1971 pamphlet with the following paragraph:

> It is not easy to estimate the influence upon his generation of the work of one quiet man. It is particularly difficult in the case of a man like Charles Daniel, who was not a beginner or finisher of things, but a go-between—one who, through the medium of the printed word, put one mind into touch with another. Daniel, by his chosen definition, was a crank—not a big thing that made a great commotion, but a little one that helped to make a revolution. One wonders how much of the revolution that has taken place this century in men's attitudes to things was furthered by people like him who, avoiding the limelight, got on quietly with the work of producing the books and pamphlets and journals that fed the minds of men.

Originally published in Raven *1 (1987).*

---

* Editor's note. NW wrote in the *Guardian*, February 10, 1990: "Denise Waltham, who has died aged ninety-three, worked as the main colleague of the great radical publisher C. W. Daniel until his death in 1955, and then ran the company until it was sold in 1971. She adopted and upheld his principles of vegetarianism, anarchism and pacifism. The rest of her life she spent with her devoted companion Mary Sweetlove in the old libertarian colony of The Chase, Ashingdon, Essex, where she died on February 9.

22
GUY A. ALDRED, 1886-1963

THE CENTENARY OF THE BIRTH OF GUY ALDRED IS A GOOD OPPORTUNITY to remember one of the most energetic and eccentric figures ever involved in the British anarchist movement.

He came from the indeterminate area between the lower middle class and the upper working class. His parents were Alfred Arthur Aldred, a former naval officer of 22 who hoped to become a playwright (and later became a theatre manager), and Ada Caroline Holdsworth, a parasol-maker of nineteen. The circumstances of their relationship are unknown, but on September 13, 1886 they married solely to legitimize the approaching birth of their child. They never lived together but separated immediately after the wedding service, and both later contracted bigamous marriages. The child was born at his mother's parents' tenement at 24 Corporation Buildings,* Farringdon Road, Clerkenwell, in North London, on November 5, 1886; he was appropriately named Guy Alfred Aldred.

He was brought up by his mother first with her parents and later with her new husband at 133 Goswell Road,** Clerkenwell. The main influence on his early development was his grandfather, Charles Holdsworth, a half-Jewish bookbinder who had radical views of politics and religion, supported Gladstone and Bradlaugh, favored Irish and Indian independence, opposed war, and encouraged Guy in all his activities until his death in 1908. Aldred was educated at the Iron Infants' School in Farringdon Road and then at the new Hugh Myddelton School in Myddelton Street (the latter still exists). He did very well, and there was some talk of his going on to take orders in the Church of England, but he left school at the usual age of fourteen in 1901.

---

* Demolished after the Second World War.
** Also demolished after the Second World War.

By this time he had already begun a public career that was to last more than sixty years, joining campaigns against smoking and drinking. His intense opposition to the Boer War soon led to his first publication in June 1902—a duplicated leaflet called *The Last Days: Peace or War*, a Christian pacifist tract that showed remarkable precocity. At the same time he adopted the style of clothes—a Norfolk suit with knickerbockers—that he retained for the rest of his life.

For six years he earned his living in a conventional way. After a few months working as a receptionist for an insurance doctor, he got a job as an office boy at the National Press Agency. He soon became a sub-editor, and seemed to be set on the traditional path to a successful career in journalism; in 1907 he moved to the *Daily Chronicle*, a leading Liberal newspaper, but he left after a few months. At the age of twenty he abandoned paid employment forever.

During the same period he traveled rapidly along a well-trodden ideological road from Christian and Liberal radicalism through secularism and socialism to atheism and anarchism. The special gifts he brought to this journey were an insatiable thirst to acquire knowledge and an equally irresistible urge to impart it, together with an extraordinary combination of extreme youth and enormous energy (the latter lasting long after the former had gone). At the same time he had the defects of a complete lack of any sense of humor or proportion and an extraordinary combination of self-confidence and self-conceit, which made him an *enfant terrible* in all the many organizations he joined and made him quarrel with almost all the many people he worked with during the next thirty years.

He began as a Christian preacher, and although he soon ceased to be a Christian he remained a preacher for the rest of his life. He was a member of his grandfather's Anglican church of St. Anne and St. Agnes (near St. Paul's Cathedral), but he soon proved too enthusiastic and too ecumenical for such a conventional institution. He took part in the Lamb and Flag Mission to the London poor. In November 1902, when he was just sixteen, he joined an evangelical preacher called Willoughby Masters as a boy preacher in the Christian Social Mission in Holloway. But his message was altogether too social, and he left after a few months. Meanwhile he met some interesting and influential religious characters, such as George Martin, a High Anglican worker priest who served the poor in the Borough district of South London and who taught Aldred about Greek literature and philosophy, and Charles Voysey, an unfrocked Anglican priest who preached to the rich at his Theistic Church off Piccadilly and who befriended Aldred until his death in 1912.

In 1903 Aldred began to attend the Peel Institute, a Quaker settlement for men in Clerkenwell, where he was soon lecturing and where he became disenchanted with Liberalism. In April 1904 he established his own Theistic Mission at Clerkenwell Green, but he quickly ran into difficulties with the attempt to combine Unitarian theology and humanistic ethics, and under the influence of T. H. Huxley and Herbert Spencer he became an agnostic. In August 1904 he took his last step away from religion, changing the name of his project to the Clerkenwell Freethought Mission, speaking several times a week at Clerkenwell Green and Garnault Place near by, and arguing and even fighting with Christian fanatics. He also began a lifelong practice of writing letters to the press and of producing his own articles and leaflets. (Incidentally, from the start he signed himself "Guy A. Aldred," always using the middle initial.)

In November 1904 he began to contribute to the *Agnostic Journal,* an established freethought weekly edited by the individualistic Scottish writer William Stewart Ross, who called himself "Saladin" (after the Muslim soldier who fought the Christians in the Holy Land during the 12th century). Saladin called Aldred "a contributor of high promise" in April 1905, and wrote in October 1905: "This Guy, born on Guy Faux day, and intent on an argumentative blow-up of the Houses of Priestcraft, has done so much at eighteen that I am sure the readers of the *AJ* would all like to see what he will have done by the time he is eighty." Aldred later said, "The *Agnostic Journal* office was my college." There in Farringdon Road, as well as Saladin he met the equally individualistic Scottish writer Morrison Davidson, who was sympathetic to anarchism, and other leading freethinkers. He learnt about the lives of Richard Carlile and Charles Bradlaugh, and tried to model himself on their examples of courage and persistence. He called himself "the Rev. Guy A. Aldred," a "Minister of the Gospel of Freethought" and later "Minister of the Gospel of Revolt." For two years he was a frequent contributor to the *Agnostic Journal,* both in his own name and as "Ajax Junior" (in imitation of the pseudonym "Ajax" used in the *National Reformer* from 1878 by Annie Besant, whom he interviewed in July 1905). But Saladin died in November 1906, and Aldred soon disappeared from the *Agnostic Journal* (which ceased in June 1907).

During this period he was also an active member of the National Secular Society, frequently speaking on its platforms, and occasionally writing in its associated paper the *Freethinker*. At the same time he was involved in the dissident British Secular League, and in 1906 he tried to form his own group, the London Secular Society (not knowing that there had been one more than fifty years earlier). But by 1907 he had turned away from formal freethought, though he continued to have contacts with the secularist and ethical movements, and he always retained a favorable opinion of Jesus and a mystical view of the world.

He had already been combining secularism with socialism. He was impressed by Robert Blatchford's non-sectarian paper, the *Clarion*. At meetings in Clerkenwell he heard Daniel DeLeon, the American socialist leader, and John Burns, the British socialist leader. He became convinced that political radicalism should parallel religious radicalism, and at the age of eighteen he embarked on a lifelong political career. In March 1905 he joined the Social Democratic Federation, the leading Marxist organization in Britain, and soon began to speak on its platforms and contribute to its papers, the weekly *Justice* and the monthly *Social Democrat*. At the beginning of 1906, when a new Parliament was elected with a large Liberal majority and 29 Members representing the new Labour Party, he became the parliamentary correspondent of *Justice*. But he was quickly disenchanted by this experience and gave up his column in disgust in May 1906, his main reasons being the respectability of the Labour MPs, the religious bias of the Liberal Government's education policy, and the evasion of the religious issue by the SDF.

In September 1906 he left the SDF, disappearing from its papers by the end of the year. He approached other socialist organizations, the new Socialist Labour Party and the newer Socialist Party of Great Britain, but he wasn't happy with either of them. He was increasingly attracted by what he called anti-parliamentary communism, by which he meant participation in electoral politics with a revolutionary program on an abstentionist basis (like the Irish Nationalists), combined with a policy of direct action in political and industrial struggles. In December 1906 he issued an anti-parliamentary election manifesto to the electors of Finsbury, and at the age of twenty he began a lifelong association with the anarchist movement.

At the end of 1906 he made contact with the Freedom Group, formed under the inspiration of Peter Kropotkin in 1886. This produced the monthly *Freedom*, which had been revived in 1895, and was just about to add the weekly *Voice of Labour* as a syndicalist supplement, produced by John Turner, Alfred Marsh, and Thomas Keell. This appeared from January to September 1907, and throughout its run Aldred was the most active (and awkward) contributor. He initiated the Industrial Union of Direct Actionists in May and the Communist Propaganda Group in June, the latter meeting in the basement of his mother's house. From June the paper commonly contained labor movement notes at the beginning by Ajax Junior and IUDA notes at the end by Guy A. Aldred, together with long feature articles in both names in between. In August he made his first speaking tour outside London, visiting Liverpool. At the same time he began contributing to *Freedom,* his articles appearing from June 1907 to November 1908, and he also had some pamphlets printed at the Freedom Press. But at the age of twenty-one, he had become firmly convinced of his own powers, and began to want his own organization and his own paper.

Aldred's involvement with the anarchists also opened a new stage in his personal life. As a non-smoking, non-drinking puritan, he had little to do with the opposite sex in his youth (though he had flirted innocently with the girl who played the harmonium at the Holloway Mission), and in 1907 he both wrote and spoke in favor of celibacy rather than contraception as the solution of the population problem. But the "life force"—which Bernard Shaw had recently dramatized in *Man and Superman* (1903)—was about to catch up with him. When he opened a benefit meeting for the *Voice of Labour* at the Workers' Friend Club in Jubilee Street, the centre of the Jewish anarchist movement in East London, on February 9, 1907, he met a Jewish girl called Rose Lillian Witcop. She had been born as Rachel Vitkopski near Kiev, the capital of the Ukraine, on April 9, 1890—so she was even younger than Aldred. She was the fourth daughter of Simon Witcop and Freda Grill, who had brought her from Russia to Britain in 1895, and like all her family she worked in the garment trade, as a milliner. Her eldest sister, Milly, was the companion of Rudolf Rocker, the German Gentile leader of the British Jewish anarchist movement; another sister, Polly, was also an anarchist; and she was herself already involved in the movement.

Rose Witcop's first known public action was the appearance of a letter in the *Voice of Labour* on March 2, 1907, criticizing the women's suffrage movement for giving too much attention to Parliament and too little to working women. Aldred, who was impressed, met her again at the May Day meeting at the Jubilee Street Club, and she soon became associated with his work and then with his life. She went to Liverpool with him in August, though they still slept apart. They don't seem to have been very popular; according to a letter to Keell from E. G. Smith of the Liverpool anarchists on September 16, 1907, there was a parody of a hymn about them:

> Praise Guy, from whom all blessings flow.
> Praise Guy, all anarchists below.
> Praise him below, ye hellish host.
> Praise Guy and Rose, but Guy the most!

They were both very young, very poor, and very determined. Both their families disapproved of their relationship, so they decided to live together without the sanction of Church or State or relations. Aldred left his mother's home, where he had based all his religious and antireligious, socialist and anarchist activities, a few weeks after his twenty-first birthday; Rose left her parents' home in Stepney; and in January 1908 they set up house together in Shepherd's Bush, West London, where they remained companions for the next dozen years.

Guy Aldred and Rose Witcop were together, but they were almost alone. Voysey characteristically and charmingly gave them his (literal) blessing. They earned a precarious living from odd jobs and hack work, supplemented by gifts from Voysey and a few other sympathetic friends. Aldred had left the *Daily Chronicle* in July 1907 in order to become a self-supporting speaker and writer. He lost the use of his mother's house for the Communist Propaganda Group, but he tried to keep it alive and spoke in every place where he was welcome and in many where he was unwelcome. He had launched his Bakunin Press in his mother's home—with the help of Karl Lahr, a German socialist later well known as Charlie Lahr, the bookseller and publisher—and he continued it in Shepherd's Bush. He began his first series of publications—"Pamphlets for the Proletarian"—mainly based on his own speeches and articles, which he rewrote and republished several times during the next forty years; the fifth in the series was his first autobiography, written at the age of twenty-one. He had more ambitious projects—a "Library of Synthetical Iconoclasts," to include biographies of various radicals and freethinkers, and a book on organization—but neither got beyond groups of pamphlets.

His main problem was that he belonged to no viable organization. He had left all those he had joined, often offending senior figures in them—G. W. Foote among the secularists, H. M. Hyndman among the socialists, Kropotkin and Rocker among the anarchists—with the comment, "Wisdom comes before whiskers!" In 1907 he had founded the Communist Propaganda Group and produced a single issue of his own paper, the *Herald of Revolt*; but the former declined and the latter took three years to be revived. By 1909 he was almost isolated in both thought and action, but it turned out to be an important moment in both personal and political life.

Guy's and Rose's first (and only) child was born on May 2, 1909 (her labor appropriately began during the May Day demonstration in Hyde Park). The boy was called Annesley, one of the names of Voysey, who was still helping them financially and emotionally. Later in 1909,

Aldred went to prison for the first time. He had been under police surveillance since 1907, when a member of the Special Branch told him
was on a list of known agitators, but he eventually got into trouble not so
much for doing something himself as for showing solidarity to someone
else. In July 1909, a member of the Indian Civil Service was assassinated in London by a member of the Free India Society, and the official reaction included the suppression of its paper, the *Indian Sociologist*.
Aldred decided to defend the principle of press freedom, and in August
he produced a new issue of the paper, reprinting much of the suppressed
material. He was arrested in August and tried in September 1909 for
seditious libel at the Central Criminal Court. Despite his skillful le-
galistic defense, he was inevitably found guilty and was sentenced to a
year's imprisonment—the judge commenting that he was "young, vain,
and foolish." He spent ten months in Brixton. Voysey insisted on visiting him as his "spiritual adviser"; Rose Witcop also insisted on visiting
him, although she refused to call herself "Mrs. Aldred." (In his absence
she began one of her many affairs, with E. F. Mylius, who shared their
house.) A new friend who added his support was Walter Strickland, a
rich and eccentric baronet who lived abroad and gave Aldred financial
help for the next thirty years.

When Aldred was released in July 1910, he began to make his own
way on the left. He resumed his work for the Communist Propaganda
Group. He and Lahr ran a Ferrer School in Whitfield Street, North
London, on Sundays from November 1910 to February 1911. And in
December 1910 he at last managed to begin the *Herald of Revolt* as
a monthly "Organ of the Coming Social Revolution," the first of the
many periodicals he edited and published for the rest of his life. He
certainly produced a lively paper, but it was marred by his personal preoccupations. By this time he was combining his early Marxism with his
later anarchism and attempting to reconcile Marx and Bakunin in an idiosyncratic synthesis. At the same time he was attacking both Marxists
and anarchists with equal abuse, incidentally beginning a feud with the
Freedom Press, which lasted forty years. He wrote most of the paper
himself. Rose Witcop wrote little at first but more later, originally over
her initials in reverse order (WLR) and then in her own name; her writing was markedly better than his. One of the more interesting features
of the paper was a series of Lahr's clumsy translations from Bakunin.
In 1912, Aldred began his second series of publications—the "Revolt
Library"—which included his second autobiography.

Aldred continued speaking as well as writing, covering the country as well as London. In 1912, he visited Scotland for the first time,

and became involved with the Glasgow anarchists. He opposed George Ballard (alias Barrett), who was editing a local weekly paper, the *Anarchist,* which was connected with the London Freedom Group; instead he helped to found a new Glasgow Communist Group, and he kept in close touch with it.

In 1911, Mylius was imprisoned for criminal libel, alleging in the *Liberator,* a republican paper published in Paris, that the new King George V was a bigamist, and he later immigrated to the United States. Aldred was caused embarrassment followed by relief.

In 1912, he was briefly involved with the *Freewoman,* the remarkable weekly paper produced by Harriet Shaw Weaver and Dora Marsden from November 1911. It began as a "Feminist Review," became a "Humanist Review" in May 1912, and in June 1912 was succeeded by the *New Freewoman,* an "Individualist Review," which in January 1914 was itself succeeded by the *Egoist,* a paper which combined philosophical anarchism with artistic modernism. Aldred was probably introduced to it by Rose Witcop, whose characteristically sour letter about marriage appeared in it on February 22, 1912. From January to July he wrote interesting articles on women's emancipation, then on the treatment of suffragettes in prison, then on civil liberties and syndicalism, and he edited a reprint of Richard Carlile's 1825 birth control tract *What Is Love?* (July 25, 1912). A Freewoman Discussion Circle began in April 1912, and he spoke to it on July 3 about "Sex Oppression"—both the oppression of one sex by the other, and the oppression of both sexes by sex itself. This was a favorite theme, and he seems to have been rather under-sexed by nature, meaning by free love free monogamous unions, whereas Rose Witcop not only preached but practised free love in its more general meaning.

Later in 1912 Aldred became involved with the Industrialist League, a syndicalist organization that had seceded from the Socialist Labour Party in 1908, and contributed to its paper, the *Industrialist.* One of its leading members, Henry Sara, soon joined Aldred as assistant editor of the *Herald of Revolt* and a leading activist in the Communist Propaganda Group (and as a lover of Rose Witcop).

In June 1914 the *Herald of Revolt* was succeeded by the *Spur,* subtitled "Because the Workers Need a Spur." Within two months the First World War began, and Aldred entered his finest hour. The *Spur* was one of the few papers that opposed the war without hesitation or qualification from beginning to end. Within two months, it was arousing complaints from the public to the authorities, and in November 1914 a Home Office internal memorandum agreed that it should be

suppressed, commenting that "it appears to dissent from all views hitherto expressed" (PRO H045/10741/263275)—a rather good summary
of Aldred's position. In fact the paper was never suppressed, but he ran
into plenty of trouble. Meanwhile he began his third series of publications—the "Spur Series." He also produced a single issue of a paper
called *War News* in 1914.

Aldred continued his busy speaking program, appearing on the
platforms of several socialist organizations and opposing the war at
every opportunity. He also opposed the imposition of conscription in
January 1916, not only in speech and writing but in bitter practice.
In March 1916, Sara was called up and refused to go, and in April he
was arrested and imprisoned, being brutally treated in both military
and civilian custody. In April 1916, Aldred was also arrested (illegally,
as it happened, since he hadn't been formally called up). At that time
only single men were liable for conscription, and he argued that he was
married to Rose Witcop according to Scots law, having lived with her
for short periods in Scotland during speaking tours; in May, a Scottish
lawyer agreed, but this argument was rejected by the West London
Magistrates' Court, and he was handed over to the Army. The resulting
ordeal lasted nearly three years.

In May 1916, he was sentenced by court martial to six months' de-
tention. In June, he was sentenced by court martial to nine months'
hard labor. In August, he accepted the status of a conscientious ob-
jector, without having to go before a tribunal, and he agreed to go to
the labor camp at Dyce, near Aberdeen. He took a leading part in the
Men's Committee, edited a prison paper called the *Granite Echo,* and
spoke in several places in Scotland. In October, he left the camp, and in
November 1916 he was arrested and imprisoned in Wormwood Scrubs.
On his release in March 1917, he was immediately rearrested and in
May sentenced by court martial to eighteen months' hard labor. He was
imprisoned in Wandsworth, where he helped to lead a brief prison revolt in February 1918, for which he was sentenced to six weeks' solitary
confinement in Brixton. On his release in August 1918 he was again immediately rearrested and sentenced by court martial to two years' hard
labor. He was returned to Wandsworth, where he refused to work or
obey orders, and helped to lead a total strike from October 1918. The
war ended in November, and the authorities were unable to impose discipline on the political prisoners. Among their many activities, Aldred
characteristically gave a series of lectures from his cell. He helped to
organize a hunger strike on New Year's Day, 1919, and after a week was
conditionally released for a month. He refused to return voluntarily to

prison, and instead began a speaking tour until he was yet again rear-rested in March. But after a few days he was unconditionally released in March 1919. He had spent more than two-and-a-half years in custody and, although his health was temporarily damaged, his spirit was never broken. He should be remembered as one of the heroes of the resistance to the First World War.

Rose Witcop continued to produce the *Spur* during his absences, and it was never directly attacked by the authorities like many other anarchist and pacifist papers. Aldred resumed control on his return to a new political situation. The war was over, and the revolution that had come in Russia in 1917 seemed to be spreading across Europe and com-ing to Britain. Aldred briefly became a prominent leader of the strug-gle in the British left to form a unified party to support the Russian Revolution and work for a British Revolution.

Among the many complex developments that eventually led to the emergence of a single Communist Party, in March 1919 the London section of the Socialist Labour Party held a Socialist Unity Conference, which established a broad Communist League with a paper called the *Communist* from May 1919. Aldred was the main organizer for the rest of the year, working again with Sara and campaigning all over the country. But this particular venture was soon swept aside by the rival ambitions of two larger parties—the Workers' Socialist Federation (the succes-sor of Sylvia Pankhurst's East London Federation of the Suffragettes), which took the title of the Communist Party in June 1919 and again in June 1920, and the British Socialist Party (the successor of H. M. Hyndman's Social Democratic Federation), which under strong Russian influence became the core of the Communist Party of Great Britain in August 1920—and the amalgamation of the two (together with other organizations) in January 1921. Revolutionary socialist parties, which didn't take the same route fell apart or fell aside, and Aldred moved on again. (Henry Sara moved in a different direction, soon joining the Communist Party and later being expelled in turn from the Labour Party for being a Communist in 1926, from the Communist Party for being a Trotskyist in 1932, and from the Trotskyist Revolutionary Socialist League for being a pacifist in 1939!)

From the beginning of 1920, Aldred concentrated his activities in Glasgow, then the main centre of revolutionary agitation in Britain, and for a time he was one of the leading propagandists, alongside such figures as John Maclean, William Gallacher, John McGovern, and Emmanuel Shinwell. In May 1920, he joined the Glasgow Anarchist Group, which had been re-formed in 1916, and other anti-parliamentarians in re-forming the Glasgow Communist Group, and after the unification of the Communist Party in January 1921 this became the Anti-Parliamentary Communist Federation (APCF). In February 1921 it published the first issue of a new paper, the *Red Commune*; Aldred was not a member of the editorial committee, because he already had the *Spur*, and he had nothing to do with the content of this issue, though it expressed his policy of abstentionist electoral politics analogous to that of the Irish Nationalists, but the authorities used it to strike at him. In March 1921, its office was raided and three of its members were arrested in Glasgow; at the same time his home was raided and he was arrested in London (illegally, as it happened, since the Scottish warrant wasn't valid) and remanded in custody. In June 1921, they were tried at the Glasgow High Court for seditious libel; he was sentenced to a year's imprisonment and the others to three months' imprisonment each. He was held in Barlinnie Prison for the full twelve months, without counting the time spent in custody on remand or any remission.

The *Red Commune* wasn't published again, and the *Spur* ceased publication in April 1921. Rose Witcop had traveled to Germany in 1920. In 1921 she seems to have traveled to Russia, partly to get support from the Third International; but apparently this was offered only on condition that the APCF joined the Communist Party, which was rejected. This episode marked the beginning of the end of the relationship between Aldred and Rose Witcop. Although he never identified himself with the Communist Party in Britain, however, he continued to support the Russian Bolsheviks for several years, even against socialist and anarchist critics.

After Aldred was released in June 1922, he stood as an anti-parliamentary socialist candidate for Shettleston, Glasgow, in the general election, coming at the bottom of the poll with a few hundred votes—an experience he was to repeat several times during the next forty years. This episode marked the beginning of the decline of his influence in the revolutionary socialist movement.

Meanwhile, Rose Witcop remained in London and concentrated on the movement for contraception propaganda and provision. When Margaret Sanger, the American pioneer (who invented the phrase "birth control"), visited Britain at various times from 1914 to 1920, Guy Aldred and Rose Witcop were among her strongest supporters and closest friends; she shared platforms with them, and she accompanied Rose to Germany in 1920. Her pamphlet *Family Limitation* was printed by anarchists in the United States in 1914 and persecuted by the authorities, and the same thing happened in Britain. From 1920 the

Bakunin Press published a series of British editions. In December 1922, the police raided the London home of Aldred and Rose Witcop and seized 1,720 copies of the third British edition. They were then proceeded against under the Obscene Publications Act—not a prosecution for the criminal offence of publishing an obscene libel, but a summons to show cause why the seized copies should not be destroyed as obscene. The case was heard at the West London Magistrates' Court in January 1923, Rose Witcop being defended by a lawyer but Aldred as always defending himself with great ability. Despite the strength of the defense and the caliber of the expert witnesses, they lost the case and also the appeal at the London Sessions in February 1923; a further appeal to the High Court was abandoned because of lack of money and unity. The police also raided Aldred's Glasgow home in February 1923 and seized more copies of the pamphlet, but no proceedings followed.

The defendants were supported by the old birth control organization, the New Generation League (successor of the Malthusian League), but were repudiated by the new Society for Constructive Birth Control led by Marie Stopes (which provoked Bertrand Russell's resignation from the latter). This was the last known court case in the long campaign for freedom of contraception propaganda in Britain, though suppliers of literature and articles were harassed by the authorities until the Second World War, and it prompted a strong reaction from the labor movement. Rose Witcop was involved in the developments which led in early 1924 to pressure on the new Labour government to allow official encouragement for birth control, an overwhelming vote from the Annual Conference of Labour Women, and the formation of the Workers' Birth Control Group, but she soon began to work independently. The prosecution in her case had concentrated not so much on the text of the pamphlet as on the explicit illustrations, and from late 1924 she published further editions without the illustrations and with a new introduction and an account of the case. She also published British editions of other works by Margaret Sanger and other material on birth control and sex education. In May 1925, she opened a People's Clinic for Birth Control and Social Welfare in West London, with support from local Labour Party and trade union members and from health officials and the local press. Later in 1925 she was threatened by the Special Branch with deportation to Soviet Russia, never having been naturalized, and Aldred reluctantly granted her a last courtesy by going through a legal marriage ceremony with her in Glasgow on February 2, 1926, giving her automatic British nationality; they had no further contact. She ran her clinic, first in Fulham and then in Hammersmith, until she unexpectedly died on July 4, 1932 of peritonitis following an operation for appendicitis. Several articles by and about her were published in the rival *Freedom*, including a long memoir by Aldred in November 1932.

From 1923, Aldred lived in Glasgow, though he used his London address until the beginning of 1926. The APCF had branches elsewhere in Scotland and one in London, but it was essentially a local organization. In May 1923, he began a new paper, the *Commune*, which lasted until May 1929, supplemented by an occasional *Special Anti-Parliamentary Gazette* from May 1926 to May 1929. For ten years, Aldred took a leading part in a series of free speech campaigns in Glasgow, frequently being arrested for speaking in public and fined for obstruction. In September 1931, the Free Speech Committee which coordinated the campaigns was transformed into a wider Council of Action, for which Aldred produced a new paper, the *Council*, in association with the APCF, from October 1931 to May 1933.

The APCF was involved in the development of what became known as Council Communism, an uneasy and unstable combination of anarchism and Marxism with an anti-parliamentarian and syndicalist flavor. It made contact with similar organizations in Europe and America, and it was involved in attempts to form a Fourth International. For a time Aldred was sympathetic with Trotskyism, and he often launched bitter attacks on anarchist individuals and organizations; according to a letter to Keell from Charles E. Ahlgren of the Leicester APCF on November 26, 1924, Aldred was "running with Communism and hunting with Anarchism." In February 1933 the APCF split, and Aldred's group seceded to form the Workers' Open Forum. (The APCF continued, producing a series of papers—*Advance, Workers' Free Press, Fighting Call, Solidarity*—and becoming the Workers' Revolutionary League in 1941, eventually joining a new Workers' Open Forum which was formed in 1942 and continued until the 1950s.)

In 1932, the Independent Labour Party disaffiliated from the Labour Party, of which it had been the largest element, and it immediately became the target of entrism from Communists, Trotskyists, and other revolutionary socialists (a process which continued until it was reabsorbed by the Labour Party half a century later). In February 1934 Aldred joined the Townhead branch of the ILP, in an attempt to support anti-Fascist unity without sacrificing his anti-parliamentarian principles. But his branch soon left the party and joined the Workers' Open Forum in forming a new group, the United Socialist Movement. Aldred had at last achieved stability in unity, but at the expense of numbers or movement, for the USM was virtually a one-man band—or rather a quartet, for he always had the loyal and loving co-operation of Jane Hamilton Patrick (who had been imprisoned in the 1921 trial and who became his companion), Ethel MacDonald, and John Taylor Caldwell—and it stagnated for thirty years, being a populist rather than a socialist or anarchist organization.

Aldred tried several times to start a new paper—the *New Spur* (December 1933–April 1934), a *Socialist May Day Special* (May 1934), the *United Socialist* (October 1934), and the *Attack* (May 1936)—but he was hampered by isolation and poverty. The beginning of the Spanish Civil War in July 1936 revived him, like everyone else on the left. He began a new paper, *Regeneración* (named after the paper produced by the Flores Magón brothers during the Mexican Revolution twenty years before), which appeared (in duplicated form) from July to October 1936 and again (in printed form) from February to March 1937, and then *News from Spain* and the *Barcelona Bulletin* in May 1937. His publications had the advantage that Ethel MacDonald and Jenny Patrick went to work for the CNT-FAI in Spain, the former becoming well-known as a radio broadcaster and then prisoner of the Communists in Barcelona, but the impulse of the Spanish Revolution failed to sustain Aldred's activity, especially as *Spain and the World* grew in influence.

Aldred produced a series of *BE Leaflets* against the British Empire Exhibition at Bellahouston from January to February 1938, and still tried to start a new paper—the *Word* in May 1938 and *Hyde Park* in September 1938 (the latter connected with a free speech campaign in London). Then his situation was unexpectedly changed by the death in August 1938 of Walter Strickland, leaving most of his fortune to be used by Aldred for peace propaganda. Only a small proportion could be recovered from the various countries where it had been invested, but this was enough for him to revive the Bakunin Press as the Strickland Press and to revive the *Word* in May 1939. In 1940, he began his last series of publications—the "*Word* Library"—which included his third autobiography; the series was also bound up as *Essays in Revolt*.

Within a few months, the Second World War began. Aldred opposed this as strongly as its predecessor, and the *Word* became a leading anti-war paper. Aldred hadn't been involved in the formal pacifist movement before (though he was elected to the Anti-Conscription Committee of the No Conscription Fellowship immediately after the First World War), but now he was for a time a leading member of the No Conscription League. He was also closely associated with the Marquess of Tavistock (later the Duke of Bedford), a supporter of Social Credit who took his pacifism almost as far as becoming a fellow-traveler with Fascism. Above all he was a consistent advocate and practitioner of free speech, making the *Word* a forum for all kinds of social and political dissent.

After the Second World War Aldred remained on the fringe of the left, an eccentric figure who jokingly called himself "the Guy they All Dread," though the emotion he inspired was exasperation rather than fear. He continued to speak regularly and to produce the *Word*, and an occasional *Word Quarterly* in 1950 and 1951. He called himself a humanist and established friendly relations with the ethical movement. He was active in the world government movement, and formed a shadowy organization of world federalists. After the death of Stalin, he once again became a fellow-traveler with Soviet Russia. He continued to abuse all and sundry on the left who broke his rigid rules of correct conduct—including many leading anarchists, and even the editors of *War Commentary* at the time of their trial in 1945. On the other hand, he fought several elections as an independent socialist candidate. He stood in Central Glasgow as a peace candidate in the 1945 general election, and came bottom of the poll. In the 1948 Camlachie by-election he stood as a world government candidate, and came second to bottom. He stood as a peace candidate in Central Glasgow in the general elections of 1950 and 1951, and twice more came bottom of the poll.

Towards the end he began to mellow, living increasingly in the past and treating old antagonists with more respect. During the 1940s and 1950s he suffered extra difficulties when the Strickland Press was blacklisted by the print unions for being a non-union shop (the ironic situation of so many left-wing printers), and he was deeply affected by the death of Ethel MacDonald in 1960. During the last eight years of his life he wrote the final though still incomplete version of his autobiography. In 1962 he stood as a peace candidate for the last time in the Woodside by-election, and for the last time came bottom of the poll.

Aldred suffered a heart attack in January 1963, but he continued to speak and write to the end, dying of heart failure in the Western Infirmary, Glasgow, on October 17, 1963. A memorial meeting was held in Glasgow on November 3, 1963, and many obituaries were published. Aldred left his body for medical research, and it was eventually cremated in Glasgow on May 4, 1964. John Taylor Caldwell continued the *Word* until May 1965 and occasional issues of the *Word Quarterly* from 1965 to 1967, and finally closed the Strickland Press in May 1968. Large numbers of Aldred's publications remained in circulation for many years, but he left no viable organization or tradition, only the memory of an extraordinarily courageous but essentially solitary man whose vanity and oddity prevented him from taking the part which his ability and energy seemed to create for him in the revolutionary socialist movement.

SOURCES

Aldred wrote four versions of his autobiography—*From Anglican Boy-Preacher to Anarchist Socialist Impossiblist* (1908); *Dogmas Discarded* (1913); *Dogmas Discarded* (2 volumes, 1940); *No Traitor's Gait!* (19 parts in 3 volumes, 1955–63)—but never got beyond 1932. Autobiographical material also appears in some of his other publications—*Socialism and Parliament* (1923), revised as *Socialism or Parliament* (1926, 1934, 1942); *For Communism* (1935), revised as *Communism* (1943); *Rex v. Aldred* (1948)—and in many issues of his various periodicals.

Unpublished manuscripts: Aldred Collection, Mitchell Library, Glasgow; Home Office Papers, Public Record Office, Kew; Nettlau and Freedom Collections, International Institute of Social History, Amsterdam; Margaret Sanger Papers, Library of Congress, Washington; Marie Stopes Papers, British Library, London. There is an unpublished biographical study by John Taylor Caldwell in three volumes—"The Red Evangel" (1976), "The Essential Aldred" (1983), "Come Dungeons Dark" (1986). First-hand biographical material appears in publications by other authors: R. M. Fox, *Drifting Men* (1930) and *Smoky Crusade* (1937); William Gallacher, *Revolt on the Clyde* (1936); John McGovern, *Neither Fear nor Favor* (1960); Hastings Russell, Duke of Bedford, *The Years of Transition* (1949); Margaret Sanger, *An Autobiography* (1938).

Originally published in Freedom, *January 10, 1981.*

23
DOROTHY DAY

THE DEATH LAST MONTH OF ONE OF THE GREATEST ANARCHISTS, PACI-fists, Christians, Americans, women—*people*—of our age has been al-most entirely ignored by the media in this country; but that is all the more reason why we should salute the memory of our old comrade Dorothy Day, the main figure for nearly half a century in the Catholic Worker movement in the United States.

She was born on November 8, 1897 in New York, and was brought up in California and Chicago. Her father was a journalist of Scotch-Irish Presbyterian ancestry, and her mother was of American Episcopalian ancestry. Neither of them had strong political or religious convictions, but from an early age their daughter combined left-wing political opinions with intense religious faith and deep personal attach-ments. When she went to the University of Illinois in 1914 she became active in the socialist movement, and in 1916 she left college without graduating to work as a journalist for various left-wing papers in New York, where she became a prominent figure in the bohemian intelligen-tsia of Greenwich Village.

In 1917 she was arrested for the first time at a suffrage demonstra-tion in Washington, and was imprisoned and went on hunger strike. In 1918, she trained as a nurse, and in 1919 she traveled in Europe. She continued to work as a journalist in Chicago and New Orleans until the success of her novel *The Eleventh Virgin* in 1924 enabled her to buy a cottage on Staten Island. There she lived for a time with an anarchist called Forster Battingham, by whom she had a daughter in 1927. By this time she had completed a long private journey from her parents' Protestantism through agnosticism and mysticism to Roman Catholicism, and at the end of the year she had herself and her baby baptized. This meant the end of her relationship with Battingham and indeed of all sexual relations; it also meant that she was ready for what became her life work of poverty, chastity, and disobedience.

For a few years, Dorothy Day concentrated on bringing up her child and continued to do various jobs (including a spell as a Hollywood scriptwriter), but in 1932 she joined the Washington hunger march that marked the worst trough of the Great Depression, and then she met Peter Maurin. He was an extraordinary talker and writer on social and political issues, who called himself "an apostle on the bum," living as a tramp and spreading the word by talking to anyone who would listen and by writing what he described as "Easy Essays." He was influenced by the radical Catholic thinkers in his native France—Péguy, Mounier, Bloy, Maritain—and by the more positive anarchists—especially Kropotkin—and he had developed a combination of revolutionary Christianity and religious anarchism, which was to be practiced by direct personal action and was labeled "the Green Revolution."

Maurin persuaded Dorothy Day to start a new paper, and in May 1933 the monthly *Catholic Worker* began with funds of less than one dollar. Within a year it was selling tens of thousands of copies, and within a few more years it was selling hundreds of thousands. It advocated Christian communism or Catholic anarchism, and was accused by Catholics of being a Communist front and by Communists of being a Catholic front. It not only survived, but became the centre of a movement, its own centre being Dorothy Day's regular column.

The Catholic Workers, led by Day and Maurin, always had difficulties with the rest of the Church and the rest of the left. They worked with anyone who would work with them, and took money from anyone who would give them money. They attacked poverty by giving free food, clothing and shelter to anyone who asked for it; they supported strikes by feeding or joining the pickets; they tried to stop unemployment by working; they tried to build a new society by rebuilding themselves; and they established independent farms in the oldest Christian and American traditions to show how it could all work. "We want no revolution," said Dorothy Day, "we want the brotherhood of man"; but what she meant by brotherhood was more revolutionary than what almost revolutionaries had in mind.

The Catholic Workers were always good Catholics in matters of faith and morals, but they were always uncomfortable. They refused to take sides in the Spanish Civil War, not being willing either to support Franco or to criticize the Church. They protested against the oppression of the blacks in the United States, which was supported by Catholic extremists. They protested against the growth of anti-Semitism in the

United States, which was similarly supported by Catholic extremists. And they not only refused to support the Second World War, but actively opposed it and the conscription that came with it. Their pacifist line hardened after Hiroshima, and they were among the founders of the American nuclear disarmament movement in the 1940s. They were also involved in the civil rights movement and the resistance to the Vietnam War.

Maurin died in 1949, and other men and women came and went, the most striking being Ammon Hennacy, who was involved from the 1930s to the 1960s and who was the best-known anarchist pacifist in the country. But Dorothy Day stayed, the one firm pivot around whom the paper and the movement revolved. As she became older, she seemed more respectable, and she received official honors from her Church, especially during the papacy of John XXIII. She also received unofficial honors from other quarters. In 1952, Dwight MacDonald wrote a profile of her in the *New Yorker* in which he called her a saint; in 1962 an atheist wrote in the *Catholic Worker*, "Thank God for people like Dorothy Day!" In 1963, she spoke to the London Anarchists during one of her rare visits to this country, and said nothing we would want to disagree with. To the end, she did more than almost anyone for the cause we have in common. In 1973, she was arrested for the, last time, demonstrating for the Chicano farm workers. She died on November 29, 1980 in New York.

As well as hundreds of articles and talks, Dorothy Day produced several books, including two volumes of autobiography—*From Union Square to Rome* (1988) and *The Long Loneliness* (1952)—and an account of the Catholic Worker movement—*Loaves and Fishes* (1963). William D. Miller produced an authorized biographical study—*A Harsh and Dreadful Love* (1973). A long obituary appeared in the *New York Times* on December 1, 1980.

Originally published in Freedom, *April 2, 1994.*

24

THE PAST FEW MONTHS HAVE WITNESSED THE DEATHS OF THREE intellectuals from Continental Europe who had idiosyncratic relations with anarchism.

Leopard Kohr died in February 1994. He was born in Austria in 1909, and studied in Innsbruck and Vienna. He witnessed the Spanish Civil War as a journalist, learning about anarchism at first hand, and then worked in Paris. When Austria was annexed by Nazi Germany he fled into exile across the Atlantic, working in the United States, then Canada, and then the United States again. He worked from 1946 to 1954 at Rutgers University, where he specialized in the problems of political size, advocating much smaller units than nations, let alone empires. His book, *The Breakdown of Nations,* was published in Britain through the initiative of Herbert Read in 1957, at a time when large size was in fashion, and he never received the credit he deserved. One of his chapters was "The Beauty of the Small," but it was the book by his pupil Fritz Schumacher, *Small is Beautiful* (1973) that caught the change in fashion and became a popular slogan.

Kohr worked from 1955 to 1973 at Puerto Rico University, where he contributed to local papers a series of essays later collected as *The Inner City* (1989). He then worked from 1968 to 1972 at University College Aberystwyth, where he advocated independence for Wales. He also advocated the independence of the islands of the West Indies, but Anguilla's secession from St Kitts in 1969 led to a British invasion by Harold Wilson's government! He wrote several more books—*The Overdeveloped Nations, Development without Aid, The Academic Inn*— and eventually saw his ideas coming into fashion. He called himself an anarchist, but was really a latter-day distributist, being more interested in the scale and spirit of institutions than their shape or structure, and he was aligned with *Resurgence* and the Fourth World movement rather than the anarchist movement. He retired to a Gloucestershire village, where his last years were marred by persecution from local vandals—supporting his thesis that our "mass society" destroys the "translucent communities" which regulate social behavior. He was a very convivial man, with a wide circle of friends and a growing circle of admirers.

Paul Feyerabend also died in February 1994. He was born in Vienna in 1924, and during the Second World War served in the German army on the Eastern Front, being permanently crippled by wounds received during the retreat from Russia. He completed his education in Austria and was first a distinguished theoretical physicist and then an eccentric philosopher of science. He worked in England for a time and then at the University of California, Berkeley, from 1958 to 1990. He was influenced by Karl Popper and then by Imre Lakatos, and moved away from scientific and philosophical orthodoxy towards unorthodoxy and indeed perversity. At the same time he drifted politically to the left, and turned away from the academic community to the young people of the New Left, in Europe as much as America. In 1975 his book *Against Method* made him famous and infamous, and he became one of the intellectual leaders of the growing unorthodoxy of the past twenty years. He called himself an anarchist, but was closer to Dadaism and nihilism than to traditional anarchism, and he approached irrationalism and obscurantism. His later books included *Science in a Free Society* (1978) and *Farewell to Reason* (1987). He taught that there are no rules and that nothing can be known, but resented it when his own ideas were treated accordingly. He was as eccentric in his behavior as in his work, but was widely liked as a person even by those who disliked his doctrines.

Alfred Reynolds died in December 1993. His real name was Alfred Reinhold, and he was born in Hungary in 1907. As a young man he was involved in the literary and artistic life of Budapest, but in 1936 he emigrated to escape the Horthy dictatorship and settled in Britain. During the Second World War he worked for military intelligence, and in 1944 he was given the job of de-Nazifying young German prisoners of war. His method of patient argument succeeded in converting several of them not only from Nazism but also to his own idiosyncratic form of philosophical libertarianism. He earned his living as a minor civil servant, and when he retired he founded the Cambridge School of English. During the 1940s he gathered some of his colleagues and disciples in the Bridge Circle, a private discussion group with an internal magazine, which for a time during the 1950s and 1960s played a small but significant part in the radicalization of a new generation. Reynolds would make contact with young people, draw them into correspondence or conversation, and gently try to clear their minds of cant. As a result the Bridge Circle involved more participants, the *London Letter* was circulated to more readers, and Reynolds himself occasionally spoke at public meetings (using the name Alfred Rajk). Some of his associates later became well known (Colin Wilson often wrote about him), and a few became anarchists. He himself never changed, reading very widely, thinking very deeply, and writing a series of essays and books. The most accessible of the latter was *Pilate's Question*, published in 1964 and in a revised and enlarged form in 1983. His models were such paradoxical thinkers as Heraclitus and Lao Tzu, Jesus and Nietzsche, and he himself exerted a quiet influence on several people who were repelled by all the orthodoxies of our age.

At the very end of his life he unexpectedly became famous in his native country, following the rediscovery of the *First and Last Book of Poetry*, which he had published in 1932. He was hailed as the greatest living Hungarian poet, and invited back in the last weeks of his life to attend readings of his writings and make a television program about his life.

Originally published in Freedom, *November 30, 1963.*

25
THE ASSASSINATION OF PRESIDENT KENNEDY: DOES IT REALLY MATTER?

ANYONE WHO BELIEVES WHAT THE PAPERS AND THE PRIESTS AND THE POL-iticians say might think that the assassination of President Kennedy on November 22 was a major event in the history of the United States, of the West, of all mankind even. The papers and the priests and the politicians have repeated the stale platitudes we hear whenever a famous man dies (just wait until Churchill's long and wicked life ends at last), and some have excelled themselves. From what we have been told during the last week, Kennedy was a world savior and his death is a world disaster.

Fortunately for our sanity, there have been some good moments in all this nonsense. There was *Pravda* calling Kennedy "an outstanding statesman," and Khruschev calling his death "a heavy blow to all who want peace." There was the Archbishop of Canterbury calling him "a statesman of Christian ideals," and Franco calling his death "a great loss for all the Christian world of the West" (hear that, Jesus?) There was John Masefield, the Poet Laureate, at his worst—or best—in the *Times*. And there was the poor old *Daily Worker* getting its wires crossed: President Kennedy's assassination is the result of the vicious hate campaign worked up by the US racialist barbarians. In this atmosphere that was also poisoned by the US nuclear maniacs, the assassin's blow was delivered in the traditional cowardly way of US reaction (hear that, Czolgosz and Zangara, you cowardly reactionaries!)

Now *Freedom* is written by and for people who don't believe what the papers and the priests and the politicians say. We didn't think Kennedy was a major figure, and we don't think his death is a major disaster. Of course there was a tragedy—for his friends and family, for those who liked or loved him—but this is the human tragedy that recurs when the least of men dies. There is no political tragedy, except the proof that so many people are still slaves to the cult of personality, and still project their emotions on to stars instead of relating them to the real world. Kennedy's death was a "happening," not a real event. As Mr. Macmillan once said about something else, it was all got up by the press. It is only important because so many people make it important, because they prefer fantasy to facts.

Let's look at the facts. Kennedy wasn't a very bad President, but he wasn't a very good one either. About freedom, he talked big and acted small. He was prepared on two occasions to sacrifice our lives to save— that is, to destroy—Cuba, but he wasn't ever prepared to sacrifice his own position to help the poor, the old, the sick, and the downtrodden of his country or the rest of the world. He talked about free medical care for the aged and civil rights for the Negroes, but after three years the aged are still going without free medical care and the Negroes are still going without civil rights. He made a great noise when the East German Government tried to stop its subjects going to West Berlin, but he made no noise at all when the American State Department tried to stop his own subjects going to Cuba. He sent as much help as he could to the oppressors in southern Vietnam, and as little as he could to the oppressed in the southern states of his own country. He loved to open his mouth about the free world, but he kept it shut about old Joe McCarthy. He was a real phony. We owe him nothing.

These facts become clearer if we consider a man who died in the same country and on the same day as Kennedy. Aldous Huxley was a writer who meant what he said. When he believed that something was right, he said so and did it. He decided that it was more important to warn than to amuse, so he began writing serious books. When he believed that something was wrong, he said so and stopped doing it. He decided that it was better to be conquered than to fight, so he became a pacifist. He was a real hero. We owe him much. Two hundred years ago, Henry Fielding said that "greatness consists in bringing all manner of mischief on mankind, and goodness in removing it from them." Huxley, who was a good man, will be remembered when Kennedy, who was a great man, is forgotten.

Perhaps it is easy for us, who were never taken in by Kennedy's life, not to be taken in by his death. We can just say we aren't sorry he died. But it isn't so easy for us to speak about the manner of his death. We can't just say we aren't sorry he died that way. In the past, anarchists shave assassinated many rulers—such as President Carnot of France, Prime Minister Canovas of Spain, Empress Elizabeth of Austria, King Umberto of Italy, and President McKinley of the United States—and, though most anarchists have always condemned the technique of terrorism, few have ever condemned an individual terrorist. We think that anyone who tries to rise above his fellow men deserves to be pulled down again, and we know that rulers have been responsible for more violence than all the assassins there ever were.

Today we see assassination as a crude and clumsy way of removing a ruler who isn't actually a dictator—as Castro said, "we shouldn't consider this method a correct form of battle." It is different for dictators. When David Pratt tried to assassinate Dr. Verwoerd, we said it was "too bad he missed" and we expressed the hope that no dictator would sleep in peace. We don't welcome Kennedy's death as we would have welcomed—and would still welcome—Verwoerd's. He wasn't a bad ruler, as rulers go, and he certainly wasn't a dictator. He was just a figurehead, like Khrushchev, with a lot less power than he and everyone else thought, and a lot more prestige than was good for him or anyone else. It was his pretension that made him so unbearable. But his assassination seems rather irrelevant.

Nor quite irrelevant, though. We can't help drawing some sort of lesson from the sudden downfall of one of our enemies. We can't help noticing how all the king's horses and all the king's men couldn't put Humpty together again. The resources of modern science and security couldn't save Kennedy from his assassin nor he from Kennedy's "avenger." The bombs and bullets our rulers threaten us with threaten them, too. They're only human, just like us. They're only there because we all put them there and keep them there. If we really wanted to, we could take away all their lives. But there's no need to do that—we could take away all their power, if we really wanted to.

If assassination is a crude and clumsy way of removing rulers, we must work out a better way. If we don't consider it a correct form of battle, we must use the correct form. Until then, we can't condemn someone who goes out and does what we just talk about. We shouldn't cry for Kennedy or crow over him. We should consider why Johnson is there in his place. Adenauer to Erhard, Macmillan to Home, Kennedy to Johnson—will it never end? People will go on believing what the papers and the priests and the politicians say until they are persuaded to believe the truth. Who shall persuade them? Next year there will be a general election in this country. The people of Britain will go out in their millions and vote for new rulers. What, short of assassination, are we going to do to stop this happening next year and in the years to come? How do *we* propose to get rid of rulers? The assassination of President Kennedy doesn't really matter, unless it becomes an excuse for more McCarthyism. What does matter is the survival of all the other rulers of the world.

Originally published in Freedom, *October 4, 1997.*

26
DIANA AS STAR AND SPECTACLE

MOST SOCIALIST AND ANARCHIST COMMENT HAS MISSED THE MOST REL-
evant point about the life and death of Princess Diana. This is that
Diana was the most spectacular example of the "spectacular society"
since the concept was launched.

When the Situationist International was formed by a handful of
intellectuals, forty years ago, the most important negative item of its
ideology was that we are no longer subjected to material and economic
so much as to intellectual and cultural oppression, that we are no longer
deprived of a sufficient standard of living so much as of a satisfactory
style of life, that we no longer experience the world directly in our own
actions and reactions so much as observe it indirectly through the im-
ages manufactured and projected by the mass media, that we are no
longer integrated members of a living community so much as isolated
spectators in a society of spectacle.

Thus when Guy Debord, the main ideological figure among the
Situationists, published his book *The Society of the Spectacle*, thirty years ago,
he opened it with a parody of the opening of Karl Marx's *Capital*: "The
whole life of the societies in which the conditions of modern production
prevail is presented as an immense accumulation of spectacles. Everything
that was once directly lived has moved away into a representation."

The Situationists described and denounced a wide variety of spectacular representations in advertising, periodicals, cinema, and television; we could now add more in videos, computers, lotteries and sport.
The mass media have become the main medium through which more
and more people perceive the world and even perceive themselves. The
image of the world transmitted through films and plays, pop songs and
soap operas, advertisements and interviews, scandals and disasters tends
to become more significant to many people than the world itself.

This isn't a new phenomenon. It is a common human characteristic to find more sense of reality in literature or music or art than in everyday life, because imaginary adventure and beauty and truth are more reliable and often more intense than ordinary events. Nowadays it is increasingly common to find a sense of virtual reality through various electronic means, because of the increasing technical efficiency and economic advantages of such means.

It is also a common human characteristic to make sense of critical episodes of life and death through fairy tale and myth rather than factual narrative and through collective ceremony rather than individual reflection. Fantasy is easier than fact, stories are easier than histories, ritual is easier than reality, symbols are easier than things themselves. Nowadays, as traditional forms of discourse and drama and belief and behaviour lose their force, many people feel the need for other kinds of displacement activity to discharge affect and anxiety.

Unfortunately the Situationists, as avant-garde intellectuals, brought into their ideology so much personal and political confusion and behaved in such disruptive and destructive ways that they became little more than a spectacle themselves, though they had their brief encounter with glory in the French "events" of 1968. But the concept of the spectacle still has great force, and without adopting all the rest of the Situationist baggage it should be adapted to the developing pathology of our society.

Unfortunately the Situationists, as left-wing intellectuals, made the mistake of supposing that the mass media are part of some kind of class conspiracy, of a process of brainwashing, of conscious manipulation of the masses. But this approach tells us nothing about the true nature of cultural life in modern society, and if we can't understand this aspect of the world we can't hope to change it.

It is too simple to refer just to media hypocrisy and mass hysteria. The people who produce and consume the mass media are not just hypocrites and hysterics. The media manipulate themselves as well as the masses, and are in turn manipulated by the masses in a process of mutual mystification. The whole gigantic phenomenon is not to be understood in terms of political paranoia.

Consider on a much smaller scale the amount of hypocrisy and hysteria involved in editing and reading *Freedom*. Consider how much anarchism is affected or infected by fantasy and myth. Consider how much so-called anarchist so-called activity is unrealistic and irrational. Consider how each of us actually engages with other people and wider society, and actually responds to the ups and downs of everyday life.

Diana is a much more complex figure than may be supposed. She belongs to a growing pantheon of celebrities who are not icons, as they are sometimes called, because they represent only themselves, but are stars, of the sky as well as the screen, very distant but also very close. Debord saw the celebrity, the star as the supreme illustration of the spectacle, the final and fatal attempt to overcome the banality of everyday life:

> By concentrating in himself or herself the image of a popular role, the celebrity, the spectacular representation of a living human being, concentrates this banality. The condition of the star is the specialization of the apparently lived; the object of identification with shallow apparent life, which must compensate for the fragments of actually lived productive specializations. Celebrities exist in order to represent various types of life-styles and styles of comprehending society, free to express themselves globally. They incarnate the inaccessible result of social labor by miming the sub-products of this labour, which are magically projected above it as its goal: power and holidays, decision and consumption, which are at the beginning and end of an undiscussed process. On the one hand, governmental power personalizes itself in a pseudo-celebrity; on the other, the star of consumption gets itself elected by plebiscite as a pseudo-power over the lived.

(The Hegelian/Marxist style is sadly typical.)

The cult of Diana alive wasn't just invented by the ruling class or the mass media; after all, it did great damage to both. It was conjured up from a general and genuine yearning for a vision of beauty and youth and wealth and health and glamor and glory beyond what is possible or practicable in our ugly and brutal age. And the cult of Diana dead, however much it was manufactured and manipulated, provided a catharsis of genuine grief and guilt and real regret and resentment. The extraordinary scenes before, during and after the funeral were extraordinary not just in themselves but in the fact that they were unpaid, unplanned, unformed, unorganized, unregulated, unstructured, unsponsored. Deep and strong social forces were at work for a moment.

Many of us felt much, most of us felt something, few of us felt nothing. Whatever we may feel about it, the spectacle of Diana is an essential part of the life of millions of people in capitalist societies at the end of the twentieth century. As with religion, if we can't understand what happened and what it means we are doomed to perpetual obscurity.

Originally published in New Society, *June 14, 1979.*

27
THE RIGHT TO BE WRONG

I WANT TO MAKE A STAND AGAINST THE LAWS LIMITING FREEDOM OF EXpression; and in particular against the law limiting freedom of expression on the subject of race—partly because it happens to be the newest, partly because it is supported by so many people who ought to know better, and finally because it does no good.

My interest in these laws is not that of a professional lawyer who uses them or a professional agitator who abuses them, but that of an ordinary person who finds that he has broken nearly all of them in the normal course of argument and journalism. Indeed it is difficult not to break them, often without knowing it, if you want to say or write anything about anything worth saying or writing anything about. Just look at them.

The law of defamation—or personal libel—would make sense if it were a matter of protecting innocent individuals from malicious and inaccurate insult. But it is far more a matter of the rich frightening the poor with civil actions, or of the strong frightening the weak with criminal prosecutions, involving huge costs rather than damages or fines. Ordinary people hardly ever get satisfaction from libel proceedings. Rather than try to make it easier for them to do so, it would be better to see how other liberal countries manage with a feebler law and a freer press. There is a legal fiction that defamation involves arousing unjustified hatred, ridicule or contempt. But in practice much hatred, ridicule and contempt is aroused with justification and without litigation. Much so-called defamation involves nothing more than telling the truth.

The law of obscenity—or sexual libel—would make sense if it were a matter of protecting innocent individuals from intolerable and unavoidable offence. But it is far more a matter of preserving traditional morality against new ideas, and of persecuting unpopular minorities.

Obscenity is in the eyes of the beholder; to the pure, all things are impure. It is a matter of taste; and what can be said about the taste of people who hunt pornography just to condemn it?

There is a legal fiction that an obscene publication is one which tends to deprave or corrupt those into whose hands it is likely to fall. But in practice there is no need to show that anyone has been or will be depraved or corrupted; and what matters is whether magistrates or jurors feel shocked or disgusted. Most of what is prosecuted as obscene neither depraves nor corrupts; and most of what both depraves or corrupts is never prosecuted. On the other hand, there is the defence of public good, if the obscene publication has literary, artistic, scientific or scholarly merit. Whatever lawyers may think, it is obvious to outsiders that something likely to corrupt or deprave will do so more rather than less effectively if it is well-written or clever or beautiful.

The law of blasphemy—or religious libel—would make sense if it were a matter of protecting innocent individuals from intolerable and unavoidable offence. But again it is far more a matter of preserving traditional doctrine against new ideas and of persecuting unpopular minorities. The authorities have wisely been reluctant to use this law for nearly two centuries, so it has generally been left to religious fanatics to use it. After the House of Lords judgment, dismissing the *Gay News* appeal in February, it now seems stronger than for more than a century. There is apparently no need to prove any intention to blaspheme, or any tendency to a breach of the peace. All that is necessary is to shock or outrage believers in, or sympathizers with, the state religion. The situation would be made worse rather than better by extending such protection to all religions.

The law of sedition—or political libel—would make sense if it were a matter of protecting the community from civil strife. But it, too, is far more a matter of preserving traditional obedience against new dissent and of persecuting unpopular minorities. This is another bad old law which has fallen out of use; but it could be resurrected without any difficulty. In the meantime, it operates through other more recent laws—such as those against "incitement to disaffection," or in defense of "official secrets" or "public order"—though at least the cases that the authorities win in the courts of law, they lose in the court of public opinion.

But now there is a new branch of the law of sedition—or social libel—in the special area of race. The traditional definition of sedition includes such actions as "to raise discontent or disaffection in Her Majesty's subjects, or to promote feelings of ill-will and hostility between different classes of such subjects." So incitement to race as well as class hatred could always have been dealt with under the sedition law. Indeed it was, in the case of a blatantly anti-Semitic editor in 1947—but the prosecution failed. Public incitement to race hatred, as well as class hatred, could also have been dealt with under the Public Order Act, 1936. Indeed this act was passed for that very purpose, when the victims were Jewish rather than colored. Nevertheless, after pressure for thirty years, this form of libel got a law to itself in the Race Relations Acts from 1965 to 1976, all brought in by Labour governments.

These acts include provisions not just to deal with racial discrimination by pressure and agreement, but also to deal with incitement to racial hatred by prosecution and imprisonment. This part of the law is disguised as an amendment to the Public Order Act (though it goes beyond public order), and it is limited by allowing cases to be brought only by consent of the Attorney-General, which has restricted its use. The 1965 act banned "threatening, abusive or insulting" words, uttered or published with "intent to stir up hatred" against any race. During the twelve years it was in force, there were only seventeen prosecutions (several involving more than one person), and only eleven convictions.

The rate of both prosecutions and convictions fell after a few years, when the Conservatives came to power. But the law was strengthened after a few more years, with the return to a Labour government, and the element of intent was removed. The 1976 act bans "threatening, abusive or insulting" words uttered or published "in a case where, having regard to all the circumstances, hatred is likely to be stirred up against any racial group in Great Britain." Since the 1976 act came into force two years ago, there have been only a dozen prosecutions; and again some acquittals in the face of the evidence. This has led to more proposals to make the law even stronger and wider—although that would make it even more unpopular, and although that is unlikely to happen with a change back from a Labour to a Conservative government.

I think that the solution lies in the opposite direction, and I suggest that the law should be repealed. I am depressed to find that so many people who oppose the enforcement of political, religious and sexual orthodoxy by law support the enforcement of social and racial orthodoxy. (I suppose the next step will be to extend the Sex Discrimination Act to cover incitement to sex hatred.) I am depressed to find that opposition to this law comes mainly from the right, from people who believe not so much in freedom of expression as in freedom for racism.

In theory it seems to make sense to say about something unpleasant that there ought to be a law against it. But in practice such laws generally do more harm than good. For fifty years, a few people who believe in civil liberty as well as racial equality have warned that such a law would indeed be harmful. I think it is time to listen.

It is argued that the law draws a line, and sets an example. I argue that it draws the wrong line by directing attention at a few extreme racists, and that nothing is gained by making an example of Colin Jordan and Michael Abdul Malik in the 1960s, or of Kingsley Read and Martin Webster in the 1970s.

It is argued that racial hatred led to the slavery of blacks in America and the extermination of Jews in Germany. I argue that there is no evidence of such an effect here and now, and that our problem is not overt but covert racism.

It is argued that racists should not be allowed to express their views. I argue that everyone should be allowed to express any view, and that the time to take action is when views lead to actions.

It is argued that freedom should not be given to those who threaten freedom. I argue that this is the test of freedom.

It is argued that juries are reluctant to convict racists because of common racism. I argue that it might be because of common sense— that ordinary people can see the absurdity of using the law against states of mind and the danger of turning it against all sorts of things from Professor Eysenck's research to Dave Allen's jokes (or this article).

It is argued that the law against racial discrimination needs to be balanced by a law against racial hatred. I argue that the constructive work of the Race Relations Acts in educating people out of discrimination is not supported, but undermined, by their negative work in punishing people for prejudice.

It is argued that racist parties should not be allowed to hold public meetings or to make political broadcasts. I argue that all organizations should have the same freedom of expression, right or left, nice or nasty.

It is argued that racial hatred is a bad thing. I argue that, although this is true, it is not illegal, and that incitement to racial hatred should not be illegal either.

It is argued that some things go beyond what is acceptable. I argue that, although this is true, it is a matter of social morality rather than political censorship.

The criminal law of racial—as of all other kinds of—libel creates not repentant sinners but defiant martyrs. Punishing racists makes both them and us worse rather than better. It projects on to scapegoats the guilt for the prejudice that pervades our society. It points at other people's beams to hide our own motes. The punishment and prevention of racism are not complementary but contradictory. What keeps racism alive is not what a person like Robert Relf says, or what the National Front does, but what is said and done to them—not their pathological actions but our equally pathological reactions to these.

I have no doubt that the law against incitement to racial hatred has increased rather than decreased racial hatred; has polarized, rather than pacified, the two sides, and has made this country more intolerant, rather than more tolerant. More people have been hurt and killed in race riots since than before the Race Relations Acts. More of them will be killed if we don't learn to behave sensibly.

I think we have been making a mistake for fourteen years. Freedom of speech means the freedom to say unspeakable things. Liberty means license, and freedom is real only when it is abused. We must learn that mere words don't harm anyone, and that we should turn to the much more serious evils in our midst. The way to get rid of racism is not to make laws against it, but to take away the reasons for it.

Originally published in Raven *25 (Spring 1994).*

28
ANARCHISM AND RELIGION

FOR THE PRESENT PURPOSE, ANARCHISM IS DEFINED AS THE POLITICAL and social ideology which argues that human groups can and should exist without instituted authority, and especially as the historical anarchist movement of the past two hundred years; and religion is defined as the belief in the existence and significance of supernatural being(s), and especially as the prevailing Judaeo-Christian system of the past two thousand years. My subject is the question: Is there a necessary connection between the two and, if so, what is it? The possible answers are as follows: there may be no connection, if beliefs about human society and the nature of the universe are quite independent; there may be a connection, if such beliefs are interdependent; and, if there is a connection, it may be either positive, if anarchism and religion reinforce each other, or negative, if anarchism and religion contradict each other.

The general assumption is that there is a negative connection—logical, because divine and human authority reflect each other; and psychological, because the rejection of human and divine authority, of political and religious orthodoxy, reflect each other. Thus the French *Encyclopédie Anarchiste* (1932) included an article on Atheism by Gustave Brocher: "An anarchist, who wants no all-powerful master on earth, no authoritarian government, must necessarily reject the idea of an omnipotent power to whom everything must be subjected; if he is consistent, he must declare himself an atheist." And the centenary issue of the British anarchist paper *Freedom* (October 1986) contained an article by Barbara Smoker (president of the National Secular Society) entitled "Anarchism Implies Atheism." As a matter of historical fact the negative connection has indeed been the norm—anarchists are generally non-religious and are frequently anti-religious, and the standard anarchist slogan is the phrase coined by the (non-anarchist) socialist Auguste Blanqui in 1880:

"*Ni dieu ni maître!*" (Neither God nor master!) But the full answer is not so simple.

Thus it is reasonable to argue that there is no necessary connection. Beliefs about the nature of the universe, of life on this planet, of this species, of purpose and values and morality, and so on, may be independent of beliefs about the desirability and possibility of liberty in human society. It is quite possible to believe at the same time that there is a spiritual authority and that there should not be a political authority. But it is also reasonable to argue that there is a necessary connection, whether positive or negative.

The argument for a positive connection is that religion has libertarian effects, even if established Churches seldom do. Religion may check politics, the Church may balance the State, divine sanction may protect oppressed people. In Classical Greece, Antigone (in the Oedipus myth) appeals to divine law in her individual rebellion against the human law of the ruler Creon.* Socrates (the greatest figure in Greek thought) appealed to the divine demon within him to inspire his individual judgment. Zeno (the founder of the Stoic school of philosophy) appealed to a higher authority than the State. Within Judaism, the Prophets of the Old Testament challenged Kings and proclaimed what is known as the "Social Gospel." One of the most eloquent texts in the Bible is Hannah's song when she conceives Samuel, which is echoed by Mary's song when she conceives Jesus—the *Magnificat*:

> My soul doth magnify the Lord; and my spirit hath rejoiced in God my Savior . . . He hath shewed strength with his arm; he hath scattered the proud in the imagination of their hearts. He hath put down the mighty from their seats; and hath exalted the humble and meek. He hath filled the hungry with good things; and the rich he hath sent empty away.

Within Christianity, Jesus came for the poor and weak, and the early Christians resisted the Roman State. When Christianity became the established ideology in its turn, religious heretics challenged both Church and State. Medieval heresies helped to destroy the old system—the Albigensians and the Waldensians, the Brotherhood of the Free Spirit and the Taborites in Bohemia, the Anabaptists in Germany and Switzerland.

---

* In Sophocles's play *Antigone* (c. 440 BC), Creon actually says in response to her rebellion, "There is no greater evil than anarchy"—one of the earliest uses of the word in the pejorative double sense.

This pattern may be seen in Britain. John Ball, the ideologist of the Peasants' Revolt of 1381, was a priest who proclaimed in a sermon to the rebels: "Things shall not go right until there is neither master nor slave." Later religious dissent led to political dissent, and the extreme Puritans in the English Revolution of 1649–59 were the pioneers of the native tradition of anarchism. Gerrard Winstanley, the ideologist of the Diggers or True Levellers, who came nearer to anarchism than anyone before the French Revolution, moved within a few years from quoting the Bible to invoking "the great Creator Reason." The tradition was continued by the Ranters and Seekers, the Quakers and Shakers, and later the Universalists and Unitarians, and may be seen in the modern peace movement.

The argument for a negative connection is that religion supports politics, the Church supports the State, opponents of political authority also oppose religious authority. In Classical Greece and Rome, the religious sceptics—Protagoras, Diogenes, Epicurus, Lucretius, Sextus Empiricus—were the real liberators (and the same is true in Ancient India and China). Within Judaism, God is the archetypical figure of (male) authority, the Jewish State was a theocracy ruled by priests, and the few good prophets (and the good rabbis who followed them) should be seen as dissenters. In Christianity, Paul told his followers that "the powers that be are ordained of God," Church and State stand together as the "two swords" of the Gospel of Luke, and the good Christians have been rebels against ecclesiastical as much as secular power—the heretics and sceptics, *esprits forts* and *libertines*, the freethinkers and *philosophes*, Jean Meslier and Denis Diderot (who both wanted to see "the last king strangled in the guts of the last priest") and Voltaire (whose motto was "*Ecrasez l'infâme!*"), Thomas Paine (the pioneer of freethought and also of free society, the opponent of Priestcraft as well as Kingcraft) and Richard Carlile (who led the shift towards both atheism and anarchism), and so on to the historical freethought movement.

Within the historical anarchist movement, these two attitudes exist together. Revolutionary anarchism, like revolutionary socialism, has quasi-religious features—expressed in irrationalism, utopianism, millennialism, fanaticism, fundamentalism, sectarianism, and so on. But anarchism, like socialism and liberalism, also has anti-religious features—all of them modern political ideologies tending to assume the rejection of all orthodox belief and authority—and is the supreme example of dissent, disbelief, and disobedience. All progressive thought, culminating in humanism, depends on the assumption that every single human being has the right to think for himself or herself; and all progressive politics, culminating in anarchism, depends on the assumption that every single human being has the right to act for himself or herself. (A point worth mentioning is the connection of anarchism, as of liberalism and socialism, with the alternative religion of Freemasonry, to which several leading anarchists have belonged—Proudhon, Bakunin, Louise Michel, Ferrer, Voline, and so on.)

There is no doubt that the prevailing strain within the anarchist tradition is opposition to religion. William Godwin, the author of the *Enquiry Concerning Political Justice* (1793), the first systematic text of libertarian politics, was a Calvinist minister who began by rejecting Christianity, and passed through deism to atheism and then what was later called agnosticism. Max Stirner, the author of *The Individual and His Property* (1845), the most extreme text of libertarian politics, began as a Left Hegelian, post-Feuerbachian atheist, rejecting the "spooks" of religion as well as of politics—including the spook of "humanity." Proudhon, the first person to call himself an anarchist, who was well known for saying, "Property is theft," also said, "God is evil" and "God is the eternal X." Bakunin, the main founder of the anarchist movement, attacked the Church as much as the State, and wrote an essay which his followers later published as *God and the State* (1882), in which he inverted Voltaire's famous saying and proclaimed: "If God really existed, he would have to be abolished." Kropotkin, the best-known anarchist writer, was a child of the Enlightenment and the Scientific Revolution, and assumed that religion would be replaced by science and that the Church as well as the State would be abolished; he was particularly concerned with the development of a secular system of ethics which replaced supernatural theology with natural biology. Errico Malatesta and Carlo Cafiero, the main founders of the Italian anarchist movement, both came from freethinking families (and Cafiero was involved with the National Secular Society when he visited London during the 1870s). Elisée and Elie Reclus, the best-loved French anarchists, were the sons of a Calvinist minister, and began by rejecting religion before they moved on to anarchism. Sébastien Faure, the most active speaker and writer in the French movement for half a century, was intended for the Church and began by rejecting Catholicism and passing through anti-clericalism and socialism on the way to anarchism. André Lorulot, a leading French individualist before the First World War, was then a leading freethinker for half a century. Johann Most, the best-known German anarchist for a quarter of a century, who wrote ferocious pamphlets on the need for violence to destroy existing society, also wrote a ferocious pamphlet on the need to destroy supernatural religion called *The God Plague* (1883). Multatuli (Eduard Douwes Dekker), the great Dutch writer, was a leading atheist as well as anarchist. Ferdinand Domela Nieuwenhuis, the best-known Dutch anarchist, was a Calvinist minister who began by rejecting religion before passing through socialism on the way to anarchism. Anton Constandse was a leading Dutch anarchist and freethinker. Emma Goldman and Alexander Berkman, the best-known Jewish American anarchists, began by rejecting Judaism and passing through populism on the way to anarchism. Rudolf Rocker, the German leader of the Jewish anarchists in Britain, was another child of the Enlightenment and spoke and wrote on secular as much as political subjects. In Spain, the largest anarchist movement in the world, which has often been described as a quasi-religious phenomenon, was in fact profoundly naturalistic and secularist and anti-Christian as well as anti-clerical. Francisco Ferrer, the well-known Spanish anarchist who was judicially murdered in 1909, was best known for founding the Modern School which tried to give secular education in a Catholic country. The leaders of the anarchist movements in Latin America almost all began by rebelling against the Church before rebelling against the State. The founders of the anarchist movements in India and China all had to begin by discarding the traditional religions of their communities. In the United States, Voltairine de Cleyre was (as her name suggests) the child of freethinkers, and wrote and spoke on secular as much as political topics. The two best-known American anarchists today (both of Jewish origin) are Murray Bookchin, who calls himself an ecological humanist, and Noam Chomsky, who calls himself a scientific rationalist. Two leading figures of a younger generation, Fred Woodworth and Chaz Bufe, are militant atheists as well as anarchists. And so on.

This pattern prevails in Britain. Not only William Godwin but nearly all libertarians have been opposed to orthodox religion as well as orthodox politics—William Morris, Oscar Wilde, Charlotte Wilson, Joseph Lane, Henry Seymour (who was active in the National Secular Society before he helped to found the British anarchist movement), James Tochatti (who was active in the British Secular Union before he turned to socialism and anarchism), Alfred Marsh (the son of the son-in-law of G. J. Holyoake, who founded the secularist movement), Guy Aldred (who rapidly moved from evangelical Christianity through secularism and socialism to anarcho-syndicalism), A. S. Neill (whose educational work was opposed to religious and ethical orthodoxy as much as to political and social orthodoxy), and so on. And of course Shelley is the poet laureate of atheists and anarchists alike.

There have been few serious studies of anarchist psychology, but those that do exist agree that the first step on the way to anarchism is frequently the rejection of religion. Nevertheless, there are plenty of exceptions to this rule. In Britain, for example, Edward Carpenter was a mystic, Herbert Read saw anarchism as a religious philosophy, Alex Comfort moved from scientific to quasi-religious humanism, Colin MacInnes saw anarchism as a kind of religion; in the United States, Paul Goodman rejected Judaism but retained some kind of religion, and New Age nonsense has infected anarchists as well as so many other radicals. But the great exception is the phenomenon of Christian anarchism and religious anarcho-pacifism. Above all, Leo Tolstoy, who rejected all orthodoxies of both religion and politics, exerted a powerful double pressure towards anarchism—although he always repudiated the anarchist movement—and towards religion by pushing Christians towards his idiosyncratic version of anarchism as much as he pushed anarchists towards his idiosyncratic version of Christianity. He influenced the Western peace movement (including such figures as Bart de Ligt and Aldous Huxley, Danilo Dolci and Ronald Sampson), and also movements in the Third World (especially India, including such figures as M. K. Gandhi and J. P. Narayan). A similar development in the United States is the Catholic Worker movement (including such figures as Dorothy Day and Ammon Hennacy).

So the conclusion is that there is indeed a strong correlation between anarchism and atheism, but that it is not complete, and it is not necessary. Most anarchists are non-religious or anti-religious—and most take their atheism for granted—but some anarchists are religious. There are therefore several valid libertarian views of religion. Perhaps the most persuasive and productive one was that expressed by Karl Marx (before he became a "Marxist") in the famous passage from his essay "Towards the Critique of Hegel's Philosophy of Right" (1844):

> Religious distress is at the same time an expression of real distress and a protest against real distress. Religion is the sigh of the oppressed creature, the heart of a heartless world, the soul of a soulless situation. It is the opium of the people. The abolition of religion as the illusory happiness of the people is required for their real happiness. The demand to give up the illusions about their condition is the demand to give up a condition which needs illusions. The criticism of religion is therefore in embryo the criticism of the vale of tears whose halo is religion.

The true anarchist attitude to religion is surely to attack not faith or the Church so much as what it is in so many people that needs faith and the Church, just as the truly anarchist attitude to politics is surely to attack not obedience or the State so much as what it is in most people that needs obedience and the State—the will to believe and the will to obey. And the last anarchist hope about both religion and politics is that, just as the Church once seemed necessary to human existence but is now withering away, so the State still seems necessary to human existence but will also wither away, until both institutions finally disappear. We may yet end with *Neither God nor master!*

Based on a talk at the South Place Ethical Society, July 14, 1991.

29
FACING DEATH

ONE OF THE GREAT STRENGTHS OF PEOPLE WHO HAVE A RELIGION IS THAT they look forward to something beyond death—perhaps a continuation of life, in some kind of world above or below or beyond this one; or perhaps a renewal of life through some kind of resurrection or reincarnation after this one; or at least some kind of significant change, an absorption into a universal spirit or will.

One of the most common questions asked of people who don't have any religion is: "How do we face death?" One answer is not to think about it, and this is probably more common than you might think among non-religious people and indeed among religious people, too.

Another answer is to think there is something after death, and this too is probably more common than you might think among non-religious people, as well as religious people.

But the answer of most Humanists who have thought seriously about the subject is this: we think death really is the end of life; there really is nothing afterwards; the only kind of existence we shall have after we die is to be followed by our children and remembered by other people, for a time; and all we can do about it is make the best of our time before we die.

This sounds good in theory, but what does mean it in practice? Oddly enough, it doesn't make all that much difference. Religious and non-religious people live in pretty much the same way for most of their lives, and they die in pretty much the same way for most of their deaths. If there is a difference, it's that Humanists who have no belief in life after death realize we must put everything we have into life before death.

If we aren't going to meet our friends and relations at another time, we must make sure we enjoy our meetings this time. If we aren't going to be rewarded or punished in another place, we must make sure we do the right things for the right reasons in this place. If there'll be no future chance to say *sorry* or *thank you*, we must say it here and now. As the English poet Matthew Arnold put it: Hath man no second life?—Pitch this one high!

But what about the actual business of being ill and getting old and dying? The French thinker Blaise Pascal said more than three centuries ago: "The last act is bloody, however fine the rest of the play." And this is true of most of us, whatever we believe. But if there's no future consolation, it's all the more important to reduce present suffering—to cure illness, relieve old age, make death as easy as possible. As for those of us who are ill and old and dying, we can learn to face our predicament at least with dignity, if possible with humor, even at times with joy.

I've been very ill with cancer, I've been crippled by the treatment for it, I shall die fairly soon. But this makes my life more precious, not less. Every day is a new gift, to be relished. Every time I look at my wife is a new look, to be cherished. Every time I meet a friend is a new occasion, to be celebrated. Every time I see my children, and now my grandchildren, I observe new life and love carried on down the generations. Every time I'm helped, I appreciate the human fellowship. Even traveling in a wheelchair can be fun, because there's more chance to slow down and look around as I go. Not to be able to enjoy live plays and concerts any more is a blow, but I can read books and listen to music at home, remember how much I've enjoyed, and realize how much I've missed. For the first time, I have the chance to stop and think.

I shall end by quoting two things said about this subject more than a century ago. The American orator Robert Ingersoll gave this as his creed: "Happiness is the only good; the time to be happy is now; the place to be happy is here; the way to be happy is to make others so." And the English scientist William Kingdon Clifford, giving a lecture on life and death, taking the same line as mine, ended as follows: "Do I seem to say, 'Let us eat and drink, for tomorrow we die'? Far from it; on the contrary, I say, 'Let us take hands and help, for this day we are alive together!'"

Originally given as a talk on BBC World Service, printed in Freethinker, *July 1996.*

BOOKS AND PAMPHLETS BY NICOLAS WALTER

The RSGs, 1919–1963. London: Solidarity, 1963.
Non-violent Resistance: Men against War. London: Nonviolence 63, 1963.
About Anarchism. London: Freedom Press, 1969; new edition, 2002.
Blasphemy in Britain: The Practice and Punishment of Blasphemy, and the Trial of "Gay News." London: Rationalist Press Association, 1977.
Blasphemy: Ancient and Modern. London: Rationalist Press Association (with the Committee against Blasphemy Law), 1990.
Humanism: What's in the Word. London: Rationalist Press Association (with the British Humanist Association and the Secular Society, G. W. Foote Ltd), 1997.
Goodway, David, ed. *The Anarchist Past and Other Essays.* Nottingham: Five Leaves, 2007.

EDITED BY NICOLAS WALTER

Bakunin, Michael. *The Paris Commune and the Idea of the State.* London: CIRA, 1971.
Lane, Joseph. *An Anti-Statist, Communist Manifesto.* Sanday, Orkney: Cienfuegos Press, 1978.
Wilson, Charlotte. *Three Essays on Anarchism.* Sanday, Orkney: Cienfuegos Press, 1979.
Kropotkin, Peter. *Anarchism* and *Anarchist Communism.* (London: Freedom Press, 1987.)
(with Heiner Becker) Kropotkin, Peter. *Act for Yourselves: Articles from "Freedom" 1886–1907.* London: Freedom Press, 1988.
Foote, G. W. *Secularism: The True Philosophy of Life: An Exposition and A Defense.* London: G. W. Foote, 1998.
Shelley, Percy Bysshe. *The Necessity of Atheism.* London: G. W. Foote, 1998.
Forster, E. M. *What I Believe and Other Essays.* London: G. W. Foote (with the British Humanist Association and the Rationalist Press Association), 1999.
Wilson, Charlotte M. *Anarchist Essays.* London: Freedom Press, 2000.

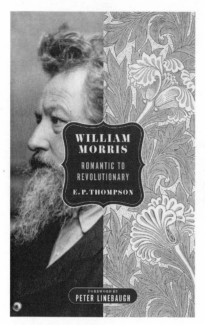

WILLIAM MORRIS:
ROMANTIC TO REVOLUTIONARY
E.P. THOMPSON
FOREWORD BY PETER LINEBAUGH
978-1-60486-243-0
$32.95

William Morris—the great 19th century craftsman, architect, designer, poet and writer—remains a monumental figure whose influence resonates powerfully today. As an intellectual (and author of the seminal utopian *News From Nowhere*), his concern with artistic and human values led him to cross what he called the 'river of fire' and become a committed socialist—committed not to some theoretical formula but to the day by day struggle of working women and men in Britain and to the evolution of his ideas about art, about work and about how life should be lived.

Many of his ideas accorded none too well with the reforming tendencies dominant in the Labour movement, nor with those of 'orthodox' Marxism, which has looked elsewhere for inspiration. Both sides have been inclined to venerate Morris rather than to pay attention to what he said. Originally written less than a decade before his groundbreaking *The Making of the English Working Class*, E.P. Thompson brought to this biography his now trademark historical mastery, passion, wit, and essential sympathy. It remains unsurpassed as the definitive work on this remarkable figure, by the major British historian of the 20th century.

Praise:
"Two impressive figures, William Morris as subject and E. P. Thompson as author, are conjoined in this immense biographical-historical-critical study, and both of them have gained in stature since the first edition of the book was published... The book that was ignored in 1955 has meanwhile become something of an underground classic—almost impossible to locate in second-hand bookstores, pored over in libraries, required reading for anyone interested in Morris and, increasingly, for anyone interested in one of the most important of contemporary British historians... Thompson has the distinguishing characteristic of a great historian: he has transformed the nature of the past, it will never look the same again; and whoever works in the area of his concerns in the future must come to terms with what Thompson has written. So too with his study of William Morris."
—Peter Stansky, *The New York Times Book Review*

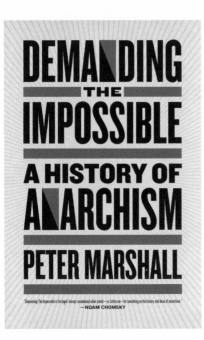

DEMANDING THE IMPOSSIBLE:
A HISTORY OF ANARCHISM
PETER MARSHALL
978-1-60486-064-1
$28.95

N avigating the broad 'river of anarchy,' from Taoism to Situation-
ism, from Ranters to Punk rock-
ers, from individualists to communists,
from anarcho-syndicalists to anarcha-
feminists, *Demanding the Impossible* is an
authoritative and lively study of a widely
misunderstood subject. It explores the
key anarchist concepts of society and the
state, freedom and equality, authority
and power and investigates the successes and failure of the anarchist
movements throughout the world. While remaining sympathetic to anarchism, it presents a balanced and critical account. It covers not only
the classic anarchist thinkers, such as Godwin, Proudhon, Bakunin,
Kropotkin, Reclus and Emma Goldman, but also other libertarian figures, such as Nietzsche, Camus, Gandhi, Foucault and Chomsky. No
other book on anarchism covers so much so incisively.

In this updated edition, a new epilogue examines the most recent developments, including 'post-anarchism' and 'anarcho-primitivism' as well as the
anarchist contribution to the peace, green and 'Global Justice' movements.
Demanding the Impossible is essential reading for anyone wishing to understand
what anarchists stand for and what they have achieved. It will also appeal to
those who want to discover how anarchism offers an inspiring and original
body of ideas and practices which is more relevant than ever in the twenty-first
century.

Praise:
"*Demanding the Impossible* is the book I always recommend when asked—as I often
am--for something on the history and ideas of anarchism."
—Noam Chomsky

"Attractively written and fully referenced…bound to be the standard history."
—Colin Ward, *Times Educational Supplement*

ANARCHIST SEEDS BENEATH THE SNOW:
LEFT-LIBERTARIAN THOUGHT AND BRITISH
WRITERS FROM WILLIAM MORRIS TO COLIN WARD
DAVID GOODWAY
978-1-60486-221-8
$24.95

From William Morris to Oscar Wilde to George Orwell, left-libertarian thought has long been an important but neglected part of British cultural and political history. In Anarchist Seeds beneath the Snow, David Goodway seeks to recover and revitalize that indigenous anarchist tradition. This book succeeds as simultaneously a cultural history of left-libertarian thought in Britain and a demonstration of the applicability of that history to current politics. Goodway argues that a recovered anarchist tradition could—and should—be a touchstone for contemporary political radicals. Moving seamlessly from Aldous Huxley and Colin Ward to the war in Iraq, this challenging volume will energize leftist movements throughout the world.

Praise:
"*Anarchist Seeds beneath the Snow* is an impressive achievement for its rigorous scholarship across a wide range of sources, for collating this diverse material in a cogent and systematic narrative-cum-argument, and for elucidating it with clarity and flair… It is a book that needed to be written and now deserves to be read."
—*Journal of William Morris Studies*

"Goodway outlines with admirable clarity the many variations in anarchist thought. By extending outwards to left-libertarians he takes on even greater diversity."
—Sheila Rowbotham, *Red Pepper*

"A splendid survey of 'left-libertarian thought' in this country, it has given me hours of delight and interest. Though it is very learned, it isn't dry. Goodway's friends in the awkward squad (especially William Blake) are both stimulating and comforting companions in today's political climate."
—A.N. Wilson, *Daily Telegraph*

FRIENDS OF

These are indisputably momentous times—the financial system is melting down globally and the Empire is stumbling. Now more than ever there is a vital need for radical ideas.

In the three years since its founding—and on a mere shoestring—PM Press has risen to the formidable challenge of publishing and distributing knowledge and entertainment for the struggles ahead. With over 100 releases to date, we have published an impressive and stimulating array of literature, art, music, politics, and culture. Using every available medium, we've succeeded in connecting those hungry for ideas and information to those putting them into practice.

Friends of PM allows you to directly help impact, amplify, and revitalize the discourse and actions of radical writers, filmmakers, and artists. It provides us with a stable foundation from which we can build upon our early successes and provides a much-needed subsidy for the materials that can't necessarily pay their own way. You can help make that happen – and receive every new title automatically delivered to your door once a month – by joining as a Friend of PM Press. And, we'll throw in a free T-Shirt when you sign up.

Here are your options:

• $25 a month: Get all books and pamphlets plus 50% discount on all webstore purchases.

• $25 a month: Get all CDs and DVDs plus 50% discount on all webstore purchases.

• $40 a month: Get all PM Press releases plus 50% discount on all webstore purchases

• $100 a month: Sustainer. - Everything plus PM merchandise, free downloads, and 50% discount on all webstore purchases.

For those who can't afford $25 or more a month, we're introducing Sustainer Rates at $15, $10 and $5. Sustainers get a free PM Press t-shirt and a 50% discount on all purchases from our website.

Just go to **WWW.PMPRESS.ORG** to sign up. Your Visa or Mastercard will be billed once a month, until you tell us to stop. Or until our efforts succeed in bringing the revolution around. Or the financial meltdown of Capital makes plastic redundant. Whichever comes first.

PM Press was founded at the end of 2007 by a small collection of folks with decades of publishing, media, and organizing experience. PM Press co-conspirators have published and distributed hundreds of books, pamphlets, CDs, and DVDs. Members of PM have founded enduring book fairs, spearheaded victorious tenant organizing campaigns, and worked closely with bookstores, academic conferences, and even rock bands to deliver political and challenging ideas to all walks of life. We're old enough to know what we're doing and young enough to know what's at stake.

We seek to create radical and stimulating fiction and non-fiction books, pamphlets, t-shirts, visual and audio materials to entertain, educate and inspire you. We aim to distribute these through every available channel with every available technology—whether that means you are seeing anarchist classics at our bookfair stalls; reading our latest vegan cookbook at the café; downloading geeky fiction e-books; or digging new music and timely videos from our website.

PM Press is always on the lookout for talented and skilled volunteers, artists, activists and writers to work with. If you have a great idea for a project or can contribute in some way, please get in touch.

PM Press
PO Box 23912
Oakland CA 94623
510-658-3906
www.pmpress.org